Think-Tanks of the New Right

ANDREW DENHAM
University of Nottingham

Dartmouth

Aldershot • Brookfield USA • Singapore • Sydney

Published by
Dartmouth Publishing Company Limited
Gower House
Croft Road
Aldershot
Hants GU11 3HR
England

Dartmouth Publishing Company
Old Post Road
Brookfield
Vermont 05036
USA

British Library Cataloguing in Publication Data
Denham, Andrew
  Think-tanks of the new right
  1.Conservatism - Great Britain 2.Political science -
  Research - Great Britain
  I.Title
  320.5'2'0941

Library of Congress Cataloging-in-Publication Data
Denham, Andrew.
  Think-tanks of the New Right / Andrew Denham.
    p. cm.
  Based on author's thesis (doctoral)--University of Southampton,
  1992.
  Includes bibliographical references.
  ISBN 1-85521-868-2
  1. Conservatism--Great Britain. 2. Great Britain--Social
  policy--1979- 3. Research institutes--Great Britain. I. Title.
  JC573.2.G7D45 1996
  320.5'2'0941--dc20   96-24901
                                                        CIP

ISBN 1 85521 868 2

Printed in Great Britain by
Antony Rowe Ltd, Chippenham, Wiltshire

Contents

Preface

This book began life as a doctoral thesis, completed and examined in the Department of Politics at the University of Southampton in 1992. (My interest in the New Right actually began in 1989 as a postgraduate student at the University of Kent, reading for a Master of Arts degree in Political Thought.) In 1994, the thesis was awarded the Walter Bagehot Prize by the Political Studies Association. This book, like the thesis, examines the ideas and policies advocated by think-tanks of the New Right in contemporary Britain.

The book is organized in the following way. Chapter 1 profiles the Institute of Economic Affairs (IEA) and discusses various schools of liberal economic thought on which authors published by the IEA have drawn. The Institute's strategic objectives are identified as the dissemination of ideas (following Keynes's famous dictum in his *General Theory of Employment, Interest and Money*), unencumbered by considerations of political feasibility in the short term.

Chapter 2 profiles the Adam Smith Institute (ASI), a policy-oriented research institute concerned to offer realistic and practical solutions to problems of the public sector via a series of techniques known collectively as micropolitics. The ASI is contrasted to the IEA, whose characteristic aloofness from day-to-day politics the ASI does not share. The two institutes thus have very different strategic purposes and frequently disagree as to how market liberal thinking can and should be applied in economic and social policy, as demonstrated in the three policy case-studies contained elsewhere in this book (Chapters 5-7).

Chapter 3 profiles the Centre for Policy Studies (CPS), a policy centre closer in terms of its strategic purposes to the ASI than to the IEA. This chapter discusses the origins and rationale of the CPS and explores the tension between Thatcherism's economic ideal, on the one hand, and its moral/cultural ideal, on the other. A further problem highlighted in this chapter is whether (and how) a think-tank which enjoys close links with the leadership of a particular political party can continue to 'think the unthinkable' when the party in question moves from opposition into government.

Chapter 4 profiles the Social Affairs Unit (SAU), an off-shoot of the IEA whose strategic purposes are similar to those of the latter, but whose ideological affinities are closer to those of the conservative (rather than the liberal) New Right. This chapter continues the exploration (begun in Chapter 3) of the tension between economic individualism, on the one hand, and social authoritarianism (or bourgeois virtue), on the other.

Chapter 5 discusses the measures advocated by New Right think-tanks in the area of education policy and assesses what impact (if any) such groups may have had on the policy thinking of, and/or legislation introduced by, the Thatcher governments in Britain during the 1980s. This chapter also explores the tensions within the contemporary British Conservative programme for educational reform and concludes that such tensions remain at the heart of that programme in the 1990s.

Chapter 6 discusses the policy thinking and advice of New Right groups in respect of the National Health Service (NHS) and assesses their impact (if any) on the 1988 Review of the NHS and the resultant White Paper, *Working for Patients* (HMSO 1989). This chapter also contains discussion of the public health issues beyond the structure and finance of health services raised by the SAU, and notes the dissatisfaction of the IEA with the Conservative government's proposals for an internal market within the NHS.

Chapter 7 examines how New Right think-tanks have addressed the issue (or dilemma) of welfare-dependency (the argument that the very existence of a welfare state undermines personal and family responsibility and encourages morally inappropriate and socially destructive values). The sense in which underlying theoretical differences between the liberal and the conservative New Right poses something of a dilemma on the question of dependency is outlined and explored. The final chapter discusses a number of theoretical issues that continue to divide the New Right in Britain and briefly considers the prospects for British New Right think-tanks in the 1990s and beyond.

Acknowledgements

In carrying out the research for this project and preparing the book for publication, I have incurred a large number of personal debts that I want to repay here. My postgraduate studies were supported for three years by the Economic and Social Research Council (ESRC), first at the University of Kent at Canterbury (MA Coursework Competition Award, 1988-9) and then at the University of Southampton (Research Award, 1989-91), where the doctoral research which provides the substance of much of this book was undertaken. Members of the Department of Politics at Southampton University were supportive throughout my time there and I should particularly like to thank Peter Johnson, Liam O'Sullivan and Sandy Wilkins for their help.

In researching this book, I conducted interviews with, or received significant input or assistance from, the following: Geoffrey Alderman, Digby Anderson, Baroness Caroline Cox, Ian Forbes, Andrew Gamble, Michael Goldsmith, John Gray, David Green, Lord Harris of High Cross, Peter Hennessy, the late Lord Joseph of Portsoken, Sheila Lawlor, Graham Mather, Calum Paton, Madsen Pirie, Roger Scruton, Arthur Seldon, Marjorie Seldon, Stuart Sexton, Sir Alfred Sherman, David Willetts and Barry Wintour. Special thanks are due to my supervisor, Professor (now Lord) Raymond Plant, for his considerable intellectual contribution to this project and characteristic warmth and good humour during its lifespan.

In preparing the book for publication, I received advice and various forms of technical expertise and support from three colleagues at Nottingham University, Paul Heywood, April Pidgeon and Maxine Simms. I should also like to thank Sonia Hubbard, Ann Newell, Amanda Richardson and Valerie Saunders at Dartmouth for dealing so patiently and efficiently with my enquiries, John Irwin for commissioning the book in the first place and all those who have helped in the production process. My greatest debt, however, is to Patricia, Nadine, Elizabeth, Anjelica, Jim and Ruth Denham, for putting up with me, for doing what they do and for being who are they are. To all of these, I am profoundly grateful. Needless to say, none of them bears any responsibility for any errors, whether of fact or interpretation, that remain.

1 The Institute of Economic Affairs

Introduction

The Institute of Economic Affairs (IEA) was formally created in 1955 and began regular publication in 1957 as a (charitable) 'research and educational trust' to study the role of markets and pricing in allocating resources and registering preferences. The assumption and rationale behind much of its work is that the 'climate of opinion' has an important, and ultimately decisive, influence on politicians. 'They are puppets on a string in the way they respond to fashions', according to its former Deputy Director, the late John Wood (quoted in Kavanagh 1990: 80). The Institute assumes, in other words, that ideas (and intellectuals) play a formative role in policy change. Its pamphlets and monthly Hobart lunches are intended to influence 'opinion-formers' and 'to supply intellectuals in universities, schools, journalism and broadcasting with authoritative studies of the economic theory of markets and its application to practical affairs' (Fisher 1974: 103).

The IEA regards itself primarily as a publishing house for market liberal thinking and the opinions expressed in its publications as those of individual authors and contributors. In short, there is no official or corporate IEA point of view. There are, however, two recurring themes across its publications to date (Kavanagh 1990: 83). The first is that the role of government (central and local) should be severely limited in economic affairs. The second emphasizes the technical (and moral) superiority of markets and competitive pricing in the allocation of resources. Significantly, both themes stand in opposition to the assumptions of the 'Keynesian welfare state consensus' in post-war Britain (King 1987).

According to its former Editorial Director, Arthur Seldon, the IEA 'may perhaps claim to have created the post-war focus for the demonstration that market analysis was indispensable for understanding and solving economic tasks and problems' (Seldon 1981a: xvii). In contrast to the view that governments can deal with any and every economic problem by regulation or direct management, the IEA adopted a very different approach and, in doing so, re-opened the prospect of services being supplied not by government, but by individuals coming together as buyers and sellers in markets. The IEA approach recognized that some goods and services had to be supplied by government and that markets were not always feasible. In general, however, its papers argued that markets should be reintroduced into 'the mass of British economic activity unnecessarily controlled by government' (Seldon 1981a: xxvii).

As Kavanagh (1990: 81) has pointed out, the IEA has drawn on various schools of liberal economic thought in order to challenge Keynesianism - notably, perhaps, the Chicago and Austrian schools, as well as the Virginia school of public choice. As will soon become clear, there are significant methodological differences between these schools of thought. Before these can be explored, however, we must first consider what is common to all three, namely their (neo-classical) economic liberalism.

Economic Liberalism

As Norman Barry (1986: 44) has argued, the 'science' of economics, has unquestionably provided the dominant intellectual foundation of twentieth-century liberalism and libertarianism. This, Barry continues, has tended to mean that, inasmuch as economic science is itself a utilitarian discipline, concerned with investigating the consequences of various courses of human action, subject to the existence of more or less necessary constraints, the prevailing forms of justification for classical liberalism and libertarianism in the twentieth century tend also to have been utilitarian, because consequentialist (Barry 1986: 44).

Indeed, Barry argues, it can even be claimed that liberalism is actually implicit in the diagrams and equations of neo-classical micro-economics. 'Economic man', around whose 'free' choices the economist builds theories of economic order, can surely only be 'liberal man' (a freely-choosing individual). Hence, Barry argues, while no classical liberal or libertarian has yet entertained the absurd notion that human beings are ruled solely by narrowly economic considerations, it is certainly the case that the 'classic' liberal writers of the twentieth century have been those who have adapted the style of economics to social explanation; that is, they have emphasized the *wertfrei* nature of economic 'science' and have regarded reason as competent only to ascertain the connection between means and ends. There is, on this view, 'no such thing as a liberal end for man' (Barry 1986: 44).

Liberalism, then, tells us precisely nothing about which particular ends human beings 'ought' to pursue, but merely informs them how they can reach a plurality of ends - each particular end being the necessarily subjective and rationally undemonstrable choice of the individual. In arguing thus, Barry argues, liberal writers have inherited David Hume's meagre account of reason and his scepticism concerning the ultimate foundation of human values. As we shall see shortly, however, twentieth century classical liberals and libertarians have also significantly altered the emphasis of this approach (Barry 1986: 45).

For Barry at least, the two most important schools of economic liberalism this century have been the Chicago and Austrian schools. While quite dissimilar in their methodological foundations, each has adopted a typically 'Enlightenment' approach to social affairs in which tradition and experience are subordinated to the 'dictates' of a particular kind of 'economic rationalism'. Although von Mises (Austrian school) and Friedman (Chicago school) represent dramatically opposed positions in the foundations of economics and social science, there is, for Barry at least, an important sense in which both may be called 'children of the Enlightenment'. True, Friedman presents his liberalism as fact unleavened by reason, while von Mises presents his as reason unleavened by fact, but neither has much respect for any form of knowledge which is 'neither exclusively a generalisation from observed fact, nor the conclusion of *a priori* reasoning' (Barry 1986: 45).

Rationalism aside, there is a further point of similarity between the Chicago and Austrian varieties of twentieth-century liberalism. This is that both are positivistic in relation to ethics and self-consciously eschew metaphysical speculations about the meaning of freedom or about the ultimate validation of the claims of liberalism. Mises, in particular, argues that although (or perhaps because) liberal economics is a 'scientific' social doctrine, there are 'no such things as absolute values independently of the subjective preferences of erring man' (quoted in Barry 1986: 45). As Barry notes, similar observations can also be found in virtually any book on political economy by an author in the Chicago tradition. Both schools, then, trade heavily on the idea that in most communities there is agreement about ends, and that liberalism 'informs us only of the means towards those ends' (Barry 1986: 46).

For both Austrian and Chicago economists, then, liberalism is simply the 'science' of economics applied to socio-political questions. Accordingly, the liberalism of economists of both schools stands or falls on their ability to show that liberalism can be sustained on a 'scientific' basis alone. That said, our discussion of twentieth-century 'consequentialist' liberal doctrines begins with the utilitarianism of the Chicago school, before moving on to consider the writings of the Austrian school, which represent arguably the most sophisticated and sustained (if ultimately flawed) attempt to construct a political theory of liberalism out of a *wertfrei* social science (Barry 1986: 46).

The Chicago School

Insofar as the Chicago school has provided a social philosophy, that philosophy can be said to constitute a spectacular example of what might be termed 'economism'. For Norman Barry at least, this means not that Chicago economists regard human beings as being driven solely by narrowly economic impulses, but that they attempt to treat those problems of social and political theory that interest them with the dissolving power of (a particular form of) economic analysis. At a more substantive level, Barry argues, Chicago economists are 'economistic' in claiming that liberty depends ultimately on capitalist economics and that political activity *per se* is destructive not merely of economic liberty, but of liberty itself. The suggestion is, then, that economic 'science' can demonstrate some causal connection between capitalism and freedom. In this way, as Barry suggests, the justification for both can be presented in purely 'consequentialist' terms, without any reference to the intrinsic moral value of liberty or to any metaphysical conception of the individual (Barry 1986: 47).

Chicago economists' demonstration of the virtues of the liberal individualist system therefore depends on how they explain the 'causality' which is said to govern economic and social order. Their explanation of this is characteristically positivist, in that the laws said to describe the social world are inductive generalisations. In a famous statement of the methodology of 'positive economics', for instance, Friedman accepts the distinction (from Logical Positivism) between purely analytical statements that do not convey information about the world but which enable us to organize knowledge, and observational statements which provide empirical data for the otherwise empty tautologies of 'pure' theory (Barry 1986: 47).

Causality in economics, then, is said by Chicago economists to be constructed out of regularities in the social world revealed by observation, the purpose of economic 'science' being to provide a system of 'generalisations' that can be used to generate accurate predictions about the consequences of any change in circumstances (Friedman 1953). In this way, the alleged insecurity and subjectivism of *a priori* reasoning is replaced by the notion of objective 'fact' in the explanation of events. At this point, it is worth noting that the methodology of Chicago economics faces the familiar 'problem of induction' first posed by David Hume - namely, that no amount of observations of a regularity in the past can guarantee that it will be repeated in the future. Because the regularities that constitute the data of economic laws exist in the world - and are not, for instance, the intellectual reconstruction of an active mind ordering the complex data of that world - such regularities are always and everywhere *contingent*, not necessary (Barry 1986: 48).

The connection between all this and classical liberalism is simple. Chicago economists argue that the methods of economic 'science' can be used to refute the claims of 'statism' (state intervention in free markets) if those claims can be formulated in ways that can be empirically tested. Empiricism, Chicago economists argue, vindicates liberalism. If, as Friedman and Stigler separately assume, there is - in Western industrialised societies at least - sufficient agreement on the values of liberty and prosperity for the role of reason to be limited to that of matching means to ends, then, Chicago economists argue, economic 'science' can objectively 'prove' that these are better maximized in systems characterized by liberal institutions (limited government and free markets) than by any alternative set of institutions known to the world (Barry 1987: 26).

Chicago economists argue, then, on empirical grounds, that only free markets can co-ordinate effectively the disparate elements in a complex society and that attempts on the part of the state to improve on the market will destroy both freedom and prosperity. The work of Stigler, in particular, has enquired not simply into the traditional liberal's question of the legitimate role of the state but also into the question of its actual performance in whatever activities it has engaged and has discovered that governmental regulation of electricity rates and the securities market (among others) has made no appreciable difference to economic behaviour (Barry 1986: 49).

Chicago economics is thus relentlessly empiricist, an approach which, Barry argues, has been of immense strategic importance in policy arguments with their collectivist opponents in an increasingly empiricist age (Barry 1986: 53). The Chicago school's approach, however, has a number of serious theoretical deficiencies and methodological limitations. The first of these is that observational statements can tell us only that interventionist policies have *contingently* failed; because of the 'problem of induction' mentioned earlier, empiricism cannot predict with absolute certainty that such policies must fail in the future, even if it can be shown that they have always and everywhere failed in the past. No theoretical reason is offered as to *why* the failure of particular interventionist measures should not lead to demands for still more interventions (Barry 1986: 49).

The way out of this dilemma for Chicago economists would be either to construct some general *a priori* explanation of the social world which could overcome the problem of induction, or to develop a moral argument prohibiting such interventions, irrespective of utilitarian (consequentialist) considerations. In practice, however, Friedman's implicit positivism means that neither option is available. The former would require the abandonment of the rigid distinction between analytic and synthetic statements on which the Chicago economists' entire epistemology rests, while the latter undermines their subjectivist view of ethics which holds that there cannot be 'rational' argument about moral values (Barry 1986: 49).

A further difficulty is that any rigidly empiricist methodology generates a conception of the person at odds with the liberal tradition in general, and one wholly unacceptable to Austrian economists in particular (see later). The problem here is that the determination to discover predictive regularities with a high empirical content in the social world suggests a metaphysical conception of the person whereby he or she is merely a passive respondent to mechanical processes, an agent that only reacts to external stimuli, a creature and not a creator of the world. A fundamental requirement both of 'positive' social science in general and of Chicago economists' liberal political economy in particular is that the behaviour of human beings is entirely *predictable*. A key insight, indeed axiom, of Austrian economics, on the other hand, is that this is simply not so.

Moreover, insofar as Chicago economists seek to evaluate policies, laws and institutions only by reference to their measurable consequences, other forms of social analysis and appraisal are effectively precluded (Barry 1986: 52). As we shall see shortly, it is crucial to the success or otherwise of Austrian economics that there are complexities in social systems that cannot be captured in simple empirical relationships, and that there exist forms of knowledge besides the raw data revealed to us by our senses. Chicago economists' 'pure' empiricism, then, tells us precisely nothing about the *unintended consequences* of any particular course of human action. Austrian economics, on the other hand, does suggest insights of this kind, and in doing so rejects the characteristic 'scientism' of Chicago economics.

The Austrian School

A second school of liberal economic thought on which the IEA has drawn is the Austrian school, a study of whose work and its relevance to government policy in Britain in the last quarter of the twentieth century was provided by Stephen Littlechild in a seminal Hobart Paper first published in 1978. *The Fallacy of the Mixed Economy* examined whether recent economic thinking and policy in Britain, dominated as it had been by 'mainstream neo-classical' and 'welfare' economics, remained vulnerable to an Austrian critique. The important contribution to thinking and policy that Britain could have drawn from the

Austrian economists, Littlechild argued, had been 'largely overlooked' (Littlechild 1986).

Austrian economic thinking is based on the individual, who provides both the method of reasoning and the source of the valuations on which policy must rest. Its critique of 'welfare' economics is that it ignores the central importance of imperfect knowledge, the pervasive uncertainty that overshadows all decisions, whether taken in private markets or by government. In the Austrian view, it is a 'myth' to suppose that governments necessarily have access to more or surer information than is available to participants in free markets. Austrian economists also reject the idea that 'market failure' provides sufficient warrant for replacing markets by government (Littlechild 1986: 8).

In his critique of the mixed economy, Littlechild argued that 'market failure' arises not from the defects of the market but from an imperfect framework of laws and institutions within which markets operate. The intellectually more compelling solution to such failure is therefore not the replacement of markets by government, but the refinement of this legal and institutional framework to make property rights easier to identify as the best incentive to the efficient use of resources. This analysis has strong implications, not only with regard to policy on competition, but also for the treatment of externalities, national planning and nationalized industries.

Littlechild, however, is chiefly concerned to draw attention to the central ideas and insights of the Austrian tradition in economics, an approach which, he argues, is quite distinct from the 'neo-classical mainstream' of economic theory. For the latter, the economic problem facing society concerns the efficient allocation of resources in the light of preferences, techniques and resource availabilities, knowledge of which is supposed somehow to be 'given'. Austrian economists, on the other hand, see this problem as including the *discovery* of such preferences, techniques and resource availabilities. A second difference is that the 'neo-classical mainstream' in economics tends to see the economy as in (or near) a state of equilibrium. Economists in the Austrian tradition, by contrast, see the economy as involved in a continuous *process* of discovery, adaptation, co-ordination and change (Littlechild 1986: 12).

These contrasting views lead to differing interpretations of the role of government in economic affairs. Neo-classical 'welfare' economists, according to Littlechild, ask whether the market provides the right incentives to allocate resources efficiently, and where it does not - wherever 'market failure' occurs - see a role for government, either in correcting the incentives of the market, or in replacing the market entirely. Austrian economists, on the other hand, ask whether the market provides the right incentives to *discover* whether there is scope for increased co-ordination, and hence to improved efficiency in the allocation of resources. Austrian economists concede that the market frequently (indeed always) makes mistakes, but conclude, on the whole, that governments cannot hope to acquire sufficient information to improve on the market. The question they ask is therefore what *kind* of government policies best encourage the co-ordinating process of the market (Littlechild 1986: 12).

In contrast to the 'neo-classical mainstream' of economic theory, then, Austrian economics has always attempted to explain behaviour in a world characterized by the lack or dispersion of knowledge (Littlechild 1986: 22). Indeed, the modern Austrian approach is sometimes described as 'thoroughgoing subjectivism' (the assertion, in other words, that the private experience of the individual is the sole foundation of factual knowledge in any society). Subjectivism, according to Littlechild, is what distinguishes Austrian economics. This is because Austrian economists have pursued its implications with a 'significantly greater consciousness and consistency' than economists in rival traditions of economic thought (Littlechild 1986: 24).

The individual's 'tastes' notwithstanding, Austrian writers have emphasized the importance of incorporating into economic theory many other aspects of the individual's personality. These include *knowledge* about one's tastes and the opportunities available, *interpretations* of events and the actions of others, *expectations* concerning future events and behaviour and *alertness* to new opportunities as yet unseen. The key point here is that individuals differ with regard to all of these aspects and hence 'subjectivism' means something much wider than merely personal 'tastes' (Littlechild 1986: 22).

The individual also provides the method of reasoning in Austrian economics. 'Methodological individualism' here refers to the consistent use of the intelligible conduct of individuals as building blocks to construct models of complex phenomena. Hence, Austrian economic theory is based on two principles - methodological individualism and subjectivism. These two principles, according to Littlechild, both describe what Austrian economists do and define what they believe good economics to be (Littlechild 1986: 75).

Two further aspects of Austrian economic theory also deserve consideration at this point. The first concerns what Hayek has referred to as the 'unintended consequences' of human action. For Austrian economists generally, many social institutions are the consequence of human action, but not of human design - an insight which has important implications for the role of government in society. A further important element in Austrian thinking is that organic phenomena (such as money and markets) can be developed only by a process taking place over time. As Littlechild points out, an appreciation of the role of time - and in particular, of the passage of time - is a vital element of the Austrian approach (Littlechild 1986: 24).

At this point, more needs to be said about Austrian methodology and on how and why the Austrian approach differs so markedly from that of mainstream neo-classical economics. Austrian methodology has been neatly summarized by Kirzner (1976). Austrians, Kirzner notes, are subjectivists, emphasizing the purposefulness of human action; they are unhappy with theoretical constructions which emphasize equilibrium to the exclusion of market processes; and they are sceptical of the idea that economic theories are ultimately capable of empirical proof. Consequently, Austrian economists have serious reservations about the validity and importance of a good deal of the empirical work being carried on in the economics profession today (Kirzner 1976: 40).

As Littlechild (1986: 25) suggests, this position is evidently quite different from that of 'mainstream' economics. As we have seen, the methodology of Friedman and the Chicago school holds that economic theorems can be established only by adopting the methods of the natural sciences, such as physics, which proceed by framing, testing and revising hypotheses about the nature of physical reality. The suggested method is that economists should frame hypotheses, then test the predictions they yield against observed behaviour. The adequacy of a theory is to be judged by the success or otherwise of its predictions, rather than by the 'realism' of its assumptions. Indeed, this approach would argue, the only test of 'realism' is the test of prediction. This (behaviouristic) approach has come to be known as 'positive economics' and is associated in particular with the work of Milton Friedman and the Chicago school of economists. One implication of positive economics seems to be that approaches to economics which do not follow its methodology are 'unscientific'. Austrian economists, however, as Kirzner's summary of their methodology clearly indicates, do not share this view. At least four reasons can be identified.

The first reason is based on the idea that, in observing the actions of others, we are assisted by a capacity to understand the meaning of such actions in a way that we cannot understand physical events. Being human ourselves, the argument runs, we have insights into the behaviour of other human beings which it is in part the task of the social sciences to explain. We know, say Austrian economists, that human beings are purposeful; that they are alert to new possibilities for increasing their satisfaction; that they take initiatives and that they do not merely respond passively to external stimuli in the same way that biological organisms do. The *purpose* of such action we know, *without* having to deduce it from others' behaviour. Indeed, it might be argued that we *cannot* deduce the purpose of human action simply by observing behaviour and that any theory (explanation) of observed behaviour is ultimately unsatisfactory unless it is consistent with such knowledge (Littlechild 1986: 26).

A second Austrian reservation is that it is difficult to generate precise testable predictions in circumstances where there is a large number of variables about which it will never be possible to obtain full information (as is usually the case in the social sciences). The suggestion here is that the economist will typically be able to predict only general patterns of behaviour, not the behaviour of each individual element. Because the economist never has sufficient information about the preferences and opportunities of individuals, he or she is limited to what Hayek (1967) has called 'prediction in principle', rather than 'prediction in detail' (Littlechild 1986: 26).

Thirdly, Austrian economists argue, it is not even clear that economic theory can be empirically tested. Consider for a moment the law of demand, which states that 'a rise in price leads to a fall in demand'. Then suppose a rise in the price of good X is followed by a rise in demand. How might this be explained? Economists will explain that consumers must have thought the higher-priced good to be of superior quality. Yet the law applies only to goods perceived as identical. In this instance, then, it would appear that what has been established is not the truth or falsity of the law of demand, but whether the observer has correctly identified identical commodities. How, then, is it possible to establish *empirically* the law of demand? (Littlechild 1986: 27).

Finally, Austrian economists object to crude empiricism in economics on the grounds that there is an indeterminacy and unpredictability inherent in the preferences, expectations and knowledge of human beings. This being so, one cannot hope to find permanent empirical regularities in economics which may be 'safely extrapolated beyond the existing data at hand to yield scientific theorems of universal validity' (Littlechild 1986: 27). There can, according to Austrian economists, be no unchanging parameters in the social sciences of the kind that exist in the natural sciences (Kirzner 1976).

For these reasons, Austrian economists have argued that the nature of the social sciences is fundamentally different from that of the natural sciences, and that economics (as a social science) requires a different methodology from, say, physics. In the Austrian view, this is not in the least 'unscientific'. Rather, it is the uncritical application to economics of the methods of the natural sciences (or 'scientism') which is itself the 'unscientific' procedure. Austrian economists, then, have for the most part eschewed empirical and statistical work and concentrated on deriving propositions of a *qualitative*, rather than of a quantitative kind. Their aim in doing so has been to generate propositions that will be true at all times and in all places, rather than just for specific times and places (Littlechild 1986: 27).

The concept at the heart of Austrian economics is that of the market process. Austrian economists cannot accept the mainstream neo-classical notion of competitive equilibrium at a given point in time, characterized by perfect knowledge and fully co-ordinated plans on the part of market actors. Instead, Austrians view the market as a process taking place over time and characterized not only by lack of knowledge (and consequently lack of co-ordination) but also by 'discovery' and increasing co-ordination (Littlechild 1986: 29).

Of particular importance in the Austrian view of the market is the power of 'alertness' and the role of entrepreneurship in the continuing search for new opportunities, be they new products or better terms for existing ones. In the Austrian view, the term 'entrepreneurship' refers to the alertness to opportunities for profit not hitherto grasped by other market actors. Profit is not necessarily (or even usually) the result of monopoly power, but of successful entrepreneurship. It is the 'reward' in noticing some lack of co-ordination in the market (Littlechild 1986: 31). In the modern interpretation of the 'Austrian' tradition, the name which has become virtually synonymous with the development of a distinctive *theory* of entrepreneurship is that of Israel Kirzner. In an IEA-sponsored seminar in 1979, for instance, Kirzner outlined a 'pure theory' of entrepreneurship (Kirzner 1980).

The source of entrepreneurship, for Kirzner, is alertness to opportunity and the imagination and vision to capitalize on it. Alertness, he argues, requires certain personal qualities, including a restive temperament, the thirst for adventure, ambition and imagination. Human beings, after all, tend to notice that which it is in their interest to notice. They notice 'opportunities', rather than mere 'situations', 'concatenations of events, realised or prospective, which offer the possibility of *pure gain*'. Human interests, on which they may hope to capitalize, include fame, power, prestige, or even the opportunity to serve a cause or to help others (Kirzner 1980: 16).

One important implication of all this is that 'alertness' is nurtured (or suppressed) by the institutions created by society through the state. Entrepreneurship, in the Austrian view, leads men and women with initiative, drive and impulse to take risks with their money, their repute and their livelihood in wrestling with competitors, bargaining with suppliers and in anticipating the wants of consumers. The IEA's former Editorial Director has argued that entrepreneurship may explain why some societies have high rates of economic growth and others not, why some countries are rich and others poor, and why systems creating the widest opportunities for entrepreneurial activity are always and everywhere richer than those that suppress it (Seldon 1980b: xi).

The key Austrian insight into competition is that different people know different things. The market process gathers and transmits these discrete (and often contradictory) pieces of information, thereby co-ordinating the actions and plans of market actors. The very existence of unexploited profit opportunities which are then seized by entrepreneurs indicates that previous plans were somewhere not co-ordinated. By drawing attention to, and remedying this lack of co-ordination, competition is said to operate as an equilibrium force. Entrepreneurial alertness to hitherto unforeseen opportunities for profit leads to a revision of plans on the part of market actors and so to new discoveries and co-ordination.

All of which brings us to the Austrian view of the appropriate role of government. Austrian economists, as we have seen, are deeply sceptical of 'welfare' economics. In particular, where welfare economists prescribe interventionist policies for dealing with instances of 'market failure', Austrians doubt whether government can, in fact, improve upon the market and so question both the feasibility and desirability of a 'mixed' (or regulated market) economy. Specifically, there appear to be three main reservations.

The first is that Austrian economists cannot accept the implied description of how the market mechanism operates. Welfare economics barely even refers to uncertainty or mistakes and sees competition as a state of equilibrium with 'given' commodities and techniques, rather than as a dynamic process of searching for new commodities and better techniques. Secondly, Austrians find no detailed explanation in welfare economics of how government is supposed to obtain the information needed to carry out the tasks assigned to it. The knowledge required for an assessment of this kind, they argue, is not to be found in any one place, but is dispersed throughout the many members of the economy. Again, the relevant knowledge does not, for the most part, refer to facts about the past, but to preferences and opportunities in the future, which exist only in people's minds and are therefore highly subjective (Littlechild 1986: 42).

Thirdly, Austrian economists point out, institutions for solving social problems may in principle be of two kinds, either pragmatic (reflecting conscious design) or organic (arising spontaneously and unintentionally). In the Austrian view, it is essential to choose an appropriate pragmatic framework of regulations and government policies within which organic processes can operate. On this point, Austrian economists claim that welfare economics fails sufficiently to appreciate the nature, resilience and power of organic processes and tends to see the solution as *necessarily* pragmatic, and as requiring government to exercise conscious control. In fact, Austrians argue, there is no reason whatsoever to suppose that pragmatic institutions can or will improve upon organic processes.

Austrian economics takes as its starting point the behaviour of individual human beings with incomplete knowledge, who not only have to economise in the situation in which they find themselves, but also to be alert to new opportunities 'just around the corner' (Littlechild 1986: 75). Entrepreneurial alertness leads to the revision of plans and forms the basis of the competitive process (the element which, in many ways, epitomises the Austrian approach in economic theory). Whereas 'mainstream' economics approaches the role of government by identifying as 'market failures' situations in which 'perfect competition' is impossible, Austrian economists argue that the alleged 'failure' of markets is often due to a lack of information and that interventionist approaches cannot hope to perform any better. In the Austrian view, a more effective way of achieving the goal of an efficient, responsive and increasingly wealthy economy is to promote the competitive process by removing (government-imposed) barriers to entry and strengthening the system of private property rights (Littlechild 1986: 76).

A final argument concerns the pursuit of what Hayek (1976) refers to as the 'mirage' of social justice. As Gamble (1986) notes, Austrian economists have set out to challenge many of the assumptions of 'statism' in general and of socialism in particular. In the Austrian view, the demand for social justice raises two questions. First, does the idea of 'social justice' have any meaning, and secondly, is it possible to preserve a market economy while extending the practice whereby the needs and remuneration of different groups is decided not by the market, but by the state? (Shand 1984: 212).

For Hayek at least, the answer to both questions is 'no'. He strenuously denies that the term 'social justice' has any clear and precise meaning. According to Hayek, whenever someone complains that there is 'injustice' in the existing distribution of goods and services in a market economy, this has two implications. The first is that some group or individual is to *blame*, while the second is that an agreed *standard* of need or desert on which to base policy is available to policy-makers.

As to the first implication, Hayek denies that market outcomes are the consequence of intentional behaviour on the part of some group or individual. Instead, he argues, they are the result of a process 'the effect of which on particular people was neither intended nor foreseen by anyone' (Hayek 1976: 64). Hence, market processes 'can neither be just nor unjust, because the results are not intended or foreseen, and depend on a multitude of circumstances not known in their totality to anybody' (Hayek 1976: 70). As to the second implication, Hayek argues that there is no agreed standard of need or desert to inform policy in respect of 'social justice', since each and every member of society will have a different view as to who deserves what and on what basis (King 1987: 41). In short, moral agreement over the issues of need or desert is *necessarily* incomplete and ultimately elusive in pluralistic societies (Gray 1984).

Thus for Hayek, and for Austrian economists generally, 'social justice' is both misleading and potentially dangerous in the threat it poses to individual liberty. It also misunderstands the nature of the market economy and the extent to which market outcomes cannot be the object of policy. In the Austrian view, the market system is a spontaneous and poorly understood process, but is the primary basis of wealth generation and progress (King 1987: 44-5). The sheer complexity of the market order, and our necessarily limited capacity to know the causes and consequences of human action, suggest that no government (however well-intentioned) ever has sufficient knowledge to be able to 'plan' to secure any particular set of economic outcomes (Shand 1984: 10).

Whether the aim is to secure economic efficiency or 'social justice', then, Austrian economists claim that the state literally cannot (and therefore does not) 'know what it is doing' and deny that government intervention can improve upon the market. In the Austrian view, the state should of necessity concern itself merely with attending to (and regularly refurbishing) the legal and institutional framework within which market processes operate. Eliminating (state-imposed) barriers to entry and strengthening the system of private property rights are seen by Austrians as the appropriate (because technically feasible and morally legitimate) concern of the state (Littlechild 1986: 76).

The Virginia School

The IEA has also brought to the attention of a wider British audience the ideas of the Virginia school of public choice, a school which has been primarily concerned with the application and extension of economic theory into the realm of political and governmental choices (Buchanan *et al* 1978). Its main protagonists have been Buchanan and Tullock, whose writings have challenged the view that government or collective choice is the outcome of a disinterested group of public servants (Kavanagh 1990: 82). In particular, public choice theory has challenged the romantic view that government seeks only to do good and that it can, in fact, accomplish most of what it sets out to do (Buchanan *et al* 1978).

According to public choice theorists, governments, budgets and bureaucracies grow in large part because of the ambitions of the people concerned. Government decisions are usually the combined outcome of vote-seeking politicians, powerful and well-organized interest groups and expansionist bureaucrats. This theory of the political process, of how the role of government as employer, spender and taxer grows, is broadly in line with 'right-wing preferences for reducing the role of government and promoting the free market' (Kavanagh 1990: 82).

The American political scientist William Mitchell has identified six main innovations of public choice theory to the study of government and the teaching of political science. First, it has contributed new and more firmly-based understandings of the everyday workings of political institutions. Public choice may be summarized as the discovery or re-discovery that individual human beings should be treated as 'rational utility-maximizers' in every aspect of their behaviour (Buchanan 1978: 17). In Britain, it has been suggested, many institutions - and in particular those of the 'welfare state' - owe their existence to a very different attitude, which has tended to 'glorify' the motives of politicians and officials (Green in Mitchell 1988: 55).

A second innovation of public choice, according to Mitchell, is that it offers more systematic and formal explanations of interest groups and their search for political privileges. The term 'rent-seeking' is used to define the political activity of those who devote scarce resources to the pursuit of a degree of monopoly rights granted by government (Mitchell 1988: 23). Public choice theorists argue that organized lobbying is costly and time-consuming and therefore not worthwhile for small gains, but very cheap if the gains are substantial. This is said to explain why interest groups organize to achieve special privileges, while the dispersed mass of consumers, who lose out bit by bit, do not find it worthwhile to do so. The imbalance in the rewards to vested interests compared with consumers would suggest that the results of the depredations of interest groups have to be very bad before there is sufficient public dissatisfaction for politicians to judge it worthwhile to act (Mitchell 1988: 55-6).

A third innovation of public choice has been its discovery of an alleged 'political-business cycle'. Given that politicians are 'vote-maximizers' confronted with business fluctuations, public choice theorists predict that politicians will make 'ample and efficient use of their political power to manipulate the business cycle in their interest' (Mitchell 1988: 28). The theory is, then, that governments will cut taxes or create a boom before elections in the hope of increasing their share of the popular vote. Alternatively, governments may try to get unpalatable measures out of the way long before polling day itself (Green 1988: 57).

Fourthly, Mitchell argues, public choice has put forward new and more powerful theories to explain the growth of government. According to public choice theorists, government has an *inherent* tendency to expand. One theory has been that permanent officials seek to maximize their departmental budget, attributing to officials a 'profit motive'. Public choice has attributed a 'vote motive' to politicians and a 'budget-maximization motive' to officials (Tullock 1976). These analogies may give only a crude insight into the conduct of politicians and officials, but certainly debunk claims that public servants and politicians are single-mindedly dedicated to the public weal (Green 1988: 58).

A fifth innovation of public choice has been its anatomy of 'government failure', analogous to theories of 'market failure' in welfare economics. Public choice theorists question whether our faith in democratic political institutions is justified. They approve of democracy as a device for removing governments without resort to violence, but question whether existing Western political institutions are capable of reflecting voters' preferences accurately on all the issues currently under the control of the state. According to David Green, the ineptitude of the political process can be seen in the record of Britain's state-run education and health services (see later). The National Health Service, he argues, is 'chronically underfunded' because successive governments have set out to finance it almost exclusively from tax revenues. For as long as services are free at the point of use and financed out of general taxation, Green argues, expectations are always likely to outpace the resources government has at its disposal (Green 1988: 59).

A final innovation has been the new subject of 'constitutional economics'. Public choice theorists have advocated a variety of institutional and constitutional reforms designed to change incentives, costs and benefits and the means for making government's responsibilities towards the citizen more nearly commensurate with the incidence of political power. These include sunset laws (which specify a date of review and possible termination for a government policy), item vetoes, demand revelation (whereby citizens make known their demands for government services) and a balanced budget rule, or similar macro-economic controls on government spending (Mitchell 1988).

The thrust of the IEA's research programme has been that 'the market alternative works', while the gist of the research programme in public choice theory has been that 'the governmental-political alternative does not'. Research in public choice concentrates on how government functions and finds that government is inherently inferior to the market. The normative implications of this are twofold: first, to shift much of what is now government activity to the market, and secondly, to change the structure of government in order to improve its efficiency. The two research programmes seem therefore to converge at the level of what should be done (Buchanan and Tullock 1981: 83).

There is, however, an important difference in that public choice is more concerned with the second of these normative implications than with the first, and aims its message at the institutional structure through which policies are made and changed. Public choice, in its normative dress, suggests that mere shifts in policy are likely to be temporary, and that effective reform lies only in the modification of the rules that allow legislatures to enact policy. This involves 'much more than the limited claim that enlightened politicians should not enact legislation involving detailed interference with the workings of markets'

(Buchanan and Tullock 1981: 84). In short, public choice is, at base, a reaction to the seemingly pervasive neglect by economists and political scientists of the political-governmental institutions through which any policy (micro or macro) must be implemented (Buchanan and Tullock 1981: 90).

The IEA, then, has drawn on the work of various schools of liberal economic thought in order to challenge the 'Keynesian welfare state consensus' of the immediate post-war years. As Gamble (1986) has argued, the main propositions of New Right economics are as follows:

- *'Intervention doesn't work'*: The Chicago school of economists has emphasized the empirical evidence that 'proves' the market (non-interventionist) solution to be the one that 'works' in (almost) every case.

- *'All alternatives to markets are deeply flawed'*: The Austrian school of economists has argued that, for markets to function as a 'discovery process', they must be as decentralized as possible.

- *'Government failure is more prevalent than market failure'*: The Virginia school of public choice has argued that debates on public policy have for too long contrasted the 'failure' of market institutions with the (supposed) 'omniscience' of the state.

That said, the question this chapter will now turn to consider is this. Given its distinctive approach and its rationale of seeking to influence the 'climate of opinion', how does the IEA perceive the fundamental relationship between the evolution and dissemination of ideas, on the one hand, and policy and events, on the other?

'Politically Impossible ...?'

As its former Editorial Director has recalled, the IEA has often been asked to show how the policies emerging from its authors' analyses might be put into practice, and why some of their analyses seem to have influenced thinking in business and government, while others appear to have been ignored. His response to this is as follows. First, there is, and should be a division of labour between the economist who analyzes, the politician who judges and the administrator who implements. Secondly, the economist is not equipped, and has no authority, to judge which of his (or her) conclusions are 'politically practicable' or 'administratively feasible'. Thirdly, economists 'risk pre-judging the relevance or efficacy' of their prescriptions and, worse, avoid pursuing their analyses if they allow themselves to be influenced by consideration of what is 'politically possible' (or 'administratively practicable'). For these reasons, he argues, the IEA has 'no intention of venturing beyond severe economic analysis into judgments on political acceptability or administrative feasibility. Its constitution as a charitable trust would in any case preclude it from such a close concern with public policy' (Seldon in Hutt 1971: vii).

An intimate concern with public policy is not, then, the IEA's paramount consideration. Advice from economists to politicians 'diluted' by political (or administrative) considerations is seen as 'second-best' to the (undiluted) 'best that economics can teach' (Seldon in Hutt 1971: ix). As Seldon recalls, authors commissioned to write for the IEA were instructed to apply economic analysis 'ruthlessly, with recognition of current conditions, but without regard for "administrative practicability", because that could not be ascertained except by practical trial, or for "political impossibility", because that could be a pretext developed by politicians or bureaucrats who resisted reform that did not suit them, however good the argument, and in any event because reasoned ideas could themselves make the "impossible" possible' (Seldon 1981a: xix-xx).

As Culyer (1981: 115) has argued, the IEA has taken 'the long rather than the short view of policy-relevance'. Its hallmark is 'the thinking through of a policy issue in specific publications and, by a cumulation, the exposition of a general mode of thinking applicable to a wide range of policy issues' (Culyer 1981: 115). For Culyer at least, although authors published by the IEA may in some cases have had a short-term impact on contemporary policy issues, its main audience is not so much people with day-to-day policy-making responsibilities as those who help to frame the context in which policy-making takes place, or 'those who teach and are taught and those whose opinions "count" - the politically aware intelligentsia' (Culyer 1981: 117).

The Emerging Consensus ...?

As Bradley (1981: 186) has argued, the IEA was the first institution seriously to question the ruling Keynesian, Beveridgite, Fabian intellectual consensus in post-war Britain. For virtually the whole of its first two decades of existence, however, its impact on practical policy-making was negligible. In fact, just about the only major piece of legislation to follow a paper published by the IEA was the abolition of Resale Price Maintenance in 1964, and there were 'long-standing administrative and departmental reasons for that decision' (Bradley 1981: 187;

Lawson and Bruce-Gardyne 1976). The only other governmental decision which was *conceivably* 'influenced' by the IEA was that taken by the 1970 Conservative administration to introduce competition into banking and break up the cartel (Bradley 1981: 187).

Moreover, Bradley argues, in its wider role of influencing the climate of political and economic opinion, the IEA made slow progress in its early years, although leading figures from both the Labour and Conservative parties were beginning to show an interest in its publications and seminars by the mid to late 1960s (Bradley 1981: 187). As Cowling has argued, the IEA was 'marginal' during the Macmillan years. 'Though conscious of a change in economic assumptions in the Conservative Party after the general election of 1964, it felt little confidence in Mr Heath's economic conversion, was depressed by his policies after 1972 and did not begin to feel central until Lord Joseph's second conversion in 1974 and the International Monetary Fund's judgment on the economic events of the 1970s, seemed to prove that what it had been saying was true' (Cowling 1990: xxii). As Bradley (1981: 187) has argued, it was the sudden (and uncharacteristic) espousal of ideology by leading Conservatives, signalled by the creation of the Centre for Policy Studies (CPS) in 1974 and by the circulation, two years later, by Sir Keith (later Lord) Joseph of a 'bibliography of freedom' throughout the universities and colleges which included several IEA publications that put the principles of free market economics and individualism firmly back on the *political* agenda.

2 The Adam Smith Institute

Introduction

The Adam Smith Institute (ASI) was established in 1977 to develop free-market policies. The Institute's task, according to its charter, is to further 'the advancement of learning by research and public policy options, economic and political science, and the publication of such research' (cited by Kavanagh 1990: 87). The Institute is run, for the most part, by its President, Madsen Pirie, and fellow St Andrews University graduate, Eamonn Butler. This St Andrews connection is important in that it links the ASI to a number of Conservative Members of Parliament, including Christopher Chope, Michael Fallon, Michael Forsyth and Robert Jones, each of whom has written for the Institute. These MPs also form a core element within the No Turning Back group - a group of younger, right-wing Conservative MPs dedicated to the cause of 'renewing the energy of radical Tory ideas and keeping the government up to the ideological mark' (Oakley 1989).

The distinguishing features of the ASI's work are its close concern with policy implementation (see later), its preference for market solutions in public policy and the wide range of its proposals. Specifically, it has produced a number of studies on quangos, providing an extensive listing of such bodies, their budgets and terms of reference and monitoring the present government's record in abolishing them. It has also promoted policies of privatization, deregulation and the contracting-out of local authority services (Kavanagh 1990: 87). Privatization, Pirie argues, derives from a recognition that the weaknesses of public sector supply are *inherent*. Only the private sector, he argues, can impose the economic disciplines and create the incentives required to ensure that the output (supply) of goods and services is sensitive and responsive to the demands of individual consumers (Pirie 1988b: 52-3). The ASI has therefore been particularly active in promoting privatization across a wide range of services, including the nationalized industries, pensions and local authority services (Kavanagh 1990: 87).

Ideas and Events

The ASI, then, is primarily concerned with the creation and successful implementation of free-market policies - the research, in other words, of innovative ideas which it then presents as 'realistic and practical options' to decision-makers (ASI 1990). In considering next the ASI's distinctive approach, it will be necessary to explore in some detail the question of the relationship between economic theory, on the one hand, and political practice, on the other. As will shortly become apparent, the ASI has attempted to reconcile theory (ideas) and practice (events) in a particular, and quite distinctive, way.

In an intriguing discussion of this question, Pirie (1988a) begins by recalling that a Conservative administration led by Edward Heath was elected in 1970 on a broadly similar 'mandate' to that on which Margaret Thatcher's first administration came to power in 1979. Heath, he recalls, was elected nine years before Thatcher to 'curb big government and promote free enterprise'. But whereas the Heath government 'failed' to enact the various pledges contained in its manifesto, the Thatcher government after 1979 managed to implement substantial parts of its programme. The key question, of course, is *why* this was so.

Before attempting to answer this question, Pirie begins by eliminating several other theories (explanations) which have been advanced by various people at various times. He rejects, for example, the accusations of 'duplicity' which have been levelled at the Heath administration. The suggestion that the Heath government never actually believed in the ideas on which it was elected is, he argues, utterly implausible. The Heath government, after all, did attempt (initially at least) to enact some of its free-market programmes. Only later in its term of office did the government renege on its Selsdon manifesto and embark on a series of 'U-turns' (Pirie 1988a: 42).

Again, Pirie argues, the fact that the Heath administration started out on one set of policies and only subsequently changed to another also discredits the theory that Heath himself was, at heart, a member of the governing class and shared its values and preconceptions and so was 'determined... to keep to the kind of politics which was understood by the business and financial community' and with which his government felt comfortable. If so, he argues, then surely the time to reassure business and financial leaders was at the outset of Heath's term of office? (Pirie 1988a: 42-3).

Allegations that Heath lacked 'toughness', Pirie argues, are also completely untrue. In fact, Heath showed at the time (and has shown since) 'a strength of will and a determination which characterize a reluctance to give way on anything'. Two further theories, for Pirie, are also implausible. The first is that the Heath government soon discovered that some of what it had promised in opposition just could not be done and concluded that it was simply unrealistic in modern times to think in terms of 'less government'. This explanation, Pirie argues, was the most plausible (and perhaps the most widely believed) until, that is, the advent of the Thatcher administration showed that it was possible, after all, to enact major parts of a free-market programme (Pirie 1988a: 43-4).

A more complex and sophisticated version of this latter theory is that, while the battle of ideas had been won, it had not been won in the right places. The suggestion here is that, even with a popular mandate, the Heath government was 'unable to fly in the face of what appeared to be virtually all informed opinion'. The battle of ideas, on this view, had to be won *there* before success would come. Despite the merits of this theory, Pirie argues, it ultimately collapses because the 'battle of ideas' had *still* not been won among the intellectual classes by the time of the 1979 General Election (Pirie 1988a: 44-5).

For Pirie at least, the failure of Heath and the success of Thatcher in enacting their respective free-market programmes is ultimately explicable in terms of policy technique. The Thatcher government, he argues, was 'concerned to have a battery of policy techniques ... which showed acute sensitivity to that which is politically acceptable' (Pirie 1988a: 51). If so, the question nevertheless remains as to why the earlier (Heath) government should have been so seriously 'deficient' in policy-making technique. According to Pirie, the reason is that opinion in the early 1970s 'lacked a coherent theory of policy application, and thought that the task of political leaders was simply to implement ideas'. It was only after the fall of the Heath government, he argues, that some economic liberals came to understand that without detailed policies to give effect to them in a way which succeeds, ideas 'may change our thinking, but they will not change the world' (Pirie 1988a: 52).

In particular, Pirie argues, the 1970s saw the emergence on both sides of the Atlantic of policy research institutes whose function became not merely the advocacy of free enterprise, but 'the investigation and preparation of the detailed policies which might secure it in practice throughout the different areas of government'. These new 'think-tanks', he argues, were an important difference between the situation of the 1960s and that of the 1970s (Pirie 1988a: 65):

> The new institutes took as their starting point the failure of the nominally free enterprise governments of the early 1970s to put market-oriented ideas into practice. They learned how the political system worked, and how to solve the problems it posed to would-be legislators. They researched ways in which choice and enterprise

might be extended in practice, as well as advocated in theory. They gave policy-makers what they were looking for: *policies*.

The Public Sector

Since 1977, then, the ASI's primary concern has been with policy innovation, policy technique and policy implementation. In this connection, the Institute has developed a new style of policy formulation known as *micropolitics* - the 'creative counterpart' of public choice theory, or the economics of politics (EP). As we saw in Chapter 1, public choice is not, first and foremost, a theory of economics, but of *politics*; it applies economic ideas to political behaviour, and shows how certain economic principles can be used to explain and interpret behaviour in the political 'realm' (Pirie 1988a: 70).

Public choice theory, for Pirie at least, is particularly effective in explaining certain aspects of the public sector which would be difficult to understand or explain using any of the conventional models of politics. Public choice, for Pirie, explains, for example, the public sector's tendency to oversupply goods and services. For Pirie, in particular, people tend to consume more goods or services when paying for them collectively than when they pay individually.

The reason for this, Pirie argues, is that when individuals pay directly for goods and services, they have to decide how best to allocate their limited resources, and must therefore limit their demands. In the public sector, on the other hand, there are no such restraints and demand is therefore (at least, potentially) infinite. In particular, Pirie suggests, restraints on demand are less effective in the public sector of the economy for two reasons: first, because restraints are felt less strongly; and secondly, because they are less visibly connected to supply or output. For Pirie at least, public choice explains why it is that the public sector tends to misallocate (oversupply) goods and services. In particular, Pirie argues, public goods and services are supplied in greater quantities than individuals would have chosen - whether or not the goods and services thus supplied are higher in quality or even responsive to the needs and demands of consumers (Pirie 1988a: 84).

For Pirie, however, it is not only consumers who perceive benefit in the oversupply of public goods and services. Those who administer the production of public goods and services, he argues, acquire additional status and responsibilities as that service expands; those employed in the public sector also gain opportunities for promotion and increased earnings as demand increases; legislators themselves gain the support of the groups whose services are overproduced, without at the same time losing the support of the taxpayers who foot the bill. The result, he argues, is 'a massive, one-sided support *for* additional service, with scarcely any effective pressure *against*' (Pirie 1988a: 85).

Moreover, Pirie argues, the service itself, although produced at greater levels than would be chosen or supported by individual consumers in private markets, is by no means responsive to their demands and needs. Instead, he writes, output (supply) 'responds instead to the pressures of the political process'. In a private market, Pirie argues, consumers can limit the quantity of goods or services purchased by 'deciding to spend resources elsewhere'. He or she selects or rejects the goods and services which meet, or fail to meet, his or her requirements. As a result of this process, Pirie argues, producers of goods and services who fail to meet consumer preferences risk bankruptcy (Pirie 1988a: 85).

For Pirie, however, the public sector is subject to entirely different pressures. In the public sector, the consumer cannot limit the quantity of goods and services supplied or the amount paid for them. Moreover, he writes, consumers of public goods and services have no choice but to pay for them because the funding for the most part comes from taxation. In addition, he argues, consumers of public goods or services have no effective alternative source of supply, for two reasons: firstly, because the public sector is often characteristically monopolistic; and secondly, because - having been forced to pay in taxes for the supply of public goods and services - very few can afford to pay again for a private supply (Pirie 1988a: 85).

For Pirie at least, what this means is that consumers have no opportunity to make economic in-puts into the public sector and thus have little impact on public goods and services (Pirie 1988a: 85-6). Consumers of 'public' goods and services *do* have periodic *political* in-puts into the public sector, but these form part of a very large package of measures in which spending on any particular item of service is very small indeed. The political system, Pirie argues, favours overproduction, not consumer responsiveness. The producers of public services, on the other hand, exert very considerable influence. In particular, he argues, those engaged in administering the service at management level, as well as those directly employed in its production, 'have a direct stake in the type of service which is produced' (Pirie 1988a: 86).

In addition, Pirie argues, the bureaucracy of a public service has an interest in running services in ways which are convenient to administer and which 'maximize career opportunities among the administrative and managerial class'. The bureaucracy also 'has the power to impede, to delay and to thwart changes which would adversely affect its own status and position'. The workforce of a public service, for Pirie, has an interest in minimizing effort and discomfort, while maximizing job security and reward and 'can interrupt, or threaten to interrupt, the service and bring public protest down upon elected leaders' (Pirie 1988a: 86).

The result, for Pirie at least, is that public services are 'captured' by the producers. Over a period of time, he argues, public goods and services show an increasing tendency to 'meet the needs of the producers rather than those of the consumers' (Pirie 1988a: 86). The producers, for Pirie at least, have 'real power' within the system; consumers, on the other hand, do not. The producers of public services, he argues, 'have more influence to trade' than does the individual consumer. For Pirie at least, the phenomenon known as 'producer capture' is 'explicable, indeed predictable' in terms of public choice theory. In particular, he argues (Pirie 1988a: 87):

> Throughout the public sector, the tendency is for the convenience and needs of the producers to take priority over those of the consumers. None of this is immediate. It is a pattern which builds up over the years as the pressures are exerted and the results of them emerge.

Public choice, for Pirie, is also particularly effective in accounting for the behaviour of the bureaucracy. Traditional models of politics, he argues, have long seen the bureaucracy as an 'instrument of government, which itself reflects popular will within certain limits'. On this basis, he argues, a picture has emerged of 'the dedicated and dispassionate Civil Service whose function is to put into effect the policies determined by their political masters' (Pirie 1988a: 93).

For Pirie, however, whilst it may be true that civil servants are indeed 'dedicated' and form 'an essential and valuable part of the machinery of government', public choice regards them not as 'machines', but as people motivated by aims and aspirations similar to those which motivate other people. In public choice theory, Pirie argues, civil servants are treated as 'a distinct minority group with assets of value to trade in political markets' (Pirie 1988a: 93). By treating civil servants as tending, for the most part, to operate like private businessmen who seek (always and everywhere) to maximize their own advantage, a much more detailed picture of their response to given situations and an altogether more comprehensible account of their behaviour is revealed (Pirie 1988a: 93-4).

In the public bureaucracy, Pirie argues, reward comes partly from seniority, partly from responsibility. It is thus in the personal (career) interest of bureaucrats to extend, as far as possible, personal 'status' and responsibility. It is, on the other hand, against the interests of the public bureaucracy to preside over a reduction in the size of any or all bureaux, if no compensating advantages are offered in return to offset the reduction of responsibility which this implies. According to Pirie, if no such advantages are offered, public choice would predict that departments will suggest 'new' areas of activity, calling for expansion of both budgets and personnel (Pirie 1988a: 94).

It is also, for Pirie at least, very much in the interest of senior civil servants to 'add new programmes to their field of responsibility and ... to compete with other departments to be the one selected to do so' (Pirie 1988a: 94). This, he argues, is the origin of the process known as 'empire building' within the Civil Service - a process in which senior civil servants act to expand their own areas of activity, the size of the staff under them and the salary scale open to them; this process, for Pirie at least, parallels that in the private sector, in which senior executives in a private corporation compete with each other for influence and status within the firm, each seeking to have 'as large a number as possible responsible to them and dependent on them' (Pirie 1988a: 94-5).

For Pirie at least, the behaviour of the public bureaucracy often mirrors the situation in which senior executives in the private sector 'move into new areas and ... suggest moving into new markets, led by their own section of the company'. It may be true that civil servants are 'dispassionate and dedicated', but a more accurate explanation of how they behave is 'generated by the assumption that they behave like businessmen, bidding and trading in a political market instead of an economic one' (Pirie 1988a: 95).

Public choice theory, then, for Pirie at least, has introduced a key 'difference' into the analysis of the behaviour of civil servants and the public bureaucracy, in that it 'deals with the bureaucracy as an interest group and takes into account their own motivations' (Pirie 1988a: 95). Instead of treating bureaucrats and officials as the traditional view has tended to do - as referees, standing outside to administer the rules in a fair and unbiased way - public choice treats them instead as players *in* the game, as 'yet another group dealing and trading in political markets'. Public choice, for Pirie, recognizes the bureaucracy's interest as *participants,* as well as their role as administrators.

For Pirie, however, public choice does more than merely offer explanations of certain features of the public sector (its lack of cost-effectiveness and inefficiency) and of the behavioural tendencies of the bureaucracy (such as the empire building that goes on within departments, the struggle between departments to take on areas of responsibility and constant pressures towards the expansion of the state sector). Public choice also sets out 'a detailed and clearly woven pattern of explanation which tells us how and why that system has been able to resist so many of the attempts to reform or to improve it' (Pirie 1988a: 98).

According to Pirie, before the public choice type of analysis was put forward, it had long been assumed that the problems within the public sector and the bureaucracy which administers it were accidental - rather than essential -

features of the public sector. It had long been assumed, he argues, that the adverse features of the public sector were contingent activities which could be eliminated (rather than *inherent* defects of the public sector itself) and that these could be corrected by introducing appropriate measures (Pirie 1988a: 100).

So, for example: If the public sector was 'overmanned', the suggestion was that manpower levels 'should be trimmed'. If the public sector used antiquated and dilapidated equipment, then the public sector 'should be re-equipped with new material'. If the public sector was inefficient and lacking in cost-effectiveness, then new management practices would be brought in to improve it. Finally, if the public sector was unresponsive to the needs and requirements of consumers, then some mechanism should be put in place which would bring these to the attention of management so that changes could be made accordingly. The assumption was always that, if there were faults within the public sector, these could be corrected by the introduction of remedial measures (Pirie 1988a: 100).

According to Pirie, the same was also assumed to be the case with the public bureaucracy. Here too, he argues, it had long been assumed that, once the adverse practices were correctly identified, it was simply a question of introducing remedial measures. If the public bureaucracy tended to be larger than that sustained by equivalent private sector operations, then the suggestion was that it should be 'cut down to size'; if it generated an excessive amount of paperwork and duplication, 'new systems should be established which would make much of it no longer necessary'; if bureaucrats were inclined to build empires, then 'circumstances should be established in which they could no longer do so'. Finally, if departments were always pushing out to extend the range of their responsibility, then 'measures should be adopted to limit it'. Here too, Pirie argues, it was assumed that what was wrong could soon be put right (Pirie 1988a: 100-1).

If so, then, for Pirie at least, 'one would have expected the public sector to be very much better than it is'; after all, he argues, the defects of the public sector and of the bureaucracy 'have been known about for some time'. The key question, then, for Pirie, is why - after being studied and known about for so long, and with appropriate remedies suggested - these 'adverse practices' are still a feature of the public sector. The answer, for Pirie at least, is that the remedies 'failed'. Although, he writes, the remedies were 'tailor-made to remove specific defects', they did not succeed in doing so when they were implemented (Pirie 1988a: 101).

If so, then the key question, for Pirie at least, is why the remedies failed. The reasons, he claims, are in themselves highly instructive. Pirie notes, for example, the problem of 'overmanning' in the public sector, arguing that attempts to reduce manning levels meet with more resistance than they encounter in the private sector. In the private sector, Pirie argues, there is an ultimate threat of closure. There are, he suggests, 'limits beyond which the workers *cannot* push without losing everything'. Private companies, Pirie argues, 'must be competitive' and so cut manning levels from time to time. The cuts, for Pirie, are initially opposed, but eventually accepted after some negotiation concerning conditions, since they are in the *interests* of the workforce as well as management (Pirie 1988a: 101).

Yet, for Pirie, none of this is true of the public sector. In that sector, he argues, there is not normally a risk of closure or bankruptcy; nor is there a need to be competitive; nor is it in the interest of either workers or management to acquiesce in cuts in manning levels. Those who work in the public sector, after all, 'value the security of a job in the public sector', especially when it is accompanied by fringe benefits more generous than the private sector could afford, including perhaps index-linked pensions (Pirie 1988a: 101-2).

For Pirie, then, it is not in the interest of workers in the public sector to accept job cuts. Union leaders, he argues, lose unless they keep manning levels, and potential membership, to a maximum. In addition, he argues, managers in the public sector, normally paid on the basis of responsibility, lose if they end up in charge of a smaller operation. Moreover, Pirie argues, workers, trade union leaders and managers can 'thwart' any attempt to impose job cuts. They control the service, have access to the media via protest and demonstration and access to the general public and thus to legislators via strike action or the threat of it (Pirie 1988a: 102). For Pirie at least, the level of resistance encountered in practice to job cuts is often such that much has to be endured to achieve very little. Legislators, he argues, 'soon learn that the costs in political terms exceed the gains in economic terms' (Pirie 1988a: 102).

The same is true, for Pirie at least, of the various attempts which have been made to reform the bureaucracy. Given that the procedures of the Civil Service are more complex and cumbersome than those of private industry, Pirie argues, it has long been suggested that the solution is to study the practices of the private sector and introduce them into the public bureaucracy. In many advanced economies, Pirie argues, public sector administration has been subject to detailed and repeated study of its operations; experts from the private sector have been called in to carry out management efficient studies; time and motion specialists have been brought in to investigate the practices and procedures. Recommendations have been made, as have declarations of intent.

Yet the result, for Pirie, is that the practices continue, 'perhaps with some token and temporary improvement in some areas'. At the end of all this activity, he writes, there is *still* a public bureaucracy which engages in empire building, expands its operations and extends its areas of responsibility. Reform of the Civil Service, he argues, is 'a tide which washes backwards and forwards, but the rocks are still there each time the tide recedes' (Pirie 1988a: 105).

The question remains, however, as to why this is so. In this connection, Pirie argues, the fundamental error of all previous attempts to reform the public sector and the public bureaucracy has been to assume that the public sector is ultimately *capable* of behaving like the private sector (Pirie 1988a: 105). For Pirie at least, there is no reason to suppose that the public sector *can* behave like its private counterpart, since it is a totally different kind of animal. The public sector, he argues, is subject to pressures which are totally different from the ones that bear on the private sector, and so behaves in a different way (Pirie 1988a: 105).

For Pirie at least, it may well be - as public choice theory would suggest - that the 'motivating forces' within the public and private sectors are essentially the same, namely: people's ordinary aims and aspirations; their desire to 'maximize their advantage' and improve their position in life; their conditions of work and the rewards which accrue to them. At the same time, he argues, the rules and conditions which prevail in the two sectors are so different that these same motivations *inevitably* produce different outcomes (Pirie 1988a: 106).

The public sector, then, for Pirie, is structurally different to its private counterpart, and so produces a different outcome. The public sector, he argues, behaves as it does not because of any accidental feature which has crept in by chance during its growth, but because of *inherent* structural aspects of it. The public sector's supply of goods and services, he continues, is less cost-effective than private industry can achieve, because the public sector does not *have* to be efficient. The pressures leading towards efficiency are also - for Pirie at least - weak in the public sector compared with those which lead towards 'overmanning and the adoption of restrictive practices' (Pirie 1988a: 107).

All previous attempts to improve the public sector and remove certain of its adverse features have thus been misconceived, in assuming that the public sector defects are accidental ones and are susceptible to removal. For Pirie, in particular, the major disadvantages of the public sector, as compared with its private counterpart, are necessary, rather than accidental; they are, in short, an 'inevitable consequence of the way the public sector is set up and of the way in which it operates' (Pirie 1988a: 108).

For Pirie at least, the same is true of the public bureaucracy. Public administration, he argues, 'does not operate like private management, nor does it achieve its levels of efficiency', since it does not have to:

Public administration faces none of the penalties which fall upon inefficiency in the private sector, and faces instead pressures which lead to expansion of staff and extension of function. The top executives of private firms might similarly compete for influence and try to expand their own areas of influence. The difference is that in the private sector there is the ultimate test of the market. If it results in better sales or greater savings or a more competitive company, it may last. Otherwise the pressures will take it out. There is no equivalent test by which to measure success in the Civil Service.

Pirie goes on to give a purely hypothetical example of the way the public bureaucracy, using certain techniques and practices, can 'thwart attempts to make the state sector behave more like private industry'. The case, he argues, might be one in which the study of government reveals that opportunities exist to make savings - to achieve, that is to say, the same output or better, while 'cutting back on the inputs' (Pirie 1988a: 109).

For Pirie at least, when a political decision is made to seek major economies, this 'signals the start of in-fighting between the various departments as each one struggles to make sure that the cuts are imposed elsewhere'. With each department fighting to maintain or increase its budget, the pressures collectively brought to bear on government 'militate against major savings'. In the first place, Pirie argues, the top bureaucrats in each department produce projections showing the 'dire consequences' which will follow from major budget cuts. Ministers, in turn, fight within the Cabinet for *their* departmental budget, using briefs prepared by their civil servants. The bureaucrats are perfectly aware that it is not in their interest to have less spending within their section or on their overall departmental budget (Pirie 1988a: 110).

For Pirie at least, 'two methods have been tried in an attempt to overcome the pressures which lead each section and department to seek to maintain its own appropriation and make the cuts fall elsewhere'. The first of these has been the device of 'imposing cuts equally across the board and requiring, for example, that every department reduce its spending by perhaps 5%'. The second method, he argues, has been to impose total cash limits on each department and leave it to the department itself to decide how these shall be achieved (Pirie 1988a: 110).

Behind both strategies, Pirie argues, lies an assumption that if unnecessary spending and wastage can be identified, they can be eliminated, or at least curbed, if sufficient discipline can be brought to bear. The reality, he argues, is different:

> The bureaucrats find it easier in practice to push through the limits than to achieve savings within them. Ministers respond to the suggestion of across-the-board cuts with the response that this is fine in general, but should not apply to the essential work of their own department: there should not be cuts in the vital area of health, for example, or education, or pensions, or social security. It would be false economy, they say, to attempt cuts in environmental spending. Security would be threatened

by defence cuts. A highly public defence of each department's essential work turns what was designed to be a cut falling equally on everyone into the more familiar picture of a cabinet fight for privileged position. This is a scenario in which bureaucrats feel comfortable, and which they know how to manipulate.

With cash limits, Pirie argues, the response is twofold. First, there is direct opposition to the limit imposed on each department from civil servants, who then supply budget figures showing the 'impossibility' of keeping within them. Secondly, after some degree of cash limit has been approved by government, civil servants respond with pressures which 'burst through the limits'. Finally, when cuts *are* imposed, the plans presented propose to achieve them not by administrative savings, but by cuts in *services* - 'commonly in sensitive and valued areas, with a vociferous and articulate public as their recipients, and with high media visibility' (Pirie 1988a: 113).

For Pirie, in particular, when the proposed cuts are announced, there is then 'an immediate outcry from those whose services are threatened'. The media, he argues, respond accordingly and 'the ministry feels itself under pressure as the protests mount'. The government in turn experiences unpopularity and its members show political concern. Legislators receive hostile mail and opinion polls show how much support there is for maintaining the service. The government calculates that it can afford to lose only so much support before the exercise is no longer worthwhile, and its enthusiasm for the savings diminishes (Pirie 1988a: 113).

For Pirie at least, this was indeed the effect intended by the civil servants when the cuts were proposed. The response of the bureaucracy throughout this sequence of events is - for Pirie at least - predictable in terms of public choice theory which tells us that it is against the *interests* of officials to preside over departments made smaller (or poorer) by politicians in search of 'economies'.

Micropolitics

Public choice, for Pirie at least, is 'an analytical tool which enables us to understand and to explain why it is that some things happen in the public sector in the way that they do'. If public choice is a critique, however, there is also said to be a 'creative counterpart' implicit in its findings - one which teaches politicians their limits and enables them to predict in advance which policies are unlikely to succeed. In particular, Pirie argues, by understanding how interest groups are likely to react within the system, political leaders can avoid policies doomed to fall foul of them and so construct policies which work *with* interest-group 'pressures', instead of trying to override them. For Pirie at least, if interest group pressures are known of in advance, the possibility emerges that policies can be devised which either work with them, circumvent them or overcome them (Pirie 1988a: 121).

In this connection, *micropolitics* is the name given by Pirie to 'a new style of policy formulation geared to the workings of the political market'. Its aim is to construct new policies which will contrive circumstances in which interest groups acquiesce in and thereby lend their support to those policies. Micropolitics, for Pirie at least, considers the behaviour of individuals and groups in political markets:

> Micropolitics ... involves the formulation of policies which acknowledge the findings of the public choice theorists, and which use them to redirect the behaviour of the individuals and groups involved. Instead of trying to act on the large scale against the benefits which groups enjoy at the general expense, micropolitics sets about creating policies which alter the choices people make by altering the circumstances.

The starting point for micropolitics, then, is the self-interest of individuals and groups in the public sector. The suggestion here is that if such groups are to acquiesce in the removal of some or other benefit which they presently enjoy, they must be offered something of greater value to them in return; after all, Pirie argues, those who now enjoy an entrenched benefit of some kind from the state 'will fight to defend it, feel aggrieved at the innovation which threatens it, and find a suitable ideology to justify their stance' (Pirie 1988a: 128).

Micropolitics, Pirie argues, is thus 'more sympathetic to the point of view of those who receive benefits from the state' and aims to construct policies which offer them something in return for their loss (Pirie 1988a: 129). Micropolitics is also, however, less confrontational and less holistic than conventional policy, in that it seeks to work with, rather than against, the grain of entrenched interest groups. And it is, for Pirie at least, more conservative than conventional free-market policies, 'because it is more piecemeal and more gradual' (Pirie 1988a: 130).

Micropolitics, Pirie argues, rarely produces policies designed to achieve sudden change or have an immediate impact; rather, it attempts to set in motion a chain of events that lead finally to the desired goals. These chains of events, for Pirie at least, are the trades and exchanges made in political markets (Pirie 1988a: 131):

> Instead of ignoring these trades or seeking to end them, it works with them, making

offers available which seek to influence the outcome which results from them. Traditional or long-standing benefits are not attacked, but bid for on the basis of more attractive offers. Individual groups are invited to exchange a continuing state transfer benefit for a short-term gain or an equivalent private sector advantage.

This process, Pirie argues, takes time. Its cumulative effect, however, is said to be to increase the degree of spontaneity in society and to expand the area of decision left outside the ambit of government and within the realm of choices made by individuals and groups. While not a revolutionary programme by any means, it *does* seek steady and consistent movement in one direction (Pirie 1988a: 131).

Beginning in the 1970s, Pirie argues, there was an increasing concentration on the part of some free marketeers not on the 'battle for ideas', but on policy engineering (Pirie 1988a: 265). Instead of simply waving free-market flags and shouting the traditional battle cries, he argues,

attention ... turned instead to the technical and mechanical details of policies which could circumvent the public choice objections. A new awareness of the power and role of interest groups led to the formulation of policies designed to prevent them from thwarting the introduction of market elements into the state sector. In some cases, this involved a rejection of the conventional market alternative on the grounds that it took insufficient account of the forces at work in political markets. In other cases, it took the form of working for partial market solutions on the grounds that these would not only succeed, but would establish a base on which more market elements could be constructed later.

For Pirie, then, the emergence during the 1970s of a radical new method of policy formulation - micropolitics - made available to the Thatcher government a range of detailed applications (Pirie 1988a: 134).

Instead of running headlong into the opposition of interest groups under threat, they were able to introduce policies which offered such groups the opportunity to trade for greater advantage. The Conservative programmes of the early 1970s met with failure. Those of the early 1980s met with some successes. The difference between the two was policy technique. It was the entry of ideas concerning political markets into the activity of policy formulation.

For Pirie, at least, there are significant differences between the conventional policy proposals put forward by free marketeers and those which have emerged from the treatment of the political process as a market. These differences, he argues, are clearly visible in the case of the delivery of local government services. In this connection, he argues that two solutions to the problems of oversupply, lack of cost-effectiveness and 'producer capture' have been put forward on what he calls the conventional paradigm. Significantly, however, *neither* of these has secured in practice the effects intended by free marketeers.

The first, he argues, was the suggestion that the entire system of local government should be *reorganized*, in the belief that amalgamation into larger units would make possible economies of scale and new peaks of business efficiency in the provision of services. This policy, Pirie recalls, was enacted in the early 1970s but achieved precisely the reverse effect to that intended. In particular, he argues, the new 'giantism' left voters with the feeling that the new authorities were too large, too powerful and too remote from their influence. Inefficiency and waste increased and abuse soon became endemic (Pirie 1988a: 136-7).

This failure, Pirie argues, led to an alternative proposal, namely that 'user charges' for local services should be introduced in order to counter the lack of 'consumer pressure'. The point was to make consumers more cost conscious and to 'put pressure on the area authority to provide value for money in each case'. The problem here, Pirie argues, is that user charges leave the production of the service entirely within the state sector, taking only the finance of it into private hands; the problems of public supply (its comparative inefficiency, overmanning, lack of choice, 'producer capture' and so on) remain intact (Pirie 1988a: 138).

A further objection, for Pirie, is that the introduction of such charges provokes angry opposition in some quarters - not least, perhaps, from those who continue to believe that 'other people' pay for the services they receive and who fail to see that they are paying themselves for services through taxation. There is also, for Pirie at least, a further point to be made concerning the *political* impact of user charges, which is that their introduction requires the price of services to be set by the local authority and must be subject to an annual review by the local legislature. The problem here, for Pirie, is that the legislators themselves - who have both to consider and to decide upon price increases for services - come under intense pressures from every minority group which thinks it has a deserving case, or whose lobbyists and spokesmen do so. For Pirie, then, 'user charges are probably a non-starter' as a solution, because they fail to appreciate the strength of political markets (Pirie 1988a: 139).

As an alternative to the introduction of user charges, Pirie argues, the exponents of micropolitics (the ASI) developed the idea of inviting private business to bid for the provision of local services - a process known as contracting-out. This process, Pirie argues, 'involves the local authority retaining responsibility for the services, and continuing to pay for them out of public funds received from national and local sources. The difference is that instead of providing its own staff and labour force, the local government authority pays private firms to perform the services, having them bid against each other to secure the contracts' (Pirie 1988a: 140).

For Pirie, in particular, 'contracting-out' has a number of positive advantages, but with none of the disadvantages which accompany the conventional solution of charging. In particular, he argues, contracting-out generates competition among would-be suppliers, and removes certain features of public sector supply (inefficiency, overmanning, under-capitalization). Contracting out, he argues, makes 'producer capture' very much more difficult, because of 'the possibility of business being won by firms which satisfy the consumers instead and because of the consequent risk of bankruptcy' (Pirie 1988a: 141).

For Pirie, however, 'contracting-out' has the added advantage of acknowledging the findings of public choice theory and of taking into account possible objections from interest groups. In local government, as elsewhere, he argues (Pirie 1988a: 143-4):

> The methods of micropolitics show clearly through the process. An analysis identifies all of the groups in the political market in question, and traces the perceived benefit they receive. A policy is then constructed to offer as many of them as possible a bigger gain from the new method than they enjoyed before. All possible objections are anticipated, and the policy is structured so that most of them can be dealt with in advance. The result is a policy which succeeds and whose success promotes the confidence in it to have it applied elsewhere.

Contracting out, Pirie concedes, is not the 'free market' solution. Indeed, advocates of a 'macropolitical' approach would criticize this proposal on the grounds that it does not go far enough, and would point out that a true free market situation would have the individuals within a local government area making the decisions about which business to employ for their services, and how much service they wanted. Although a just criticism, this objection, he argues, misses the point (Pirie 1988a: 144):

> The problem is that public choice analysis suggests that the attempt to achieve a totally free market will fail because of the pressures of the interest groups involved, whereas the attempt to introduce contractors can succeed. While the advocates of a total [market] solution were still attempting to win the battle of ideas, the micropoliticians meanwhile managed to take the use of private contractors to such a stage of success that the British government felt confident of enough support to mandate local authorities to seek outside bids.

For Pirie, in particular, the differences between the solution developed by micropolitics and the alternative supplied on the conventional paradigm show 'how much the former is involved in the practical world'. Its concern to bring an idea to reality through political markets 'shows itself in the detail which it devotes to the development of techniques which can circumvent possible obstacles' (Pirie 1988a: 144-5).

Micropolitics, for Pirie at least, 'does not seek to apply a blanket solution, but to tailor-make a policy for each situation it encounters. It often succeeds because the policies fit better when they are tailor-made' (Pirie 1988a: 145). For Pirie at least, micropolitics 'tells us why certain policies fail. The reason is that they do not take account of political markets. The new policies produced by micropolitics, then, 'try to overcome the objections which caused other policies to fail. They take account of political markets, and are designed to work with them rather than to override them' (Pirie 1988a: 259).

Like many scientific theories, Pirie argues, 'micropolitics' originated from the perceived inadequacies of the prevailing model. For Pirie at least, the failure of the Heath government in Britain led some analysts to the conclusion that it was not enough to win the 'battle of ideas', or even to elect politicians committed to them. Instead, he argues, some free marketeers became convinced that it was as important, indeed more so, to have policies which could succeed (Pirie 1988a: 264-5).

For Pirie at least, it was the policy 'engineers', coming as they did in the wake of the 'pure scientists' of political and economic theory, who 'made the machines which changed events'. Ideas, he argues, had been necessary (to win the intellectual battle), but this was not enough. At the core of micropolitics, Pirie argues, is the idea that creative ingenuity is needed to apply to the practical world of interest group politics the concepts of free-market theory (Pirie 1988a: 267).

The basis of micropolitics, then, is working *with* interest groups, and restructuring circumstances so that it becomes to their advantage to choose the course preferred by the policy-makers. Micropolitics, for Pirie, has two advantages over the conventional style of politics: it solves problems and it is attractive to political leaders. For Pirie, in particular, attempts to replace the public sector by market solutions face two difficulties: first, that most of the attempts fail; and, secondly, that the government that enacts them makes enemies. Micropolitics, however, has neither of these drawbacks. For Pirie at least, because 'micropolitics' offers advantages to interest groups, it is popular; and because they accept it, it works (Pirie 1988a: 283).

Micropolitics, Pirie argues, is concerned with generating policies designed for the practical world. It begins by looking at the political markets which operate in each case and examines the political problems they cause. It then proposes solutions which are designed within the context of the practical, urging politicians not to resist or to oppose political markets in ways which spell failure or defeat (Pirie 1988a: 294). In short, he argues:

> It teaches politicians to enter political markets in order to trade. Rather than opposing the self-interest of the groups involved, it urges them to bid for it with more attractive offers. It represents one of the few methods of policy generation to emerge looking at the world from the point of view of the profession.

Conclusion

For the ASI, then, winning the battle of ideas (theory) is a necessary, but not a sufficient condition for securing market solutions in public policy (practice). For Pirie at least, perhaps the key insight of public choice theory is what it tells us about the force of an *interest* compared with that of a general idea (Pirie 1988a: 226). This suggests that, however similar they may be in ideological terms, the IEA and the ASI differ profoundly over the fundamental relationship between economic scholarship, on the one hand, and political interest, on the other (Seldon 1989). As David Green (1987: 153) has pointed out:

> The IEA has firmly established itself as a non-partisan research institute with a reputation for scholarly independence. Its emphasis on the production of academic research papers *and remaining aloof from day-to-day politics* is not shared by the younger Adam Smith Institute. [The ASI] eschews what it calls the 'linear' approach of the IEA and follows a more vigorous 'micro-political' strategy, diligently searching out the next incremental step which can be taken towards a more free society and, informed by public choice theory, carefully targeting the interests that might benefit from it.

What this suggests is that, despite a shared enthusiasm for the 'free market', there will be important *policy* differences between these two 'think tanks' in areas such as health and education. These will be examined in more detail in Chapters 5-7 of the present study.

3 The Centre for Policy Studies

Our Centre is a new venture. Our name, Policy Studies, indicates that we shall work towards influencing policy, rather than just producing research briefs (with no disrespect to the latter). We shall work to shape the climate of opinion - or, to be more exact, the various micro-climates of opinion ... Much of our work will be comparative. We shall see in greater detail what people are doing in other lands. We shall look at the success stories and ask why they succeeded. But the main thing is that we shall argue. In the first instance, we shall argue the case for the social market economy.

(Sir Keith Joseph)[1]

Introduction

The Centre for Policy Studies (CPS) was founded in the summer of 1974 by Margaret Thatcher and Sir Keith Joseph - then in opposition after the first of two General Election defeats for the Conservative Party (in February and October) that year. Sir Keith, in particular, was anxious to learn from the experiences of the Heath government of 1970-74 (in which both he and Thatcher had served), and to study successful 'social market' economies like Japan and West Germany (Kavanagh 1990: 89). Interviewed in 1987, Joseph explained the thinking behind the decision to set up the CPS in the following way:

> [The idea] was mine and Alfred Sherman's.... I did it to try to persuade myself and them ... the party and the country, that the German social market philosophy was the right one for the Conservatives to adopt. I set it up - with Ted Heath's understandably slightly grudging approval - to research, and then to market, social market philosophy.[2]

In particular, Thatcher and Joseph - as the Centre's former Director of Studies, David Willetts, has recalled - were far from happy with the direction policy had taken towards the end of the Heath government's period in office, and 'wanted instead to take conservatism back to what they saw as its true roots'.[3] The CPS was established with the (reluctant) permission of Edward Heath. Joseph became Chairman, Thatcher its President and Alfred Sherman its first Director of Studies.

After the Party's second General Election defeat of 1974 (this time in October), it was clear that the Conservatives would soon be looking for new leadership. Heath's personal unpopularity notwithstanding, he had now led his party to defeat in three out of four General Elections - a disappointing performance, to say the least, for the 'natural party of government'. Initially, it had been thought that, in the event of a leadership contest, Joseph would stand against Heath, but after his decision to withdraw, the CPS became instead the base from which Mrs Thatcher ran for and secured the leadership of the Conservative Party in February 1975.

After she became leader, Mrs Thatcher was, to say the least, suspicious of Conservative Central Office (CCO) and the Conservative Research Department (CRD). Many of those working at CCO and at the CRD at that time had been appointed by her predecessor and most (understandably perhaps) had failed to support Thatcher in her campaign to succeed him. A more important factor in shaping Thatcher's opinion of CCO and the CRD, however, was that the then incumbents also *thought* differently from the way she and Joseph now did. The CRD, directed at the time by Chris Patten, seemed to Thatcher and her supporters to have remained 'loyal', in many ways, to the policy 'outlook' of previous Conservative leaders - up to and including Heath. As Joseph recalled in 1991, the CRD strongly disapproved of the CPS: 'After all, we were singing new tunes. They were still intent on putting as good a face as possible on the old tunes.'[4]

After 1975, then, there ensued an intense rivalry between the CRD and the CPS for the intellectual 'soul' of the Conservative Party in opposition (Halcrow 1989, Young 1990). In the event, the new ascendancy within the Conservative hierarchy enjoyed by Margaret Thatcher, the Party leader, and Keith Joseph (to whom Thatcher, on becoming leader, gave control of its policy-making apparatus) meant that much of the work done by the Conservative Party in preparation for the 1979 General Election, both at the policy level and at the philosophical level, was carried out at the CPS under its then Director of Studies, Alfred Sherman. In his assessment of the period, Joseph later recalled that Sherman deserves particular credit for his part in 'contributing a pressure to understand the reasons for [Britain's] discontents. The CPS was at that stage a very significant and positive contributor to the re-education of the country and of the Conservatives.[5]

Modus Operandi

Since 1974, the Centre has operated by sponsoring the publication of speeches by Thatcher and Joseph, presenting evidence to parliamentary and select committees and establishing study groups to examine particular measures (CPS 1989a). The principle aim of the Centre has been, and is:

> the translation of belief in individual freedom, economic enterprise and social responsibility into recommendation of policies which governments can in practice carry out. Studies are despatched to Cabinet Ministers and Departments of State, to the media and to a wide circle of those engaged in the political life of Britain.

Interviewed in 1991, the CPS's former Director of Studies, David Willetts, identified three functions carried out by the CPS. The first has to do with conservative philosophy, 'to remind people, from time to time, what we think conservatism stands for [namely] some combination of free markets and a sense of community'.[6] Secondly, the CPS produces pamphlets and holds discussions on particular aspects of policy in areas such as education, health, social security and privatization.[7] The Centre's third role, at least in the period since the Conservatives returned to office in 1979, has been to make itself available to Conservative ministers and to offer a private resource for ministers (and members of the Downing Street Policy Unit) wanting to 'try out' ideas.[8] In pursuit of these objectives, the Centre's work proceeds as follows (CPS 1989a):

> Study groups or working parties are set up of men and women eminent in education, law, commerce, local government, nationalized industries, defence and other areas. Meetings are regularly held in Wilfred Street to discuss the problems of today and formulate the policies of tomorrow. Sometimes this - voluntary - work issues in Policy Studies, sometimes in written submissions to Ministers and Departments, sometimes in conferences and papers called in response to government proposals.

According to Lord Thomas of Swynnerton, a former Chairman of the CPS, its *modus operandi* is as follows (CPS 1989b: 6):

> We scent a problem or an interlocking series of problems; perhaps from conversations with our directors or donors; perhaps from visits to the corridors of Westminster or Whitehall. We then find an author, or set up a working party, to consider the matter. We put that author in touch with others working on the same theme, either in academic life, in business or in the Government. We draw the attention of the undertaking to Ministers who, we think, are sympathetic to our

> approach. We act as outriders, scouts, as a vanguard - who can ... if necessary be
> disavowed.

The key phrase here, of course, is 'our approach', and it is to the Centre's
approach to social and economic problems - or, to its underlying and guiding
philosophy - that this chapter now turns.

'Britain Needs a Social Market Economy'

As the citation from Lord Joseph at the head of this chapter indicates, the CPS
was established in 1974:

> to secure fuller understanding of the methods available to improve the standard of
> living, the quality of life and the freedom of choice of the British people, with
> particular attention to social market policies.

The founders of the CPS sought to reinforce this declaration of intent, by arguing
as follows:

> The Centre will state the case for a social market economy: that is, a free market
> economy operating within a humane system of laws and institutions. This case will
> be presented in moral as well as economic terms, emphasizing the links between
> freedom, the standard of living and a market economy based on private enterprise
> and the profit discipline.

The Centre's founders sought, above all, 'to change the climate of opinion to
make possible policies not now feasible'. At the outset, it was argued (CPS
1975a: 3-4) that:

> The Centre will help to redress a distortion which has come to affect British
> intellectual and political life during our lifetime. Socialist ideas and other varieties
> of collectivist, centralist or statist philosophies have come to dominate political
> thought. Although socialism and dirigisme have been uniformly unsuccessful,
> indeed calamitous where taken to their logical conclusions, their hold over educated
> opinion has strengthened from failure to failure. Conversely, though private
> enterprise and the market continue to show far greater success than dirigiste and
> state dominated economies, the climate of opinion in this country is largely hostile
> to them. Socialist assumptions in economics, social policy and education have
> gained general bipartisan acceptance with only minor modifications. As a result, the
> workings of the market have been hampered. These induced failures have been used

as excuses for even more damaging intervention, until economy and society alike have become increasingly beset by contradictions. We believe, therefore, that the time is ripe for re-examining the new conventional wisdom pragmatically in the light of a quarter century's experience in Britain and other industrialized countries. This is one of the Centre's objectives.

In arguing the case for a social market economy, the Centre's founders sought to 'transform the climate of opinion and with it the face of British society in the last quarter of the twentieth century' (CPS 1975a: 4).

The task of the CPS, then, was and is 'to build, and take to the country, policies of conviction based on the justice of giving people as much freedom as possible, and the necessity of reviving a culture of enterprise' (CPS 1989a). From its inception, the Centre has sought, above all, 'to make market economics acceptable in a society that had previously taken a measure of socialism, or at least of state intervention in the economy, for granted' (Halcrow 1989: 67). As Halcrow suggests, however:

> There was much discussion in the early days [as to] whether it might be too daring to talk overmuch about 'the market economy'. One school of thought was that it would be better to talk of the 'social market economy'. This was the literal translation of *Soziale Marktwirtschaft*, the system that had been so effective in Germany - roughly speaking, the philosophy that market economics, allowed to operate freely, provides the goods and services that people want, and does so more democratically than any system of central planning can do.

'Social market economy', Halcrow recalls, had two important advantages over 'market economy' for the founders of the CPS:

> One was that the word social conveyed the idea that market economics was not in conflict with social idealism; indeed, that social idealism was unrealistic without market economics. The other advantage came from the connection with West Germany: it gave credence to the reputation they wanted to maintain vis-à-vis Tory Central Office that they existed simply to study the workings of business economics internationally.

Why, though, did Britain need a 'social market economy'? Because, it was argued (CPS, 1975b: 3-4):

> Experience has taught us that the only real alternative to a market economy is a command economy, in which narrow short-term expedients reflecting conflicting party-political considerations dominate government economic behaviour. We are also learning - or re-learning - that a command economy means a command society;

that the state, in order to secure its uncontested domination over economic life, must increasingly dominate people's livelihoods, and limit their freedom of choice in education, health, housing, jobs, careers, savings, their access to the media of expression and later their access to information. In short, a command economy means increasing dependence for the citizen. Hence our reiterated conviction that a market economy with freedom to own property and engage in production of goods and services is an essential condition for all other freedoms.

A market economy 'within a humane framework of laws and social services', it was argued, gives 'freest scope for material, social and cultural development and the quest for happiness' (CPS 1975b: 4). Indeed, it was argued:

> The scope and quality of social services depend crucially on the health and efficiency of industry [which] alone creates the wealth which pays for social welfare. The more industry is left free - and indeed encouraged - to get on with its vital job of creating wealth, the greater will be the money that can be devoted to social purposes. Conversely, when industry is vilified and squeezed, the result is lower profits, lower wages, less employment and thus a reduced capacity to pay the taxes which alleviate distress and advance education. In short, a profitable, efficient and thriving industry is the precondition of a humane, compassionate and civilised society.

Support for the free market did not, however, imply advocacy of *laissez-faire* in the sense of wishing to outlaw government from economic and social affairs. Nor was the market system without its imperfections (CPS 1975b: 8-9):

> The market's shortcomings are well-known: it does not in itself ensure that the occasional divergence of private and social costs/benefits is reflected in prices; it often fails to provide for those who, through misfortune, cannot provide for themselves; it may bring about a distribution of income, wealth and economic power which many people find unacceptable.

There was, then, a clear need to 'complement' the market system with various social policies to help the elderly, the sick, the disabled and the unemployed; poverty and deprivation should not be tolerated where - in the absence of *any* intervention - these would otherwise occur (CPS 1975b: 9). There was, then, a need for *some* government intervention in the economy, but in a form which would limit the resulting distortions:

> Government involvement is necessary to create and regularly refurbish a framework of law in which private enterprise can be truly competitive and responsive to consumer demands. Government has a clear responsibility to curtail restrictive

practices and the abuse of monopoly power whether perpetrated by companies, trade unions, or professional associations. Government must be there, both as a forum for establishing the rules and to appoint an umpire to interpret and enforce them.

'Social market' philosophy was not, however, an egalitarian creed, for it recognized the 'fundamental conflict between equality and personal liberty'. Beyond a certain degree, it was argued, equality could only be enforced at the cost of sacrificing individual freedom (CPS 1975b: 13):

> It is certainly possible to modify by government action the distribution of income and wealth without destroying the market economy - but this process can be carried only so far. Despite the achievements of competitive capitalism in breaking down class barriers and official hierarchies, a viable market economy does entail some private individuals with wealth and incomes considerably higher than the average citizen enjoys.

Britain, then, must nourish 'a free enterprise society in which, over all but a limited area of their lives, adult individuals are left free to make their own decisions and enjoy the dignity and self-respect which comes through so doing' (CPS 1975b: 16). It is, after all, 'only through the operation - as unfettered as possible - of the free market that the life of each citizen will be enhanced' (CPS 1989b).

A Moral Issue?

> We are, of course, free marketeers but we were never *just* free marketeers ... We don't think that economics is the explanation of everything, nor believe the free market is the solution to everything.
>
> (David Willetts)[9]

The CPS has not, of course, been alone in arguing that the operation (as unfettered as possible) of the free market is a *necessary* condition for enhancing the life of each individual. As we have seen, this neo-liberal conviction is shared by both the IEA and the ASI (Chapters 1 and 2, above). In arguing the case for a *social* market economy, however, the CPS has also been concerned with the question of the moral values which, it claims, are essential to underpin and ultimately sustain the free market. As we saw earlier, the founders of the CPS sought to present the case for 'a free market economy operating within a humane system of laws and institutions ... in *moral* as well as economic terms'.

The CPS, then, has been anxious to claim not merely technical, but also 'moral' superiority for 'competitive capitalism' and its institutions - namely, limited government and a market economy (Griffiths 1985, Harris 1986). Implicit in this claim is the idea that there is a particular set of moral values or personal responsibilities which individuals should have or acquire. The notion of a 'socially responsible' market economy further implies that individuals should be, or become 'socially responsible'. In other words, the moral choices made by individuals are a matter not only of 'private' but also of 'public' concern. The question remains, however: what precisely are these virtues, and how are they to be acquired by those who have so far 'failed' to acquire them?

The starting-point here is the Centre's initial insistence that changes in attitudes and expectations were a prerequisite for the transition to a social market economy. The cultural 'problem' in the early days of the CPS (as now) was said to be 'statism'. Too many people were too 'dependent' on state provision; too few were deemed sufficiently independent or self-reliant. There was early interest, then, at the CPS, in reviving the so-called 'Victorian' values of hard work, thrift and self-reliance. 'Victorian values', as we shall now see, has been a recurrent theme in the political rhetoric of 'Thatcherite' Conservatives since the mid-1970s.

In January 1975, for example, Sir Keith Joseph argued that '*the* political objective of our lifetime' should be to encourage '*embourgeoisement*'. An important element in 'bourgeois' values was 'a further time-horizon, a willingness to defer gratification, to work hard for years, study, save, look after the family future'. Historically, Joseph added, bourgeois values had always 'rested on personal economic independence'. Anticipating his party's return to office, Joseph argued that the task of an incoming Conservative government should be 'to recreate conditions under which the values we cherish can form the cement of our society. Our job is to re-create the conditions which will again permit the forward march of embourgeoisement which went so far in Victorian times' (Joseph 1975: 56).

Interviewed on LBC radio in 1983, Mrs Thatcher also spoke at length about the need - as she saw it - to restore Victorian values and suggested that a return to such values might be a prerequisite for economic recovery:

> I was brought up by a Victorian grandmother. We were taught to work jolly hard. We were taught to prove yourself; we were taught self-reliance; we were taught to live within our income. You were taught that cleanliness is next to godliness. You were taught self-respect. You were taught always to give a hand to your neighbour; you were taught tremendous pride in your country. All of these are Victorian values. They are also perennial values. You don't hear so much about these things these days, but they were good values and they led to tremendous improvements in

the standard of living.

'Victorian values', as Jenkins (1989: 66) recalls, made their first appearance in the repertoire of 'Thatcherism' in Thatcher's address to the Greater London Young Conservatives in July 1976. On that occasion, as Russel (1978: 104-5) recalls, Thatcher insisted that:

> Choice in a free society implies responsibility. There is no hard and fast line between economic and other forms of personal responsibility to self, family, firm, community, nation, God. Morality lies in choosing between feasible alternatives. A moral being is one who exercises his own judgement in choice on matters great and small, bearing in mind their moral dimension, i.e. right and wrong. Insofar as his right and duty to choose is taken away by the State, the party or the union, his moral faculties - his capacity for choice - atrophy, and he becomes a moral cripple. A man is now enabled to choose between earning his living and depending on the bounty of the State.

In spelling out, and placing on the record, her personal moral 'vision', Thatcher left her audience in no doubt as to its origin and inspiration:

> The Victorian age, which saw the burgeoning of free enterprise, also saw the greatest expansions of voluntary philanthropic activity of all kinds; the new hospitals, new schools, technical colleges, universities, new foundations for orphans, non-profit-making housing trusts, missionary societies. The Victorian age has been very badly treated in socialist propaganda. It was an age of constant and constructive endeavour in which the desire to improve the lot of the ordinary person was a powerful factor. We who are largely living off the Victorians' moral and physical capital can hardly afford to denigrate them.

For Thatcher, in particular, Victorian values 'were the values when our country became great' (Jenkins 1989: 67). By implication, then, the departure from such values had something to do with Britain's economic decline - decline she was pledged to arrest and reverse. Economic regeneration thus implied moral regeneration (Jenkins 1989: 66):

> Not only the intellectual but the moral foundations of the *ancien regime* were crumbling, or so the Thatcherites believed. In the way of all revolutionaries or counter-revolutionaries possessed of a simple truth, they embarked upon a crusade to restore lost virtue.

For 'Thatcherism', then, this theme of 'Victorian values' has long been salient. Those close to Mrs Thatcher - and in particular those linked to the CPS - have long sought to resolve economic problems in terms of moral values (Griffiths 1984, 1989). In the context of *economic* decline, there has been particular and persistent interest at the CPS in the 'rediscovery' of certain traditional - or 'Victorian' - *moral* values.

For example, in a Summer Address to the CPS in August 1987, Gertrude Himmelfarb took as her theme 'Victorian Values - and twentieth-century condescension'. In her Address, Himmelfarb argued that 'bourgeois' or 'middle-class' values such as hard work, thrift, temperance and self-restraint, far from being a middle-class device to subjugate the working classes, were in fact 'modest virtues the Victorian working classes *themselves* aspired to'. Some historians, she argued, had interpreted the idea of 'respectability' and the values connected with it as a technique or device of 'social control' - as the means by which the ruling (or middle) class sought to dominate the subordinate (or working) class. This social-control thesis, for Himmelfarb at least, was seriously flawed and does nothing to explain the 'inconvenient fact' that a great many workers - not merely the 'labour aristocracy' but also lesser skilled and even unskilled workers - seem to have adopted these values as their own. For Himmelfarb, then, hard work, sobriety, frugality and foresight were not, and are not, exclusively middle-class or 'bourgeois' values, but mundane virtues within everyone's reach. There was nothing particularly exalted or heroic about them. They needed no special breeding, status, talent or money. In this sense at least, Victorian values were also 'democratic' values - 'common virtues' well within the reach of 'ordinary' people (Himmelfarb 1987).

The important point here is that for the CPS, a free economy and a free society ultimately *depend* on a moral citizenry - on the voluntary exercise of morality by individual citizens. In this connection, economic self-sufficiency and moral restraint are seen not just as a personal but as a *social* responsibility. Because the individual is no mere individual but an individual *and* social being, he or she must be prevailed upon to exercise particular social responsibilities; to fulfil moral duties and obligations; to recognize 'legitimacy' in authoritative social institutions and observe the 'fact' of community (Harris 1989, Gray 1991).

Social responsibility, then, is a second theme of considerable importance to the CPS. For example, Peregrine Worsthorne argued in a 1988 CPS pamphlet that 'the habits of social authority must be relearned, the arts of custodianship encouraged and the transmission of civility and all that is best in our institutions nurtured' (Worsthorne 1988). In 1989, Sheila Lawlor, a former Deputy Director at the CPS, argued that although people should be 'free' to live their lives as they wish, when it comes to the effect of their actions on children, on the state or on the community at large, government action is imperative. For Lawlor at least, this implied an active moral policy of incentive and disincentive to encourage stable family life - for example, by making divorce more 'difficult' than it is at present (BBC 1989).

As a final example, it is worth noting the interest the Centre has shown in the work of leading American 'dependency' theorists like Lawrence Mead and Charles Murray - who typically claim that poverty is not simply a question of economics, but partly also a question of the cultural attitudes and dispositions of many poor people. Under the welfare state, they argue, the poor have grown increasingly dependent on the state and have lost their sense of initiative; the work ethic has weakened; and some of the poorest have lost their sense of obligation to their families and indeed the wider community. In March 1987, a CPS-sponsored seminar was held in London, the aim of which was to bring such issues to the attention of British intellectuals and politicians (Chapter 7).

Ideas and Events

As we have seen, the IEA and the ASI, though both 'politically independent' institutions with an 'overwhelming commitment' to the free market as the best means of solving economic and social problems, tend also to perceive the question of the relationship between ideas and events in equally decisive, but also (and more importantly) in radically different ways. The IEA, as we saw in Chapter 1, was originally constituted as an educational charity, concerned primarily with educating - or re-educating - members of the intelligentsia generally and future generations of university students in particular in a particular brand of economic thought, namely free-market thought. In so doing, we argued, the IEA has always taken 'a long-term view of the relationship between ideas and events'.

As we saw in Chapter 1, the IEA has always insisted that a particular advantage enjoyed by its independent status as an educational charity is that it releases IEA authors from the constraints that might otherwise be imposed on them by short-term considerations of the politically possible, administratively feasible and socially acceptable, thereby enabling them to pursue fearlessly their investigation of the technical efficacy of markets in either solving, or failing to solve economic and social problems. As the IEA's former Editorial Director has recalled (Seldon 1981a: pp. xix-xx and xxxiv):

> Authors were asked to apply economic analysis ruthlessly, with recognition of current conditions but without regard for 'administrative practicability', because that could not be ascertained except by practical trial, or for 'political impossibility'

because that could be a pretext developed by politicians or bureaucrats who resisted reform that did not suit them however good the argument, and in any event because reasoned *ideas* could themselves make the 'impossible' possible. Above all the IEA was not deterred by the tired defences of established practices - 'politically impossible', 'administratively impracticable', 'socially unacceptable'. Its Founding Fathers saw behind the circular reasoning, for it is *ideas* that can make possible, practicable and acceptable what reason shows to be desirable, timely, overdue.

The ASI, on the other hand, as we saw in Chapter 2, has been intensely interested in what is currently politically possible and administratively practicable. In an attempt to 'reconcile theory and practice', the ASI has developed a new style policy formulation known as *micropolitics,* deliberately tailoring its proposals to suit the political circumstances of each case, by targeting the interest groups that would 'thwart' or otherwise obstruct the successful implementation of reform. The ASI, in contrast to the IEA, has engaged itself in *policy* 'innovation'. Typically, the ASI tends to adopt a 'short-term', 'gradualist' and 'incrementalist' approach. This incrementalist approach to 'policy engineering' is said by the ASI to enjoy the particular advantage of enabling further, perhaps more radical, reforms to be introduced at a later stage in the policy process. Once the initial reforms are in place, the suggestion from the ASI is that these can be refined where appropriate - and that further gradual reforms can be undertaken, as and when these become necessary and desirable.

As we have seen, the ASI claims to have enjoyed considerable success in seeing its proposals taken up and acted upon by the Conservative government during the 1980s. The reason for this, according to the ASI, is that the Thatcher government realized that it had in *micropolitics* a remarkably creative or flexible, as well as formidable tool of policy innovation, technique and implementation at its disposal - a weapon which is said to have been absent from the political armoury of previous Conservative leaders. Micropolitics, according to the ASI, demonstrates how an economic idea such as privatization can become *in practice* a political 'event' (Chapter 2, above).

The IEA and the ASI, then, hold very distinctive, yet radically different views of the relationship between ideas and events. In this connection, the question we must now consider is whether the CPS's perception of this relationship is more in line with the IEA's position or whether, in fact, it has more in common with the stance adopted by the ASI. Our purpose in the remainder of this chapter will be to examine the evidence, from a variety of sources, in order to generate a response to this question. As far as the CPS is concerned, the question of what is, and what should be the relationship between ideas and events is somewhat more complex and ambiguous than it is for either the IEA or the ASI (below). To understand why this is so, it is worth recalling how and why the Centre came into being, and thereafter to seek to trace the Centre's development from its inception in 1974 down to the present. As we shall see below, there is documentary as well as oral evidence to suggest that even the most senior among CPS personnel have often found it difficult to agree among themselves as to what the Centre's precise role and function should be, both when the Conservative Party is in Opposition and when it is in office. As a result, the CPS's perception of the relationship between ideas and events has been (and remains) ambivalent and imprecise in comparison to the IEA and the ASI.

Opposition 1974-9

> I saw it in the first place as an out-rider, an organisation that would not be in the Party and therefore would be able to ask questions, to think the unthinkable, to question the unquestioned ...
>
> (Alfred Sherman)[10]

As we saw earlier, the CPS was founded in the Summer of 1974 'to secure fuller understanding of the methods available to improve the standard of living, the quality of life and the freedom of choice of the British people, with particular attention to social market policies'. The Centre, according to an early statement of its objectives, would state the case for a social market economy, presenting it in moral as well as economic terms and emphasizing 'the links between freedom, the standard of living and a market economy based on private enterprise and the profit discipline'. The Centre's work, it was further argued, would at all times be intellectually respectable. In a statement issued to potential donors and benefactors, the Centre's founders argued that:

> Our purpose is practical. We shall seek to change the climate of opinion to make possible policies not now feasible, but we shall be realistic in what we propose.

The Centre, according to its founders, would have several tasks, including those of formulating the questions on which Government must have policies in order to achieve an effective social market; studying the answers to those questions, including those adopted by some countries abroad; appraising policies for the UK; presenting such appraisals privately to the Shadow Cabinet (and, when suitable, publicly) and arranging to help people, including MPs, in London and elsewhere to understand the arguments for and against the social market economy, private enterprise and the profit discipline. In parallel with and drawing from this work, speeches would be made presenting the case for a market economy, and opportunities sought to debate the case on television and in the universities. In addition, it was argued:

> Since the task of sustaining and adapting to current need the social market economy concept will be a continuing one, it is hoped that the Centre will exist for the foreseeable future. Certainly it should exist during periods of Conservative government.

The Centre's activities would not be 'party-political', in the sense that many of its studies would be published and so be of use to politicians and members of *all* parties. However, since much of the Centre's output would be used for *Conservative Party* discussion and preparation for government, financial donations to the CPS from interested parties should properly be declared as *Party* contributions.

In November 1974, the CPS's first Director of Studies, Alfred Sherman (later Sir) argued that the main thrust of the Centre's work should be to modify the climate of opinion through the use of studies, 'to show the failures of socialism and dirigisme of various kinds - here and abroad - the success gained by working with the market and the rationale for doing so.'[11] The success or otherwise of the CPS, Sherman argued, would be determined by the Centre's ability to 'identify the various micro-climates of opinion and engage in dialogue with them'. The job of opinion-forming to 'extend the freedom of manoeuvre' for a Conservative government was said to be a mid to long-term activity. Writing to Joseph in April 1975, Sherman argued that 'much may possibly be done to improve the Party's stance over the next few years. But little is likely to happen unless we at the Centre initiate it and see it through.'[12] The Conservative Research Department, for Sherman, had not changed substantially for the better, but was staffed by a group of low calibre opportunists whose ideas were 'fundamentally at variance with our own'.

For Sherman, then, it fell to the CPS to 'change the climate of opinion' by publishing books, papers and studies and by arranging seminars on issues of interest to policy-makers. In Spring 1975, Sherman argued (CPS 1975a) that:

> We are convinced that sound arguments, adequately documented and presented with combined perseverance and sensitivity to other viewpoints in the idiom best suited to each milieu can succeed in changing the climate of opinion. Socialistic and dirigiste ideas have had the field almost to themselves for a generation; their assumptions have been deeply assimilated into national thought ways in most institutions, not least in political life and administration [and] shape the climate of opinion within which policies are shaped. We are confident that our case is strong

enough if well prepared and presented to transform the climate of opinion and with it the face of British society in the last quarter of the twentieth century.

Again, writing in 1976 on the occasion of the Centre's second anniversary, Sherman recalled how the CPS had begun 'early in 1974' when he and Joseph had been anxious to examine what had caused the disappointment of their high hopes. At that time, Sherman recalled, it seemed to them that, whatever the merits and shortcomings of the 1970-74 government, many of that government's difficulties had stemmed from 'the prevailing climate of opinion' which had disfavoured the market economy - so creating a brittle society. With the benefit of hindsight, wrote Sherman, it could now be seen that the post-war consensus had 'contained the seeds of its own failure'. The CPS, he argued, had been set up by Joseph, Thatcher and himself to act as:

> a free-standing participant in the Conservative campaign of re-assessment and opinion-forming. In a sense, our chosen and agreed role is that of trail-blazer. We are not a research organization, in the sense of a body set up to carry out research. We are rather consumers of research, which we commission as needed. Our main job is opinion-forming. [13]

This, then, was Sherman's understanding of the CPS's role, both before and, as we shall see, after 1979. In 1978, for instance, Sherman protested vigorously at Gerald Frost's suggestion that the Centre should undertake to publish regular *Backgrounders*, or critical analyses of current policy proposals and issues (similar to the *Backgrounder* series produced by the Heritage Foundation in Washington), insisting that this implied:

> a fundamental reorientation of the Centre's aims and modus operandi. We were to be one step away from policy and to concentrate on influencing opinion-formers. We are now asked to step into the current political arena, by putting out papers... on proposed legislation. [14]

In a strongly-worded letter to Sir Keith Joseph in January 1978, Sherman pleaded:

> I really beg you - drop the idea and let us work to finance, improve and develop what we have. We must not move into political policy fields... thereby inviting attacks from Party or media enemies... A false move now could cripple, perhaps destroy, the Centre.

To Sherman at least, the suggestion that the CPS should move into *political* policy fields represented a fundamental and potentially fatal reorientation of its original aims and *modus operandi*. The Centre's original purpose, he argued, had been to remain one step removed from policy-making and to concentrate instead on the task of 'influencing opinion-formers'.

Government After 1979 -

> The Centre... is jealous of its independence. Supporting the Government in all its initiatives, however admirable a role, can with some safety be left to others. The Centre seeks to be a porcupine, not a poodle.
>
> (Lord Thomas of Swynnerton)[15]

In April 1979, a month or so before the General Election of that year, Sherman was still insisting to colleagues that it was idle to suggest that a Conservative victory should mark anything of a turning-point for the CPS. The CPS, he argued, should 'continue doing what it has been or should have been doing till now'. The Centre had never been an electioneering body; there were, in any case, other organizations whose job this was. The Centre's task had always been to change the climate of opinion - a longer term task, wrote Sherman, whose time-scale had nothing in common with the election cycle.[16] It had been agreed at the outset that the CPS should operate as 'outriders, trail-blazers', remaining 'one step away from policy'. The Centre had been envisaged as a long term venture because the climate of opinion could not be changed overnight - nor even during the lifetime of one parliament. For Sherman at least:

> We were formed from the outset to do a long-term educational job outside the Party apparatus. We were neither a shadow cabinet in exile, and subsequent extension of the leader's office, nor a Party electoral auxiliary.

Shortly after the Conservative victory in the General Election of May 1979, Sherman drew up a 'Programme of Activities' for the CPS for the next five years arguing that the return of a Conservative government would enable the CPS to 'devote the larger part of its efforts to its original purpose - changing the climate of opinion to facilitate bolder policies by a Conservative government in due course.[17] The Centre, wrote Sherman, should continue to provide a range of services - speech-writing, briefing, and expertise - to Thatcher, Joseph and 'other Ministers or Party officers who might require them' and should continue to work closely with Number 10, the (Downing Street) Policy Unit, the Prime Minister's

Political Office and the CRD. Seeking to transform the climate of opinion, however, should remain the major concern of the CPS, as had been the case in Opposition.

In particular, as Kavanagh (1990: 90) suggests, Sherman wanted the CPS to retain what he regarded as its original ginger-group function and not become too tied to the Conservative Party, retaining the capacity to criticize the Conservative government from the free-market point of view and attract other supporters or thinkers who were not necessarily pro-Conservative. The new Chairman of the CPS, Lord (Hugh) Thomas of Swynnerton, however, had a more modest view of the Centre's role, and seems to have thought that 'any criticism which its publications made of the government should be measured and constructive'. In 1983, for example, Thomas argued that in its future activities the Centre should continue as a centre of research, publication and advice; that it should maintain its good friendship with both Party and Government and continue to be institutionally independent. Its commitment, however, was to sustain the policies of the present (Conservative) government.[18]

Such views were anathema to Sherman, and led to his departure from the CPS in 1985 to establish a new research body - 'Policy Search'. The internal feud at the CPS in the early to mid-1980s between Sherman, on the one hand, and Thomas on the other is highly instructive and raises some interesting and important issues. In particular, the disagreement between Sherman and Thomas over what the Centre's function should be highlights the problem of deciding whether the CPS can properly be regarded as an organization working 'independently' of the Conservative Party, whether in Opposition or in Government. This chapter now turns to explore precisely this question, and examines its implications for the Centre's perception of the relationship between ideas and events.

The CPS: 'Independent' or Party-Political?

In 1983, Sir Alfred Sherman (as he now was) wrote to colleagues at the CPS recalling that the basic agreed objective of the CPS in 1974 had been to re-shape the climate of opinion in order to change the boundaries of the politically possible. The CPS was seen as an outrider, a trail-blazer, 'thinking the unthinkable' and 'questioning the unquestioned until the *common ground* moved in our direction.'[19] The 'whole point' of the CPS, for Sherman, was its commitment to ideas and policies *without* committing the Conservative leadership. Indeed, it was 'precisely because the Centre and I did not commit the

Party leadership that we were able to move the frontiers of debate and policy-search within which Conservative leaders are bound to operate'.

The entire *raison d'être* of the Centre, warned Sherman, would be threatened by the suggestion that it should be turned into a 'research organization' and by any change in its *modus operandi* which involved committing the Prime Minister; Research Director Elizabeth Cottrell's recent declaration that she believed the Centre's role to be to support Thatcher and her administration, and to be seen to be supportive, implied, for Sherman at least, *committing* the Prime Minister. Supporting Margaret Thatcher's administration, for Sherman, was not the responsibility of the CPS, but the official job of the Conservative Party.

Moreover, Sherman argued, it had not been explained - at least, to him - how it was possible for the CPS to 'behave like an organ of the Conservative Party, while at the same time managing to preserve its independence of thought'. The Centre, thought Sherman, would become 'redundant' if its sole purpose was to do what was, in any case, the *Party's* job. In addition, he argued:

> We have always attracted not only Party members, but non-Party people and even members of other parties who shared our ideas or approach and appreciated our way of doing things. My reputation for integrity and originality... *above* Party was one essential ingredient of our success. Hugh [Thomas] explicitly enjoined me to sacrifice it for the sake of the Party's convenience, and my refusal to do so was one reason for my being obliged to leave.

On the question of whether or not he and Thomas could ultimately agree on a compromise solution, Sherman wrote that he was unsure but conceded that he personally thought it unlikely. 'Given the conflictive situation and basic disagreements about the aims and *modus operandi* of the Centre', said Sherman, 'I think I may have outstayed my welcome'.

Interviewed in 1991, Sir Keith (now Lord) Joseph recalled that the CPS was established with aims and objectives 'parallel with those of the IEA' (Chapter 1, above). There is, however, one fundamental difference. Whereas the IEA's role has always been, and remains, to 'open the eyes' of those of every political persuasion and in all parties to the superior wisdom of free-market thought, the work of the CPS has always been, and remains, 'directed to *one* party.'[20] Interviewed in 1991, the then Director of the CPS, David Willetts, confirmed this. The CPS, Willetts argued, does not actively seek to influence *other* political parties.[21] To the extent that the CPS is a 'semi-official' organ of the Conservative Party, it cannot be said to enjoy genuine 'independence' from *party* political constraints in the same way as the IEA or the ASI.

As far as the Centre's perception of the relationship between ideas and events is concerned, this party-political factor does, however, have a further implication. This is that the Centre is bound to consider and take into account the political advantages or disadvantages for the Conservative Party and the Conservative Government of introducing particular *policies*. To the extent that CPS ideas are always and everywhere influenced by *events*, this would suggest its perception of the relationship between ideas and events has more in common with that of the ASI than with that of the IEA (Seldon 1989).

'Stepping Stones'

This last claim is further strengthened by one particular piece of evidence. Before the 1979 General Election, a particularly important CPS initiative (associated, above all, with Sir Keith Joseph but also with two of Mrs Thatcher's subsequent political 'advisers', John Hoskyns and Norman Strauss) was the concept of *Stepping Stones*. The strategic thinking behind this initiative was that the Conservative government - once in office - should introduce reforms in particular areas such as housing or trade union law but that it should do so gradually and incrementally, since it was politically unrealistic to imagine that wholesale changes could be introduced 'all at once' or 'in one go'. The suggestion, recalls Joseph, was that an incoming Conservative government should undertake such reforms in a piecemeal manner. This was to be achieved by 'building stepping stones of public persuasion, until we could reach the stage when the changes we wanted to introduce were broadly acceptable'.[22]

The suggestion here, then, from the CPS was that an incoming Conservative administration should attempt to introduce reform *gradually* by seeking to implement certain cautious reforms 'in the short run' so that - once these were in place - the way would be clear for further 'steps' to be taken in due course, if indeed these were thought necessary and desirable. To the extent, then, that the thinking behind the 'Stepping Stones' initiative closely resembles the thinking behind the ASI's micro-political method in relation to policy research and implementation, this would appear to strengthen the hypothesis that the CPS's perception of what is and/or should be the proper relationship between ideas and events is closer to the ASI than to the IEA (Chapters 1-2, above).

Conclusion

To return to the question of the CPS's 'proper' function, then, although the

Centre does operate at the level of philosophy and *does* seek to persuade Conservatives to share its own particular understanding of what it means to be 'Conservative' in politics (above), its overall purpose has at least as much, if not more, to do with the attempt to directly influence Conservative Party *policy* in the short term, as with the medium to long-term 'job' of 'changing the climate of opinion' in the Conservative Party and in the country; indeed, as the citation from Joseph at the head of this chapter indicates (above), the Centre's very name, the Centre for *Policy* Studies, suggests that the Centre mainly operates not so much at the philosophical level - in 'fighting the battle of ideas' - as at the *policy* level in servicing the Conservative *Party* in Government and Opposition.

Notes

1. 'The Politics of Political Economy' in *Reversing the Trend: A Critical Re-appraisal of Conservative economic and social policies*, Barry Rose, London, 1975: 63.
2. 'Escaping the Chrysalis of Statism', *Contemporary Record*, Spring 1987: 29.
3. Interview.
4. Interview.
5. Interview.
6. Interview.
7. Interview.
8. Interview.
9. Interview.
10. 'The Think Tank', BBC Radio 3, 21 October 1983.
11. Alfred Sherman, 13 November 1974, *Sherman Papers*, Royal Holloway and Bedford New College, University of London.
12. Memorandum to Sir Keith Joseph, 22 April 1975, *Sherman Papers*.
13. 'Our Second Birthday Paper: Two Candles to Shed Light', July 1976, *Sherman Papers*.
14. Memorandum to Sir Keith Joseph, 22 January 1978, *Sherman Papers*.
15. 'The Power of Ideas', CPS, London, 1988: 6.
16. 'The CPS and its Future', 2 April 1979, *Sherman Papers*.
17. 'CPS Programme of Activities 1970-84', 16 May 1979, *Sherman Papers*.
18. Lord Thomas of Swynnerton, 24 June 1983, *Sherman Papers*.

19. 'Preconditions for Sherman to work at the CPS in Autumn 1983', *Sherman Papers*.

20. Interview.

21. Interview.

22. Interview.

4 The Social Affairs Unit

Introduction

The Social Affairs Unit (SAU) was founded in 1980 as a (charitable) 'research and educational trust', committed to the promotion of 'lively and wide-ranging debate' on social affairs and to the 'sociological analysis of key controversies in contemporary culture'. Its general purpose is 'public education on economic and social affairs' carried out, for the most part, by the publication of books and reports. The Unit specializes in identifying academic research which is potentially informative for public debate and in making that research available to a non-specialist audience. In particular, its authors and contributors have attempted to analyze 'the factors which make for a free *and orderly* society in which enterprise can flourish'.

To date, studies published by the SAU have covered a wide range of topics. Examples include the reform of personal taxation and social security, the relationship between the culture of schools and business and enterprise, school standards, police accountability, housing, criminal deterrence, the media, the environment, family matters, health education and the churches' handling of social issues. Its personnel have written for various national daily and Sunday newspapers, including *The Times*, *The Daily* and *Sunday Telegraph* and *The Daily Mail*. In addition, the Unit has provided guest speakers for national and local radio programmes (including the BBC's World Service) and visiting speakers at academic conferences, schools and universities.

The SAU is not, first and foremost, a quasi-academic institution like the IEA, or a policy centre like the ASI or the CPS (Chapters 1-3). According to its Director, Digby Anderson, the optimum solution to social problems lies 'not in politicians, but in a better-informed public opinion' (cited in Kavanagh 1990: 86). The SAU attempts to inform 'public opinion' by 'making ideas available through its publications, through its authors' appearances in the media, and through media discussion of its publications, so that ideas originating in academic research are successively translated into common currency' (Kavanagh 1990: 86-7). The Unit's main criterion for measuring the 'success' of its activities is thus the extent to which its publications are discussed and debated in, for example, educational establishments, the media and Parliament, rather than the degree to which its authors' ideas are adopted and implemented by decision-makers.

'The Ignorance of Social Intervention'

At the outset, the SAU's immediate programme, according to one self-description at least, was to build 'a systematic literature on the practical outcome of government attempts at social engineering in the fields of education, health, social welfare, discrimination and criminal rehabilitation'. As Kavanagh (1990: 84-5) has pointed out:

> Many authors writing for the Unit have been highly critical of the status quo and many of the assumptions which dominated the public sector in general and social policy and the welfare state in particular. They have questioned and often debunked the alleged expertise of various welfare professions, especially social workers and teachers, the more exaggerated analytic and predictive claims of various social sciences, again of social work, sociology of education and criminology. A repeated theme has been scepticism about the old confident optimism in social engineering.

In particular, the SAU has set out to criticize what its Director, Digby Anderson, has called the 'ignorance of social intervention', or 'that component of - usually state - action which seeks to alter the behaviour of individuals, the characteristics of social groups and the relations between individuals and social groups' (Anderson 1980: 9). Social intervention, Anderson argues, is underwritten by an assumption that the intervenor *knows* what he or she is doing and can predict with *some* success that his or her intervention will have some of the desired effect. The 1960s and 1970s, he argues, saw a number of cases where such knowledge can be shown to have been seriously defective (Anderson 1980: 10):

> Some of the theories and evidence on which ... interventions have been based are quite simply inadequate, erroneous or irrelevant. In other cases ... intervenors seem to have no satisfactory criteria for assessing whether their knowledge is inadequate, erroneous or irrelevant, a failing we might call methodological ignorance. In yet other cases [social] intervenors neither know their own inadequacies, nor how to recognise them and even fail to take notice when errors are pointed out to them by others. Such ignorances can be differentiated as substantial ignorance, methodological ignorance and critical ignorance.

Another theme of the Unit's publications has been the argument that 'just as private industry producers have vested interests, so do producers of nationalized welfare and education'. These interests, it is alleged, are defended by the resort to claims about 'service', 'clients' and 'professionalism' which are deployed rhetorically to manipulate public funds (Anderson 1980).

'Breaking the Spell of the Welfare State'

According to Anderson, the position in sociology in 1980, when the Unit was founded, was 'akin to the position in economics a decade, or two decades before'. At that time, he has recalled, sociology did not represent a wide range of viewpoints. There was, in fact, a sort of 'consensus' in both sociology and social policy. Moreover, for Anderson at least, the position in 1980 was that:

> We were reaching a stage in English social institutions where there was a very urgent need to ask some critical questions particularly with regard to the welfare state, which was really our first topic. [1]

In this connection, among the Unit's early offerings was the seminal *Breaking the Spell of the Welfare State*, which argued that large sections of state education, health, social work, housing and other services should be 'reduced or changed to private, voluntary, tender, voucher, mutual aid, co-operative or subscription services' (Anderson *et al* 1981). Anderson, in particular, argued that:

> The urgent need [to reduce] public expenditure combined with the ever present obligation to monitor services which cost so much and affect so many people means that the welfare state is overdue for sustained scrutiny. These three papers suggest places in which scrutiny could start - priorities in the evaluation of the welfare state.

For Anderson, in particular, those wishing to subject the welfare state to 'sustained scrutiny' should concentrate their efforts on the careful and thoughtful development of a *policy* to reduce such services (Anderson *et al* 1981: 8):

> If there is to be less government and ... less nationalized welfare, health and education, there has to be a policy for their reduction. That means a thoughtful respect for the content and customers of welfare, education and health services. It also means thinking about the types of criticism that will be effective and those which ·could be ignored or neutralized. If the welfare state is a source of employment and remuneration to millions of teachers, social workers, doctors, nurses, porters, caretakers, bureaucrats, environmental health officers, academics et al, then it will not be amused by incisive criticism. It will respond to it by argument and evidence but also by abuse, appeal to sentiment, obstruction and professional manoeuvring. A criticism that is going to be more than hot air will have to anticipate these responses and be ready to answer and expose them ... no criticism will achieve actual and effective service reductions unless it makes its priority the exposure of the defensive manoeuvres of the welfare state, unless it breaks the spell of the welfare state.

Those concerned to 'break the spell of the welfare state', then, must recognize that the welfare state provides many people with their livelihood (Anderson *et al* 1981: 24):

> Many people depend on it directly for their income: teachers, lecturers, social workers, environmental health officers, youth workers, race relations officials, Manpower Services Commission employees, education advisers, employees of 'voluntary' organisations in receipt of permanent grants, and bureaucrats, central and local, DHSS and DES. Then there is the secondary welfare industry: academics who research the welfare state, publishers who sell to welfare state students, journalists who write for welfare state papers, TV and media men who 'document' the welfare state. For some of these the welfare state provides a convenient stable income. For others life would be very cold outside it.

Terms such as the 'Poverty Lobby' and the 'Race Relations Industry', it was argued, drew attention to the financial stake welfarists have in the perpetuation of a welfare state (Anderson *et al* 1981: 24). For Anderson at least:

> It is one that few electioneering politicians can afford to neglect. The welfare state is another estate, a power bloc. It is not just the recipient of taxpayers' money, but is an *active* lobby in the land through its syndicates, through civil servants and at local government level. It is a *'new class'* with its own class interest. One does not have to be a Lenin to see that such an estate will not be interested in the virtues of rational arguments that threaten it. If threatened, it will use its powers and it can be expected to use a measure of rhetoric, collusion, mystification, distraction and obstruction.

As we shall now see, the concept of a 'new class' is not unique or peculiar to the SAU, but one which has been developed, in particular, by a group of leading American intellectuals, known as the *neo-conservatives* (Steinfels 1979). In tracing the emergence of the 'new class' concept (and its significance for the SAU), it is important to examine the force of this neo-conservative critique.

The Emergence of the New Class

In distinguishing between the 'liberal' and the 'conservative' New Right, Andrew Gamble argues that the attack on the New Class 'was spearheaded by the group of American intellectuals who have been dubbed the neo-conservatives' (1988:

58). This group of intellectuals, he argues:

> criticize the assumptions and the ambitions of post-war social and economic policy. They argue that too much of modern planning by public agencies failed to observe the limits which are inherent in human action, limits both of understanding and of knowledge. They are sceptical also of the optimistic expectations held by so many of the new class about the ability of government to change both the nature of human beings and of society.

In the United States, the 'neo-conservative' movement consists of a relatively small group of intellectuals such as Irving Kristol, George Gilder and Nathan Glazer (the latter also occupies a place on the SAU's Advisory Council). For these authors, the so-called 'new class' first rose to prominence during the 1960s, the period of President Lyndon Johnson's 'Great Society' programme. According to Kristol, interviewed in 1986 (Graham and Clarke 1986: 51):

> Politicians are always looking for new ideas, new policies to sell to their public, policies that are attached to their name and which will ensure their re-election. In the post-war years, our politicians acquired staffs of bright young aggressive people from universities whose job it was to dream up programmes which no-one had ever thought of before. We have therefore produced, in this country, an educated class whose careers are linked to the state. The new class is the educated class that really wants to shift power away from the private sector and towards the government. They would deny indignantly that they were socialists, but nevertheless they want a highly regulated society.

For Kristol and other neo-conservatives, Johnson's Great Society programme was, from the outset, very much the product of the 'new class' (Graham and Clarke 1986: 51):

> It was run by university graduates with a utopian view of the future, a confidence that changing the world was easy and that people were basically nice. They came from middle-class backgrounds at the end of a post-war boom which just went on and on. The urge to do something was focused by growing public guilt about the position of black people in America. Their politics were 'liberal' in the American meaning of the term. They were what others would call social democrats.

As Kristol recalls, the neo-conservatives were sceptical from the very beginning of the Great Society programme, about the array of policies that were supposed to abolish poverty, reform education, reform all the criminals, because the programmes themselves were highly 'ambitious' and 'seemed to have such a utopian vision of human nature'. For Kristol at least, the Great Society failed because the programmes themselves and the people who designed them 'didn't understand poor people' (Graham and Clarke 1986: 51).

The intellectual consensus of the 'new class' is said to have been overwhelmingly *rationalist*. Their university education as well as their training in academic sociology 'encouraged them to locate the causes of poverty and deviance not within individuals and families but within the structure of society'. As a result, it is argued, this class believed either that an administrative solution to poverty was available to policy-makers, or that one could soon be devised and implemented. Neo-conservatives argue that the programmes can now be seen to have failed. Indeed, it is argued, statistical evidence seems to suggest that, far from achieving its objectives, the Great Society programme increased poverty, reduced employment and retarded education (Murray 1984). In locating the causes of poverty in the 'structure of society', it is argued, the 'new class' failed to understand the mechanisms which raise poor people from poverty (see Chapter 7).

The Rise of the Permissive Society

American neo-conservatives, then, argue that the Great Society programmes can be seen to have failed to realize their overall ambition of reducing poverty, reforming education, and helping the unemployed.   Neo-conservative disillusionment with welfare statism is not, however, confined to the fact that the various Great Society programmes failed on *technical* grounds. Kristol and other neo-conservatives also insist that the *moral* climate changed significantly at this time. In January 1976, Kristol explained to the magazine *Newsweek* that:

> if there is one thing ... neo-conservatives are unanimous about, it is their dislike of the 'counter-culture' which has played so remarkable a role in American life in these last 15 years.

Similarly, in a commentary on the neo-conservatives, Elizabeth Drew (in Steinfels 1979: 10) notes that they are on common ground against what they see as the 'spoiled children' and their 'indulgent elders' of the late 1960s and early 1970s. For neo-conservatives on both sides of the Atlantic, the 1960s and early 1970s were characterized, above all, by a massive revolt against authority, a 'consecration of disorder'. As Edgar has suggested, however, the problem was not merely confined to the behaviour of college students in the 1960s (Edgar 1986: 67):

Indeed, perhaps the most important ideological construct developed by the neo-conservatives is the notion that a significant proportion of the 'Vietnam generation' of college students now forms the core a 'New Class' of scientists, teachers and educational administrators, journalists and others in the communications industries, psychologists, social workers, those lawyers and doctors who make their careers in the expanding public sector, city planners, the staffs of the larger foundations, the upper levels of the government bureaucracy and so on, which, while not much interested in money is keenly interested in power, a power which it wishes to transfer from business to government, where the new class itself will have a major say in how it is exercised.

The danger was, then, that the 'revolting' students of the 1960s, who had been and presumably therefore remained 'hostile' to both capitalist free enterprise and traditional social values, might in due course occupy powerful and influential positions within the corporate state itself and encourage the expansion of public and universal welfare provision as a justification for their own existence and growth. Indeed, according to neo-conservatives in both Britain and the United States, this is precisely what happened in the late 1960s and early 1970s.

In particular, Edgar (1986: 68) argues, the neo-conservative case against the social-democratic post-war 'consensus' in sociology and social policy is that:

> liberal capitalism, unlimited by bourgeois constraints, encouraged the post-war generation in the belief that it has a right to the instant satisfaction of all appetites, regardless of effort. In the late 1960s, this conviction shifted from the purely economic into the political arena, with the consequence that a ... new class of people entered the distributive sectors of government, there encouraging its clients to believe in turn that they were entitled, as of right, to the full benefits of a consumer society, whether or not they could afford them. Thus liberal capitalism gave permission to the post-war boom generation to pursue its appetite for moral self-satisfaction regardless of the political consequences: allowing this new class in turn to foster in a new underclass the notion that it had the right to satisfy its physical appetites without economic restraint, to the point where liberal capitalism itself is threatened by social violence on the one hand or financial collapse on the other.

Under the promptings of the 'new class', then, the state itself is said to have become over-extended by expanding its activities and the range of its responsibilities to cover those areas which had previously been reserved for other social institutions. As Gamble (1988: 55) notes:

> In usurping their role the state ... overburdened itself and undermined precisely those institutions, particularly the family, on which it depends for its own support. Social democracy destroys the balance between state and society, threatening the creation

of an atomised mass society, the rise of an authoritarian state and the shrinking of the domain of private life.

The conservative New Right, Gamble argues, has been concerned 'to restore the balance between the different parts of the social order and to prevent the undermining of authority' (Gamble 1988: 60).

'The Kindness that Kills'

In 1984, the SAU produced a study which was deeply critical of the way church reports had analyzed social and economic issues (Anderson 1984). In particular, the contributors were commonly opposed to secular ideologies. Christian Socialism and Marxism were said to be 'heresies', inconsistent with 'Christian' beliefs. The same could not, however, be said of capitalism. Brian Griffiths, for example, argued that:

> Capitalism is not anti-Christian, nor need its stress on the importance of individual competition and profit be rejected out of hand. The challenge is to incorporate capitalism *within* Christianity.

On closer inspection, contributors to *The Kindness that Kills* can be seen as responding to precisely this challenge - namely, to demonstrate that capitalism is not merely compatible with a Christian outlook, but is in fact the most 'Christian' form of political economy there is, at least in relation to Marxism or Christian Socialism. The book's contributors assert, first of all, the *technical* superiority of capitalism over all other forms of political economy - and, in particular, over centralized state planning, ownership and control. Dawson's chapter on the subject of wealth creation, for example, argues that it is reasonable to believe (on the basis of historical evidence) that capitalism is the best wealth-creating system yet devised (Anderson 1984: 19).

Similarly, Lord Bauer considers but rejects four common 'myths' about Third World poverty: that Third World poverty is the result of developed countries' riches; that governments (always) act for the common good; that politically initiated income redistribution from rich to poor is necessary, and that this should involve land distribution. Poverty, Bauer explains, is caused by many factors but not by the misconduct of the rich. Governments do not always act for the common good. Political redistribution 'may aggravate poverty, not reduce it'. Land and resources are not a crucial factor compared with human attitudes and motivation. The four myths, Bauer argues, have three things in common: they would not have been perpetrated had the church worked harder at a balanced study of Third World poverty; do little to help those who suffer poverty, and 'legitimize envy' (Anderson 1984: 38).

As a further example, Robert Miller's chapter on unemployment concedes that 'joblessness' is theologically and indeed morally objectionable, but rejects the argument that state intervention provides an obvious answer to the problem. For Miller at least, the findings of 'public choice theory' suggest that a return to large-scale state intervention is unlikely to increase economic stability, and 'will do nothing to effect a permanent reduction in unemployment' (Anderson 1984: 80). Finally, Ralph Harris insists that high expenditure on universal welfare must be paid for by the poor and not just the rich. Taxation, he argues, distorts incentives to save and to work. Services supplied 'free' will prove inadequate because the articulate middle classes will do better than the poor. Finally, he argues, inefficient hospitals, schools and welfare departments will be exploited by trade unions for the benefit of those who work in them.

This same theme of the *technical* superiority of capitalism and democratic institutions over other forms of political economy is taken up by Brian Griffiths, in what is perhaps the key essay in the collection, on 'Christianity and Capitalism'. In his essay, Griffiths sets out to challenge claims that capitalism is 'anti-Christian' and that the free market is 'the institutionalization of individualism and non-responsibility'. Statements like these, from his Christian contemporaries, suggest to Griffiths that a more virulent and widespread antagonism towards the market has developed within the Church over the last quarter of a century. In particular, he argues (Anderson 1984: 105):

> The dependence of the market economic system on the profit motive, individualistic self-interest and the competitive spirit render it morally indefensible in the eyes of its critics ... the materialistic and unequal society it seems to foster is judged to be utterly at variance with the teachings of Jesus on wealth, poverty and community.

In fact, Griffiths argues, the opposite is true; as a matter of historical fact, he argues, capitalism has been responsible for the transformation of the Western world from widespread poverty and degradation to unprecedented prosperity:

> in the contemporary world the market economies of the West have been able to create wealth more efficiently and have secured for the poorest of their people a far higher level of *per capita* consumption than have the state-owned and state-planned economies of the socialist bloc.

For Griffiths, then, there is a strong *economic* case to be made for capitalism as the most efficient system of wealth creation. However, he goes on, this *technical* dimension is only one, and perhaps for many Christians, the least important aspect of the problem of the *legitimacy* of capitalism. The key problem for the Christian, Griffiths argues, is the extent to which capitalism is or is not compatible with a 'Christian' morality. This question is clearly important, but is also 'problematic' for the Christian to deal with, because (Anderson 1984: 114):

> Whether we look at Adam Smith in the eighteenth century, Herbert Spencer in the nineteenth century, or Friedman and Hayek in our own, all the major intellectual defences of capitalism as an economic system have been conducted within the context of a thoroughly secular philosophy, which is a direct product of the Enlightenment. The common feature is that they all attempt to present economic life as something which is impersonal, amoral, which can be expressed as a 'system' and which, as a system, has a natural tendency to equilibrium. God is pushed into the background and economic life becomes independent of anything divine or indeed, ultimately, anything human as well.

For Griffiths at least, it is difficult on Christian grounds to accept the ideological underpinnings of these defences of capitalism (Anderson 1984: 114):

> Firstly, economic life has to be judged within a moral framework: efficiency is not enough. Secondly, it is important to think about economics as [the] actions of individual people not systems ... belief in the system's tendency towards equilibrium emphasizes the economic machine to the exclusion of people. It is imperative therefore from a Christian point of view, to rescue the market economy from its narrow secular ideology. From an economic, theological and moral point of view there is much that is of value in the market economy: for the Christian the challenge is to incorporate those aspects within a framework that is distinctively Christian and subject to Christian values.

'Moral Aspects of Social Problems'

In common with the CPS (Chapter 3), then, the SAU has been concerned not merely with 'economic' questions but also with the moral and cultural aspects of social problems. For the SAU, no less than for the CPS, the continued existence of a market economy and of 'democratic' institutions depends on the widespread acceptance of certain values. Values, then, are seen as crucial in securing legitimacy for capitalism, and must occupy a central place in any discussion of socio-economic affairs. As Griffiths (whose work has been published by both the SAU and the CPS) argues in his book *Morality and the Market-Place* (Griffiths 1989: 11):

> Whether in the family, the school, the workplace or the community, the values ... people espouse and which guide their lives are important to our economic and political life. Mediating structures help generate and maintain values. In the battle against crime and hooliganism, in appealing for responsible stewardship of the environment [and] in helping prevent drug abuse and homelessness the need for permanent values to be transmitted from one generation to the next through the family and through schools is important. Government can achieve a certain amount through legislation. But that is, of necessity, limited. Even those who remain agnostic about personal belief recognize that the continued existence of the market economy depends on the widespread acceptance of certain values.

Which values, though, should people have? As we have seen, the contributors to *The Kindness that Kills* argue that 'Christian' (or, more precisely, perhaps, 'Judaeo-Christian') values are the ones people should have. What, though, do Griffiths and other SAU authors *mean* by 'Christian' values? The answer is provided by Griffiths in the following claim (Griffiths 1989: 40):

> for a market economy to work, the society of which it is part needs to believe in certain kinds of values: it must lay great store by individual responsibility [and] have a non-egalitarian view of what constitutes social justice.

'Christian' values, then, involve two aspects - namely, a sense of personal responsibility and secondly, what Griffiths calls a 'non-egalitarian view of social justice'. Clearly, these aspects need to be examined in rather more detail, beginning with the latter.

Here, it would seem, Griffiths' meaning is clear enough: for capitalism to secure the legitimacy necessary for its survival, market *outcomes* must be widely perceived as being fair or just. Although Griffiths emphatically rejects the idea that equality of outcome in economic affairs is either feasible or desirable it is nevertheless important, he argues, that market outcomes should be consistent with 'biblical principles of justice'. Poverty should be 'eliminated', 'injustice' remedied, and 'abuse' in the form of externalities such as monopoly or pollution rectified. 'Christian' justice also implies each family should have a permanent stake in economic life. To the extent that all of these elements are seen as necessary and desirable, then, the market is said by Griffiths to *fail* in certain respects, the suggestion being that a role can and should be set aside for government and indeed for other 'non-state' institutions (mediating structures) in eliminating poverty and ensuring that capitalism is not 'an economic system shorn of justice' (Griffiths 1989: 29).

There is also, however, a second sense in which the market is said by Griffiths to fail. This is that the free market *per se* cannot necessarily ensure that people behave in morally virtuous ways. Indeed, the market may even encourage people to behave in ways that are both personally and socially 'irresponsible'. For Griffiths and (as we shall see) other SAU authors, self-reliance and moral restraint are essential not only for markets to 'work', but also - and more importantly perhaps - in maintaining social cohesion. Again, to the extent that the free market *per se* may fail to generate these values spontaneously, this would suggest that a significant role can (and should) be set aside for other 'non-state' institutions - schools, the family, neighbourhoods, local communities, the church itself - to generate and maintain such values.

'Self-Improvement and Social Action'

SAU authors, then, have been concerned not only with 'economic' questions, but also with the 'moral' aspects of social problems. In this connection, they have emphasized the importance of the 'Judaeo-Christian' virtues of personal and social responsibility. In a contribution to the SAU series exploring the 'moral aspects of social problems', Professor Antony Flew insists that 'social' problems such as poverty, drug-abuse and ill-health are not problems which merely 'happen' to innocent victims (the poor, drug-abusers and the sick), but happen, at least in part, because of the way the victims (or those close to them) have *chosen* to act. For Flew at least, this element of choice is fundamental, in terms of the response of social policy to particular social problems (Flew 1990: 3):

> Several of the major life-threatening or disabling diseases, notably heart disease, respiratory diseases and AIDS are related to the kind of life which their victims chose to lead, whether they smoked, what they ate and what their sexual practices were. Even poverty is now increasingly linked not with an inevitable old age, but with the disruption of, or the failure to form, families. Yet single parenthood and divorce both result from the choices of individuals ... the part which individuals' choices play in allegedly 'social' problems is repeatedly seen when, of two persons or families subjected to the same unemployment rate, the same drug temptations or the same inner city deprivation, one avoids problems and the other succumbs.

Human beings, Flew argues, are creatures who can (and cannot but) make choices. Indeed, this is the ground for their pretensions to a peculiar dignity. Individuals alone, he argues, are responsible for the choices they make. Flew's report, then, is intended to redirect attention towards the need for, and possibilities of, individual action (Flew 1990: 7):

> individual action, that is, to better the condition both of individuals themselves and of other people both immediately and directly, rather than in and through some inevitably protracted and indirect political process.

For Flew at least, while much of what can and should be done can be done only or most effectively by government (or some other form of collectivity), there is also a great deal which individuals *as* individuals both can and should do, both to better themselves and (either immediately or ultimately) to benefit other people. This 'Christian' emphasis on personal responsibility has, according to Flew, been neglected by the churches in general and in particular by the contributors to *Faith in the City*, a report produced by the Archbishop of Canterbury's Commission on Urban Priority Areas (UPAs) in 1984.

Antony Flew condemns the 'collectivist assumptions, uncritical contentions and unexamined criticisms' made by the Commissioners, there being 'almost always a lot which individuals *as* individuals both can do and ought to do to better themselves and (immediately or ultimately) to benefit other people'. Ill-health, he argues, is frequently self-inflicted. Smoking, excessive drinking and drug-abuse are 'hugely damaging indulgences' which represent 'a tragic waste of human resources' and impose a 'heavy burden' on the National Health Service (Flew 1990: 14). These 'truths' about the extent of ultimately self-inflicted ill-health and about the often lamentable effects upon other people of choices endangering one's own health, he argues:

> cannot honestly be avoided or evaded, as so many would wish to do, by pointing to positive correlations between socio-economic class membership and certain of the relevant dangerous indulgences.... Everybody has the right and some opportunity to improve their own health.

Similarly, Flew argues, in relation to the issues of poverty and low pay, the same possibilities exist for self-help. As Michael Novak and his colleagues conclude, from their work on poverty in the United States (AEI 1987: 5):

> The probabilities of remaining involuntary in poverty are remarkably low for those who, first, complete high school, then, once an adult, get and stay married (even if not on the first try) and finally, stay employed, even at a wage and under conditions below their ultimate aims.

'Social Policy Cannot Be Morally Neutral'

SAU authors, then, have typically been concerned less with free-market economics *per se*, than with the 'moral aspects of social problems'. In this connection, these authors typically want to claim that 'social policy' cannot, and should not attempt to be, morally neutral (Mitchell 1990). A 'free' society, it is argued, is one whose members subscribe to certain common values - the most central of which is 'a common understanding of freedom itself'. Moreover, a free society is said to rely upon 'a comparatively high level of habitual good behaviour, and a general readiness to pursue purposes and conduct through the medium of institutions which are widely understood and recognized' (Mitchell 1990).

Freedom, on this view, requires 'a commitment by those in society to a particular set of moral values and social institutions'. In addition, government should be committed to social policies which support those values and institutions. In this connection, it is said to be vital to distinguish between a 'liberal' society and a 'plural' society. 'A free and liberal society is not the same as a 'plural' society when that term is used to mean one in which there is no conception of the common good, no agreed values or agreed means of reconciling conflict' (Mitchell 1990: 2).

A 'free' society, then, should properly be distinguished from 'pluralism' in this sense, because 'radically different policies' are implied by the two terms. In particular, pluralism suggests that social policy can and should be morally neutral. A liberal society, on the other hand, presupposes the existence of certain common values and shared assumptions about 'freedom' and the role of institutions in society - above all, perhaps, a shared view of morality itself. Furthermore, if the balance between freedom and stability is to be maintained, the suggestion is that a moral and institutional framework has to be kept in being, in which law and social policy have a part to play (Mitchell 1990: 22). Social policy, for Basil Mitchell, presupposes there is a social system to underpin:

> It is a basic precondition of all social policy that there exists a social system which exists independently of it and to which its role is supplementary. This system is based primarily on the family. If family responsibilities were to be generally disavowed, no amount of remedial action by the state could repair the damage. The general stability of marriage and the regular care of parents for their children are always presupposed, and this means that the moral obligations and moral virtues which these relationships demand are equally presupposed. In such a system people

are not free to conduct their sexual lives in any way they please; they are subject to moral constraints.

A particular concern of authors writing for the SAU has been the breakdown of family life and, specifically, of the institution of marriage. For these authors, changes in the law on divorce since 1969 - based increasingly on the principles of 'clean breaks' and 'no fault' - have weakened the institution of marriage by letting it seem as if it is of no public concern whether married couples adhere to their wedding vows or not. In a 1988 SAU report, for example, George Brown has argued that any divorce law must balance a number of priorities which may be in conflict with each other. Examples include the need to buttress marriage against the need for a quick, efficient divorce; the need to have a moral base against the need to reduce recrimination; and the need to promote the welfare of the children against the need of the parents to divorce (Brown 1988).

Conclusion

Publicly, Anderson argues, the SAU 'will be noted as the think-tank that has drawn attention to values'. Both in sociology and social policy, he argues, 'the explicit acknowledgement of the role of values in society has, to some extent, been played down.'[2] The SAU has therefore sought to re-direct attention to the importance of certain virtues. Indeed, the Unit certainly has a programme at the time of writing (April 1991), examining the sorts of moral issues that are bound up in social problems. As this chapter has tried to show, the dominant themes of SAU publications since 1980 have been those of restoring 'personal responsibility' and moral restraint and also the argument that these values can and should be acquired by individuals through institutions other than the free market. The conservative New Right tendency, we have noted, attaches most importance to the institutions that sustain capitalist economic activity (Gamble 1988).

For the conservative New Right, no less than for their liberal counterparts, the post-war 'consensus' was a major mistake and has to be reversed. New Right conservatives, as Gamble argues, make common cause with New Right liberals 'because they have a common enemy. Both see the destructive impact of social democracy upon the institutions that sustain capitalism' (Gamble 1988: 54-5). As Gamble argues:

> Liberals may express this concern in terms of freedom of the individual, while Conservatives emphasize the erosion of authority. Both, however, regard the trends

established by the growth of public sectors and the kind of government intervention practised since the 1940s as pernicious. Both focus on the rise of a 'new class' of public sector professional employees who have come to staff the agencies of the public sector and who have a vested interest in its continued growth.

For the conservative New Right, in particular, the authority of the state itself and authority within major social institutions has to be restored. Markets and free competition are thus 'not ends in themselves' for New Right conservatives, but only means to those ends. Important as it is to protect the private realm from arbitrary interference, New Right conservatives argue that social and political authority is as important as the 'rights' of individuals. For Gamble (1988: 60) at least, these two strands within the New Right:

> helped create the intellectual ferment which was part of the context in which Thatcherism emerged and played a major part in shaping its concerns and objectives. It supplied ideas for challenging the dominant ideas within British politics and the Conservative Party. It suggested a novel political strategy for the Conservatives which broke from the assumptions and limitations of the 1940s settlement; and it offered a new strategy for accumulation and reversing economic decline. In the hands of a major political leader plans for making the economy free once more and the state strong were to be welded into a powerful political programme, capable of reversing the decline in Conservative electoral fortunes and seizing the new agenda of British politics for the Right.

Notes

1.   Interview.
2.   Interview.

5 Education

Introduction

The purpose of this chapter is twofold. A first aim is to explore some of the tensions (contradictions) within conservative capitalism (the New Right) between those identified by Hoover and Plant (1989: 76-90) as traditionalists (communitarians) and individualists (free marketeers) over educational reform/policy, with particular reference to the four think-tanks (IEA, ASI, CPS and SAU) profiled in Chapters 1-4 (above). A second aim is to examine the impact (if any) of several New Right groups on Conservative education policy before and after 1979, and in particular to examine the role of such groups in either contributing, or failing to contribute, significantly to the Education Reform Act (ERA) of 1988 which, for one writer at least, represents 'the most substantial and complex piece of educational legislation since the Butler Act of 1944' (Wilcox 1989).

As Miriam David (1989: 155) has argued, the ERA is 'probably unique' in the history of educational legislation in Britain in its coverage of both schools and higher education:

> Even the 1944 Education Act, which has always been hailed as the major cornerstone of post-war educational policy, was centrally concerned with the school system - not with higher education. No previous Education Act took both together.

For reasons of space, however, the focus of this chapter is confined to those clauses within the ERA which affect schools and leaves to other authors and other occasions discussion of those aspects which affect the future of universities, polytechnics and colleges of further and higher education.

The starting-point for this chapter is with the free marketeers' 'Big Idea' for reform in the sphere of education, the education *voucher* - an idea with which the IEA, in particular, has long been identified and which IEA authors and contributors continue to support and advocate as the best, and perhaps even the only, way to secure the benefits of a 'free market' in education. As we shall see below, however, despite an impressive intellectual lineage and decades of intensive academic advocacy, a voucher scheme of the type preferred by the IEA over many years has still to be applied in British public policy by any government, Conservative or otherwise. A further aim of this chapter is to seek to explain why even the most market-oriented administration of modern times ultimately failed to introduce an education voucher scheme at any time during the 1980s (Seldon 1986).

As we shall see below, a possible - indeed, for some, the most plausible - explanation for this is that which would be predicted by public choice theory (the economics of politics). The suggestion here has been, and is, that any attempt by the Thatcher government to introduce a 'Friedman/IEA-type' voucher scheme could never have succeeded *politically* - not least, perhaps, because the implementation of such a scheme would have been bitterly opposed by powerful and well-organized vested interests. As we shall see below, it was on the strength of precisely this critique that the Adam Smith Institute (ASI) and others ultimately came to embrace and develop an 'invisible' (backdoor) voucher scheme designed to secure many of the same (economic) benefits as the Friedman/IEA education voucher but without at the same time incurring its (political) costs.

In this connection, the ASI's alternative to the Friedman/IEA education voucher (below) is seen to have been informed by the techniques of the style of policy formulation known as 'micropolitics' (Chapter 2, above). The suggestion here is that in education (as elsewhere) the IEA and the ASI perceived differently the question of what is, and what should be, the proper relationship between ideas and events after 1979 (Chapters 1-2, above). The dispute over vouchers between the IEA and the ASI notwithstanding, this chapter also reviews the proposals for reform of groups such as the Education Study Group of the Centre for Policy Studies (CPSESG) and the SAU after 1979, and seeks to trace the impact (if any) of various New Right groups on the ERA itself. In the final part of this chapter, some of the tensions (contradictions) within the Conservative programme for education reform during the 1980s are also - briefly - explored.

'Education for Democrats'

For Hoover and Plant (1989: 173), the policy proposal which accords most with the 'free-market conservative' approach to reform in education is the education *voucher*, an idea which has been espoused in particular by Milton Friedman and in Britain by the Institute of Economic Affairs. For the IEA (Seldon 1986: viii), in particular:

> There is wide agreement that one or other variants of the voucher would give parents something of the authority and choice over schools and teachers which is now

confined to the paying customers of private schools. If direct payment by all or most parents for schools (as for food, shelter, holidays) is not yet possible, the transferable voucher, perhaps under the politically more appealing name of education credit or bond, is the next best way of exerting consumer sovereignty in education.

The voucher concept itself is a simple one. Instead of paying taxes to the government in return for the promise of a 'free' school place, parents would continue to pay taxes but would receive instead a voucher for each child to the value of the (usually average) annual cost of provision. The voucher could then be exchanged for a place in the school of the parents' choice. A voucher scheme, its supporters claim, would once again restore to parents the power to control the education of their children (Green 1987: 157).

The voucher is said to be the closest to a free market in education which could be attained and has all the benefits, its supporters argue, of the free market in other spheres (Hoover and Plant 1989: 174). Specifically, its advantages are said to be that:

> It gives the consumer choice between different sorts of schools, even if the government were to set minimum standards, because within this constraint there would still be a wide variety of schools with different educational styles and traditions available. It weakens the power of professional producer-interest groups, in this case the teachers, who will have to be far more responsive to parents' demands if they are to retain the enrolment of children.

The idea of enabling, and even encouraging, all parents to break free of the state education system by 'distributing earmarked purchasing power in place of providing nil-priced schooling' was first advocated in the modern era by Professor Milton Friedman (then a relatively little-known economist at the University of Chicago) as long ago as 1955 (Seldon 1986: 12). In 1964, Professors Alan Peacock and Jack Wiseman produced their seminal IEA Hobart Paper *Education for Democrats* and so became 'the *first* economists in Britain to argue that parents should be enabled by vouchers, grants or loans to shop around in a free market' (Chitty 1989: 181).

For the IEA's Arthur Seldon (1986: 1), the education voucher is a highly flexible instrument, with many variations, which would effectively:

> replace the financing of schools through taxes under political control and bureaucratic supervision by payments direct from parents thus equipped with a new ability (for the 95 per cent with middle and lower incomes) to compare schools and move between them.

In theory at least, some eight different versions of the voucher scheme are broadly conceivable (Maynard 1975, Blaug 1984). In general, however, there seem to be two main variants (Bosanquet 1983). Under Friedman's version of the scheme, parents would receive a voucher for either the full cost or a proportion of the cost of an average place in a state school. Similarly, the IEA's Friedman-type voucher has usually had a value at the average cost of a place. Parents would be free to top up with any amount they chose; vouchers could be spent at any school, state or private, and there would be no restrictions on how schools selected pupils from any waiting-list (Bosanquet 1983: 168).

The idea of an education voucher made a considerable impact on political debate, if not on public policy, in both Britain and the USA during the 1970s and 1980s (Green 1987: 157). In Britain, the campaign to promote parent-power through the voucher began in earnest in September/October 1974, with the presentation of a motion in favour of experimental vouchers to the annual conference of the National Council of Women (NCW) in Worthing, where it narrowly failed to secure the two-thirds majority required to make it NCW policy (Seldon 1977: 193). The motion was moved by Marjorie Seldon (wife of Arthur Seldon) and seconded by Margaret Jones, herself a teacher. Although the motion was narrowly lost, the support it received encouraged its sponsors to establish an organization known as FEVER (Friends of the Education Voucher Experiment in Representative Regions) in December 1974 to transform what had hitherto been a purely academic/intellectual campaign for the voucher into a populist crusade (Knight 1990: 91).

In October 1974, the Kent County Council majority party (Conservative) expressed an interest in the possibility of an experiment with vouchers and in February 1976 announced that it would conduct a feasibility study, based on Ashford. In the meantime, a number of Conservative MPs also began to take up the cause - not least, perhaps, Dr Rhodes Boyson. In an article published in 1975, for instance, Boyson gave a glowing account of a voucher experiment in Alum Rock, California which had been inaugurated in 1972, and argued that the time was now ripe for the establishment of at least two full voucher experiments in Britain in areas where local education authorities (LEAs) were anxious to co-operate. In 1976, Boyson also initiated a motion in the House of Commons by the Conservative Opposition in favour of local experiments with school vouchers. The motion was supported (on a three-line Whip) by all Conservative MPs, including the former Prime Minister, Edward Heath - later a critic of the scheme - with only one abstention. Thereafter, experiments with vouchers became the Conservative Party's official education policy. In 1978, the Kent feasibility study revealed strong parental desire for choice in education and suggested that the number of pupils who would switch schools would not be unmanageable (Seldon

1986: 14).

Despite misgivings across the political spectrum, the prospect of political action on the voucher accelerated with the return of Margaret Thatcher's first administration in May 1979. In December 1979, a deputation from FEVER was sent to Mrs Thatcher's first Education Secretary, Mark Carlisle, to present a national petition in favour of vouchers for all schools, state and private. The voucher lobby made little impression on Carlisle, but when Sir Keith Joseph eventually succeeded him in September 1981, the new Secretary of State declared (at the Conservative Party Conference in October) that he had personally been 'intellectually attracted' to the idea of seeing whether the voucher might eventually be a way of increasing parental choice in education even further. It was now, said Joseph, 'up to the advocates of such a possibility to study the difficulties - and there are real difficulties - and see whether they can develop proposals which will really cope with them' (cited by Chitty 1989: 183).

In November 1981, two pressure groups, the National Council for Educational Standards (below) and FEVER, wrote to the Secretary of State requesting an account of the difficulties that would need to be resolved before a voucher scheme could be designed, and its implications assessed, for the purposes of education policy. Sir Keith, in turn, responded by asking civil servants at the DES to prepare a paper on the voucher. A memorandum was duly sent to FEVER in December 1981 with a covering letter from Sir Keith himself in which the Education Secretary again confirmed that he was 'intellectually attracted' to the voucher as a means of eventually extending parental choice and influence, and improving educational standards (reprinted in Seldon 1986: 36).

The memorandum itself, however, which was hardly sympathetic to the voucher plan, stated categorically in its first paragraph that 'the Secretary of State for Education and Science has made it clear that he has no plans for the general introduction of a voucher scheme'. Civil servants at the DES were, it seems, anxious to see the whole idea 'quietly dropped' (Chitty 1989: 183-4). In March 1982, FEVER responded to the DES memorandum in a fifteen-page document (signed by its Chairman, Marjorie Seldon and Vice-Chairman, the late Ruth Garwood-Scott) which drew on advice received from 11 economists, political scientists and lawyers, several of whom had direct experience of running schools. Three further academics who had been approached by FEVER also responded to the memorandum through other channels in 1982 and early 1983. There was, however, no further response from the DES and by the end of 1983 the scheme had indeed been 'dropped' (Chitty 1989: 185).

In his speech to the Conservative Party Conference in October 1983, Sir Keith Joseph declared that 'the voucher, at least in the foreseeable future, is dead'. In a later statement to the House of Commons in June 1984, Sir Keith explained that he had concluded that 'the difficulties which would arise from the many and complex changes required to the legal and institutional framework of the education system, and the additional cost of mitigating them, were too great to justify further consideration of a voucher system as a means of increasing parental choice and influence' (cited by Chitty 1989: 186). For these reasons, Sir Keith argued, vouchers were no longer on the Government's political agenda.

Two main arguments have been advanced against the voucher. The first of these is that, in Friedman's version of the scheme - but not in others - allowing parents to top up the value of vouchers would enable wealthy parents to buy superior education for their children by attracting better teachers to the better conditions and salaries available in a topped-up voucher school. Bosanquet (1983: 172), for example, has argued that:

> The Friedman scheme is likely to result in the better teachers moving away from working-class schools. There would be price competition for better teachers. Schools with more purchasing power from topped-up vouchers would be able to bid for teachers more successfully. These schools would become more efficient than the others. Many teachers would prefer to work with more teachable children. Thus the results of schools with high proportions of working-class children are likely to be worse. The supply-side effects would provide a further deterrent to working-class parents towards matching the larger purses of better-off parents. The New Right might argue that in the long run supply elasticities might draw more resources into education. But even in the long run, better teachers would tend to go where pay and teaching conditions were better.

A second objection has been that vouchers are incompatible with a sense of national community and a common culture. As Hoover and Plant (1989: 174-5) recall:

> This argument was put forward in several ways which were not wholly compatible. The first is that schools could be set up on ethnic, religious or sectarian lines and offer very narrow forms of education. At the other end of the scale it was argued that, if topping up of vouchers were allowed, then rich parents would tend to send their children to the same school, and that this would lead to a decline in social integration. Hence the ideas and values of common culture (a rather leftish notion) or community or a sense of national identity were used to argue against the voucher scheme because it could produce great educational diversity, some aspects of which would not be compatible with more *traditionalist* views (both left and right) about the common values which the educational system should serve.

The dispute between New Right traditionalists (communitarians) and individualists (free marketeers) over vouchers is one to which we shall return in due course. For the moment, however, our main concern is to examine how the IEA, in particular, has since sought to explain the decision in 1983 by 'a sympathetic, even enthusiastic Secretary of State' in Sir Keith Joseph not to proceed with an education voucher scheme - an idea to which, as we have seen, Joseph had previously declared himself to be 'intellectually attracted'.

The 'Riddle' of the Voucher

In February 1986, the IEA produced a case study of the entire voucher episode, a recurring theme of which was (and is) that, in the end, 'the concentrated, articulate producer interests of organized teachers and entrenched bureaucracy had triumphed over the dispersed, muted interests of consumer-parents'. For Arthur Seldon, in particular, the reason for Sir Keith's decision was emphatically 'not administrative impracticability but official feet-dragging and political underestimation of potential popular acclaim' (Seldon 1986: 97).

The 'purely *political*' reasons for the abandonment of the voucher in 1983, Seldon argued, had been indicated by Sir Keith himself in a television interview in May 1984 and a House of Commons statement in June 1984. In May 1984, Seldon recalled, Sir Keith had given the following four reasons for his decision not to proceed with a voucher scheme. The first of these was that governments had a statutory obligation - under the Butler Act of 1944 - that all children should be given education 'free'. Secondly, Sir Keith had argued, the habit of looking to the state had bitten so deeply into the public awareness that 'only a minority of parents appreciate the improvement that vouchers might have brought'. Thirdly, the introduction of a voucher scheme, for Joseph, would have caused 'a great deal of controversy in our own Party as well as across party lines'. Finally, Joseph had insisted, vouchers would not have brought a harvest of votes quickly enough in time to reward the political 'slog' (Seldon 1986: 61-7).

The decisive objections to adopting the voucher in 1983, Seldon argued, were 'not ultimately administrative' (as had been suggested in 1981) but essentially political:

> In short, the voucher was a challenge to the formidable fortress of paternalism, professional corporatism, monopoly and political authority that had long ruled British education. That the ramparts did not fall to the first intellectual assault was almost predictable.

For Seldon at least, if the 1983 abandonment of the voucher had been for essentially political reasons, this implied that:

its advocates may have to make more allowance for the economics of politics and the rigidity of the machinery of government if their next essay is not to end in a second failure.... Economists who see glittering prizes in the voucher must now accept that it will not come to pass simply because a Government of sympathetic politicians is furnished with the intellectual argument.

For the IEA in early 1986, then, the privatization of education 'in one go' had, perhaps, been too much for politicians and the public to accept; instead, what was needed was a more subtle way of incorporating the principle of the voucher, possibly under a different name, into education policy (Seldon 1986: 95-6):

Only an open market in school education can allow free rein for the consumers and producers to meet in voluntary exchange of information and experience to discover the optimum quantity and quality of schooling. To allow the market to re-emerge, the price of education must be restored as the link between supply and demand. And the way to restore price is through the voucher, in essence, even if another name is politically more expedient.

Education Credits: A Phased Introduction

As Clyde Chitty (1989: 230) has recalled, the IEA Hobart Paperback *The Riddle of the Voucher* (Seldon 1986: 45-54) also described various alternative schemes - three of which, by the political scientist John Barnes and by Professors Peacock and West, appeared in the IEA's journal *Economic Affairs* - which had been developed between 1981 and 1983 and which offered:

a number of suggestions for half-way houses and stepping-stones: changes in the way education was organized which fell short of the introduction of a proper voucher scheme but which would pave the way for such a move later on. One of the IEA proposals was for the central government grant-in-aid for education to local authorities to be paid as a *per capita* payment for each pupil. This was a variation of the scheme which eventually found its way into Chapter 3 of the 1988 Act. What both schemes have in common is the establishment of something approaching a fee-structure. Once this is established, the advocates of the voucher believe it will be comparatively simple to proceed to the next stage and make the *per capita* payment to the parent instead of to the school.

As we shall now see, this scheme (developed in 1982-83) to introduce the voucher in three (or four) logical stages was subsequently refined and developed at the IEA following the arrival of Stuart Sexton to run the IEA's new (albeit semi-autonomous) Education Unit, the IEAEU.

The first publication from the IEAEU, in March 1987, was a radical election manifesto for schools by Sexton himself, in which the former Special Advisor to both Mark Carlisle and Sir Keith Joseph argued that better standards in state schools would only ultimately be achieved by their eventual privatization and by 'the creation, as near as practicable, of a free market in education'. The burden of Sexton's paper, it was disclosed, was to suggest proposals which could deliver 'better education for all children through the exercise of genuine parental choice, harnessing parent-power and leading ultimately to the only true parent power: parent *purchasing* power'. For Sexton at least, only a direct financial relationship between the provider and the consumer of education could ultimately raise standards and ensure the responsiveness of schools to the choice of parents and the needs of children. Privatization, however, was now said to require a methodical, step-by-step approach. In particular, Sexton argued, the phased introduction of education credits (vouchers) would be more likely to succeed politically than any attempt to make 'a *sudden* change, nationwide, to an education credits system from the existing system of provision and finance' (Sexton 1987: 30).

For Sexton, in particular, a voucher system should be the ultimate objective of education reform. This eventual aim and ambition, however, would take 'perhaps five years' to achieve, even if the Government began to introduce the first of a series of measures immediately. In pursuit of the ultimate goal of privatization, Sexton argued (1987: 10):

> the mistake has been to assume that we can get from where we are now to where we want to be in one giant stride, and all in a couple of years. After a hundred years of state-managed education, it will take more time to accommodate the schools, the teachers and above all the parents themselves to a system of free choice: from a producer-led system to a consumer-led system, which is what it ought to be.

In March 1987, then, the IEA was still committed to the eventual introduction of a voucher scheme. For tactical and strategic reasons, however, the IEAEU, in common with other New Right groups (below), was now actively embracing a *gradualist* approach to the long-term aim of replacing a 'producer-led system' with a 'consumer-led system' through the introduction of a system of education credits (Flude and Hammer 1990: 52).

As we saw earlier, Sir Keith Joseph, in explaining his decision not to proceed with the voucher in 1983, had argued in May 1984 that any attempt to introduce such a scheme would have caused 'a great deal of controversy' both within the

Conservative Party and between parties. Moreover, Sir Keith had insisted, the voucher would not have reaped a political 'harvest' quickly enough for it to be sufficiently attractive for the Conservative Party (or indeed, for any other political party) to introduce. For Sexton, on the other hand, these two arguments were true only of a *sudden* 'switchover' to a voucher system. A phased introduction, for Sexton, with each step a gentle step, would be 'far less controversial' and would also 'bring its political harvest at each step, with the final harvest being achieved towards the end of the next Parliament' (Sexton 1987: 46-7).

For Sexton, the phased introduction of education credits should be a three-stage process, the first stage of which should seek to establish a clear, specific, *per capita* sum to be spent on each child's education sufficient to afford each child a proper and adequate education. This *per capita* sum of money, Sexton argued, should also be the minimum sum to be spent on each child's education. Local Education Authorities would be obliged to spend at least this sum of money on each child within their maintained schools. Once Stage 1 had been established, it was argued, every parent would know how much public money had been designated for his or her child's education (Sexton 1987: 31-3).

In Stage 2, Sexton argued, parents should be given an opportunity to choose to take this *per capita* sum in the form of an education credit, which they could 'spend' at any school instead of taking up state provision in the form of a 'free' place at an LEA maintained school. Having clearly established, both in practice and in the public mind, that a clear, *per capita* sum of money would be spent on each child's education at an LEA school, some parents would see the advantage of 'taking that allocation of money in the form of an education credit rather than in the form of an LEA place'. The education credit, Sexton argued, could be spent at any school. Because, however, an LEA place would remain freely available to all parents, the only point of accepting an education credit at this stage would be to 'spend' it at a non-LEA or independent school (Sexton 1987: 33-4).

In Stage 3, Sexton argued, education credits (vouchers) should be offered to every child, with parents sending the child with the credit to the school of their choice - including, of course, to an LEA school 'if so desired'. Stage 3 would therefore be one of *opting in* to an LEA school (or any other school) where Stage 2 had been one of *opting out* of the maintained sector. At this stage, the education credit would, in any case, 'buy a free place at an LEA school'. Parents wishing to send their children to more expensive, non-LEA or independent schools, however, would be required to top up the value of the education credit (voucher) themselves to meet the extra cost involved.

The precise timing of these three stages, Sexton argued, could be left open. Stage 1, however, could be introduced 'immediately' (March 1987), the second stage a year later (March 1988) and the third 'within four or five years'. By phasing the introduction of education credits, Sexton argued, a voucher system could be fully operational within the lifetime of one parliament (Sexton 1987: 31).

'The Limits of Privatization'

In the early 1980s, the Friedman/IEA education voucher scheme had also been considered, but was rejected, by the younger Adam Smith Institute (ASI). As we shall see below, the ASI's pursuit of a free-market solution to the problems of state education began in the early 1980s with an explicit recognition that there were significant limits to what free marketeers could realistically hope to achieve in seeking to privatize immediately the existing system of state education. In 1982, for example, the ASI's President, Madsen Pirie, argued that it was 'politically unrealistic' to suppose that state education could be made private 'overnight' (Pirie 1982: 36):

> The voucher scheme has been known about for at least half a century, yet nothing has been done to implement it no matter what the shade of government in office. This is not due to any inherent fault in the economics of education vouchers, but to a political fault.

The major problem with the Friedman/IEA education voucher, for Pirie, was (and is) that such a scheme involves an overnight revolution. All schools would become privately financed via vouchers and would effectively become autonomous, rather than local authority controlled. For Pirie (1982: 37), on the other hand:

> While bold members of a government might contemplate such a revolution, it is highly unlikely that any government could undertake it. Opposition from the teachers and the local authorities would be added to that from the administrators, locally and nationally, and orchestrated groups of parents who gain more from the present system. Very soon, the level of media hostility would make the government uncertain of its own majority on the issue. As with the NHS, the forces in favour of the status quo would prevail.

For Pirie (1988a: 148) at least, the Friedman/IEA education voucher has many attractive features and would, if it could be achieved, be a vast improvement on the effective state monopoly of education. Unfortunately, he argues, the evidence suggests that the voucher scheme cannot be introduced:

> Despite its undoubted economic strengths, it has political weaknesses which tell heavily against it. In its modern form, it has been discussed at various times for sixty years. It has been seriously investigated by Conservative governments in Britain, but never introduced. In the first place, there is strong opposition from those engaged as producers of education. Teachers' organizations resist it, not wishing their members to be exposed to market forces. Ministry bureaucrats are fanatical in their opposition, recognizing correctly that it would transfer power over education to parents. The parents themselves are easily alarmed at the prospect of losing the free place at the local school. They fear that they would have to pay large extra amounts to secure a decent education.

A further problem, for Pirie, is that the Friedman/IEA voucher scheme cannot realistically be introduced on a 'gradual' or experimental basis:

> Despite talk of experimental schemes, it would have to cover all of the schools within a very large area to be effective and to allow for real variety and choice. It would be prone to sabotage by those determined not to lose control over education. It is a holistic scheme, making its changes all at once. Parents would find pieces of paper arriving through the mail in place of their free school place. Schools, as well as the parents, would suddenly face uncertainty. It is easy to characterize it as some theoretical scheme, never properly tested, which would put the education of children at risk. Governments have long tried to push voucher schemes through, but have always and everywhere had to retreat in the face of political pressures exerted by interest groups.

The decision by Sir Keith Joseph not to proceed with the voucher plan in 1983 seemed to confirm Pirie's earlier (1982) prediction that it was 'highly unlikely' that any government - of whatever political complexion - could or would undertake the scheme. As Pirie has since recalled (1988a: 148):

> Even the combination which saw strong supporters [of the voucher] as Secretary of State and Junior Minister at the Education Department [Sir Keith Joseph and Rhodes Boyson] was insufficient to bring it into practice.

'Omega Education Policy'

In 1983-84, the ASI put forward an alternative set of proposals designed to 'short-circuit' the various obstacles which (for the ASI) would *necessarily* have thwarted any attempt by the Thatcher government to introduce the voucher, and suggested instead three separate - but, as we shall see, interrelated - reforms. In the first place, it was argued, parents should have an effective choice between state schools. The ASI therefore proposed that there should be complete 'open entry' within the state sector so that, in future, a child could be sent to any school willing to accept it. Schools which were oversubscribed, for the ASI, would henceforth have every incentive to expand. Schools which were undersubscribed, on the other hand, would be encouraged to copy those which had been more successful in attracting demand (Butler *et al* 1985).

This reform, as Pirie has since argued, was calculated to be popular with those parents who found themselves trapped by location in the catchment area of a bad school. Choice of school, for the ASI, would enable those parents to escape (Pirie 1988a: 149-50):

> This choice in the absence of open entry is limited to those who can afford to move house into the catchment area of a good school. Indeed, it is not unknown to have a premium of several thousand pounds for houses on the side of the street in the good school area, compared with identical ones opposite them. The policy of open entry still leaves parents to cope with problems of transport to and from school and would see good schools heavily over-subscribed and unable to accept many of their applicants. However, it represents an improvement, and is a popular one.

The ASI's second reform was a policy of making schools much more independent in operation. This, it was argued, could be achieved by ensuring that the policy of each school be determined by its own board of governors (consisting overwhelmingly of parents with children at the school, elected by postal ballot) which should negotiate fixed-term contracts of employment with the headteacher and other teachers. The headteacher's fixed-term contract, it was suggested, could be for five years and could also be made subject to certain conditions of satisfactory performance being met (Butler *et al* 1985: 271).

The head would become the equivalent of a chief executive, answerable to a board of directors. Henceforth, the head would be answerable not to his or her local education authority (LEA) but to the school's governing body, subject to whose approval he or she would also control the curriculum (within certain national guidelines) and other matters such as the school timetable, its policy on discipline and school uniform and the general conduct of the school. The head would also be expected to evaluate each member of staff annually and, in consultation with the board, negotiate with individual teachers and other staff their terms and conditions of employment. The head, again in consultation with the board, would also be authorised to suspend and dismiss teachers 'subject to a written rule that they must first receive written warnings endorsed by the board'

(Butler *et al* 1985: 271).

The ASI's third proposal called for the direct funding of schools from central government on the basis of the number of children enrolled. Henceforth, it was suggested, central government should provide LEAs with a grant which would represent a *per capita* contribution to education in each area. The more pupils there were in any given locality, the larger would be the central government grant. This reform, Pirie has since argued (1988a: 150-1) would, in effect:

> cut the local bureaucracy out of the picture [by] permitting schools to opt out of local authority control and allowing schools funds from the centre according to enrolment. Of course, this incurs the hostility of the local education committees, but these are very small, and have little to trade in political markets. There is more support from the central bureaucracy, which perhaps sees more openings for its members in the administration of such a scheme, and sees no potential job losses or drop in status for them.

Schools wishing to opt out of LEA control, for the ASI, could eventually receive their funding directly from ministerial bureaux within the central education ministry (DES), which would allocate funding on the basis of the same *per capita* formula as before. These ministerial bureaux, it was envisaged, would (eventually) establish 'a local presence for the national authorities and help to bring unbiased information about local needs to the central decision-making process'. *Per capita* funding, for Pirie (1988a: 151) at least:

> should be based on the cost of the education for each group, and might have exceptions to allow a higher rate for inner city schools with language problems [or] isolated village schools with [fewer] economies of scale. Two groups who might have felt threatened by the move over to direct funding are thus taken care of. Parents as a whole have nothing to lose by direct funding of schools and gain the saving which results by eliminating an entire layer of administration, leaving more available to be spent on actual education.

The combined effect of these three reforms, for the ASI, would be to achieve a 'market' in education. Schools controlled by their governing bodies would pursue a variety of different educational priorities and would 'vary in quality and type of education'. A policy of open entry would mean that parents could 'choose for their children the type of education they prefer'. The direct funding of schools on a *per capita* basis implied that schools attracting extra demand would also receive extra funding. Unpopular schools, on the other hand, would either make changes or face the threat of closure (Pirie 1988a: 151).

For the ASI at least, the great advantage of this package of *micropolitical* reforms (Chapter 2, above) was that each of its 'steps' could be supported independently by different interest-groups. Their combined effect, however, would be to secure in practice the results long desired by free marketeers:

> No sudden change is forced upon parents against their will, in that for those who want nothing more than the free place at the local school, this is still available. Choice is there for those who want it: no-one is forced into it. Of course, as the system developed, increasing numbers of people would take advantage of what is offered. Extra techniques have to be incorporated into the new system to allow for the establishment of new state schools where there is demand for them, and to attract additional sources of finance from the private sector.

This policy would not produce a total market situation. Indeed, the ASI scheme promised to do so less than the Friedman/IEA education voucher, in that the former was concerned *only* with state schools:

> It leaves the fee-paying schools as they are, unaltered by the new system, and not participating in it. It aims straight at the state system on which 93 per cent depend, and aims to improve it by transferring power from producers to consumers. The schools are still state schools, still funded out of tax revenues for the most part. New schools founded by parents and teachers are also still state schools, attracting the direct funds from the centre.

The ASI's 'new' scheme, however, also promised to deliver major changes. State schools would become independently run, but would stay in the state sector. Parents' choices would determine where the funds should go to pay for their children's education. Only those schools which responded to demand would attract the enrolment on which their budgets would now depend:

> The clear boundary which exists under the old system between the state sector and the private schools blurs a little under the new system. Forces and pressures are set in motion whose effect is to bring gradual improvement in standards of education achieved within the state sector. They are brought in by reforms calculated to command the support of some of the groups which have a direct interest in state education.

For the ASI, however, there were also key differences between this 'new' approach and the Friedman/IEA education voucher:

> One of them is that the new policy does not involve the use of vouchers. The money follows the child as its parents make choices between a variety of schools. Another difference is that the alternative proposal represents practical politics, working with

the grain of the political market. It is capable of being brought in by stages, and of developing gradually into a system of education which shows more flexibility, more variety, and more responsiveness to the wants and needs of parents. It may not be perfect, but it is a viable solution to the problem. And it is significant that, whereas the voucher system was rejected for years, the new system was in the Conservative election manifesto of 1987, its elements introduced in the Queen's Speech following the Conservative win and similar proposals outlined for Scotland a few months later.

'Save Our Schools'

In 1986, an almost identical scheme to that suggested by the ASI was put forward by members of the Conservative 'No Turning Back' Group. Among the twelve Conservative MPs who put their names to the document were Christopher Chope, Michael Fallon, Michael Forsyth and Robert Jones. In an earlier pamphlet, published by the Conservative Political Centre (CPC) in 1985, the Group had called for a radical package of education reforms, including a scheme to allow parents and teachers to start their own schools and receive state monies for doing so. On lines similar to 'magnet' schools, it was envisaged that these schools would offer greater specialization and would bring extra choices into areas which were badly served by existing schools (Brown *et al* 1985).

In a second pamphlet in 1986, the Group developed and extended this 'radical agenda' for educational reform. For the Group, as for the ASI, the key to a successful education system lay in 'the introduction of opportunities for consumer input'. Improving the quality of education for the majority of parents, however, was said to require more thoroughgoing change than merely expanding the independent sector. Here too, the Friedman/IEA voucher was rejected as 'politically unrealistic':

> It alienates or deters the various interest groups involved, and does not immediately construct interest groups on the other side to outweigh them. It changes everything all at once, and forces change on those who might not feel equipped to handle it. A more viable system might seek to provide opportunities for change and allow the incremental decisions of parents to build the new reality cumulatively, instead of overnight.

The Group, like the ASI, proposed three separate (but interrelated) reforms. Newly-constituted school governing bodies, it was argued, should have responsibility for administering schools and for determining educational priorities. Secondly, it was suggested, schools should henceforth receive their funding directly from central government (as well as from private sources) to give effect to the independence of the school by changing the method of finance. Finally, it was argued, parents should be free (via open entry/enrolment) to send their children to any school willing to accept them (Brown *et al* 1986). Within this package of reforms, financial delegation to schools was regarded as crucial if schools were eventually to operate as independent and fully autonomous units. The Group's three interrelated reforms, then, like those which had earlier been suggested by the ASI, can be seen as the constituent elements of 'an incrementalist strategy for liberating consumer interests and establishing something approaching an *internal market* within state education by simulating market conditions within the framework of a state-financed education system' (Flude and Hammer 1990: 55).

'The Right to Learn'

After a meeting at the House of Lords in the Spring of 1987, a few months before the presentation to Parliament of his Great Education Reform Bill (GERBIL), the Secretary of State for Education, Kenneth Baker, was overheard telling his political adviser that 'these are the people who are setting the educational agenda'. The people in question were members of the Education Study Group of the Centre for Policy Studies (CPSESG), including Baroness (Caroline) Cox and John Marks, Fred Naylor, Lawrie Norcross, Marjorie Seldon and Stuart Sexton (Wilby and Midgley 1987).

The CPSESG was set up in 1980 to translate ideas like diversity, choice, freedom, responsibility and accountability in education into coherent political programmes. The same year, Caroline (now Baroness) Cox and John Marks, Chairman and Secretary of the Group respectively, in one of several reports co-written for the National Council for Educational Standards (NCES), called for greater parental choice in education, the relaxation of school enrolment limits and for some kind of alternative, non-government funding for schools. Cox and Marks, as Wilby and Midgley (1987) recall, first came to public notice following the publication in 1975 of *Rape of Reason*. Written with Keith Jacka, this was the authors' own account of how students, staff and governors at the Polytechnic of North London (PNL) had sought to subvert academic integrity (Knight 1990: 115). The NCES was launched (initially as the Council for the Preservation of Educational Standards, or CPES) in 1972 to campaign for the protection of 'standards' in education, following the publication of the early *Black Papers* (Cox and Dyson 1969a, 1969b, 1970).

As we saw in Chapter 3 (above), the Centre for Policy Studies (CPS) was established in 1974 by Sir Keith Joseph and Margaret Thatcher to review (and, they hoped, to reverse) Conservative Party thinking/policy after the 'U-turns' of the Heath administration of 1970-4. In 1977, the CPS commissioned, and subsequently published, a study which suggested that the educational standards achieved by Britain's 'non-academic' children were significantly below those achieved by their European counterparts in France and West Germany and that there were lessons Britain could learn from educational practice elsewhere in Europe (Wilkinson 1977).

Some of the contributors to the later *Black Papers* (Cox and Boyson 1975, 1977), including Caroline Cox, John Marks and Fred Naylor, were subsequently associated with the NCES, before joining the CPSESG in 1980. Over the next few years, Cox and Marks (with their colleague Maciej Pomian-Srzednicki) produced a series of reports for the Council, suggesting that standards in selective schools were significantly higher than those in comprehensives. In 1982, the first major publication from the CPSESG proposed a number of reforms designed to raise educational standards and called - in particular - for 'centres of excellence' specializing in particular subject areas, the introduction of a system of education vouchers and student loans and a reassessment of the system of academic tenure (Cox and Marks 1982).

'Whose Schools'?

In the mid-1980s, four members of the CPSESG - Caroline Cox, John Marks, Lawrence Norcross and Jessica Douglas-Home - and Professor Roger Scruton (below) came together to form the Hillgate Group with a similar brief to that of the CPSESG (Wilby and Midgley 1987). In December 1986, the Group issued a 'radical manifesto' for change in Britain's education system, public confidence in which was said, in many places, to have broken down. In its manifesto, the Group recommended changes in four key areas of education policy, namely: the curriculum; ownership of schools; the role of the state and the duties of teachers. The key proposal of *Whose Schools?* was for the ownership of schools to be transferred from local education authorities (LEAs) to independent self-governing trusts, whose trustees would also be responsible for appointing the headteacher. Britain's schools, it was argued, should be released from the control of local government and financed by direct grant from central funds. This direct grant, it was suggested, should be provided on a *per capita* basis, according to the number of pupils enrolled in each school. This proposal, the Group disclosed, had been 'designed to transfer freedom of choice to parents, by giving them partial control over the financing of the schools which their children attend' (Hillgate Group 1986: 13, 16).

On the question of how such a scheme would work, the Group suggested the following two possibilities. First, that parents be offered a choice between a place in a state school (funded by direct grant at the local *per capita* level) and an education credit at the national *per capita* level which parents could then use to 'buy' a place in a private school. Capital expenditure in state schools would be provided by special grant. To avoid a large increase in public expenditure, it was argued, credits could also be 'taxed for all who pay tax above the standard rate: a proviso which could be waived for an initial period ... to encourage the foundation of new schools'. Alternatively, it was suggested, Britain could follow the Japanese model. Here again, the ultimate objective of reform should be to 'erode the distinction between public and private education by funding all schools at a *per capita* rate, but subsidizing the private schools at a *per capita* rate which covers only a part of the total annual cost'. The point of this exercise, the Group suggested, would be to reduce the cost of private education and to 'ensure that the *per capita* expenditure in the state system bears comparison with that in the private sector' (Hillgate Group 1986: 16).

For the Group, however, an important feature of both schemes was that either would produce a situation in which parents would decide, through their patronage, how much money a school should receive. As the differential between the private and the public sector narrowed, it was argued, more and more families would be able to afford private schools. The educational opportunities available to poorer parents would also 'markedly improve'. In addition, the Group argued, all those receiving the benefits of state education would henceforth enjoy a right of *exit* - whether to other state schools or to private schools - which would give parents 'something more than a merely nominal freedom'. The beneficial effect of this on state education was said to be 'obvious'. Henceforth, it was argued, schools would have to work in order to stay in business. The worse their results, the more likely they would be to 'go to the wall'. The Group's proposals would also, however, secure a range of other benefits (Hillgate Group 1986: 18):

> Local Education Authorities will no longer be able - as now - deliberately to deny educational opportunities to the less well-off, by restricting access to the better schools. Local government will be freed from the administration of a service that, in many places, it currently lacks the ability to manage competently. A whole section of the self-feeding local bureaucracy will be eliminated.

Not least, it was argued, 'politicized' LEAs would be 'deprived of their major source of power and of their standing ability to corrupt the minds and souls of the young' (Hillgate Group 1986: 19).

'Away with LEAs'

The suggestion from several New Right groups that schools be allowed, and encouraged, to opt out of local authority control following a democratic decision by parents and staff and that schools should henceforth receive their funding by direct grant, on a *per capita* basis, from the central education ministry (DES) was presented in the mid-1980s as a way of enabling schools to 'escape from what was considered to be the malign influence of Labour-controlled local education authorities' (Hoover and Plant 1989: 175). In calling for the abolition of the Labour-controlled Inner London Education Authority (ILEA), the Hillgate Group argued in 1987 that:

> The ILEA incurs excessive costs; it displays overall poor standards of attainment, which moreover vary enormously from school to school; it has tolerated or even encouraged a politicized curriculum and the introduction of politicized appointments and teachers.

Having survived previous attempts (in 1979, 1981 and 1983) to abolish the Authority, ILEA became a directly-elected single-purpose authority in 1985, following the abolition of the GLC. In its Education Reform Bill consultation papers in 1987, the Government proposed that individual boroughs should be able to apply to become LEAs for their areas and that ILEA should continue to be the local education authority for the areas of those boroughs choosing 'not to take advantage of this opportunity'. Between the publication of the Bill and the passing of the ERA in July 1988, however, the Government's legislative provisions for education in Inner London changed significantly. At the Committee stage, Michael Heseltine and Norman Tebbit (both former Cabinet Ministers in the Thatcher government) joined forces to move an amendment to replace the Bill's opting-out clause with a single proposal for ILEA's immediate abolition and for the transfer of the Authority's existing powers to individual boroughs. 'Faced with the prospect of defeat at the hands of their own backbenchers, Ministers bowed to the inevitable and submitted their own amendments along these lines' (Maclure 1988). Thirteen new borough-based LEAs for Inner London would be established on 1 April 1990 (Flude and Hammer 1990: xv).

In 1988, the CPS's Deputy Director of Studies, Sheila Lawlor (1988a) argued that the abolition of ILEA, while a necessary and desirable first step in the right direction, also presented the Government with an opportunity to tackle:

> one of the most serious threats to education reform, the dominance of [LEAs] in running the system. As long as LEAs continue to control the life of individual schools through their extensive bureaucracy and support services, the aims of reform will be frustrated. Higher standards for pupils, greater responsibility for schools and more choice for parents will remain illusory. The root of the problem is the LEA itself, which must not be left intact... Abolition of [ILEA] provides the occasion for the necessary reduction of the powers, scope and role of the LEAs.

In a second pamphlet in 1988, Lawlor claimed that too many of the functions of LEAs had 'diverted resources and attention to social aims and away from education proper'. Many of the services which were currently provided by LEAs - transport, school meals and so on - should therefore be put out to tender and funded for each school on a *per capita* basis. The role of LEAs, Lawlor argued, should henceforth be limited to the distribution of monies to schools, the provision of an information service and to ensuring that every child be found a school place (Lawlor 1988c).

'Trials of Honeyford'

In December 1985, the CPS published a pamphlet whose intention it was to provide 'a backcloth for informed discussion of what is agreed, on all sides, to be one of the most important and difficult social questions of the day'. Andrew Brown's *Trials of Honeyford* recalled how, in the period 1982-84, Mr Ray Honeyford (Headmaster of Drummond Middle School in the predominantly Asian Manningham district of Bradford) had published a series of articles in *The Times Educational Supplement* and *The Salisbury Review* which led directly to allegations of racism against Honeyford and to his 'persecution at the hands of extreme political factions'. In 1982, an article of Honeyford's had been published in the TES attacking some of the theories current in multicultural thought. In September 1983, Honeyford published a second article in the TES describing a week in the life of his school, which had drawn 'intemperate criticism' from anti-racists. In the summer of 1983, Honeyford produced a third article, this time in *The Salisbury Review*, in which he again attacked multicultural thought and followed this with a further piece in the Winter 1984 issue of the *Review* which led to calls for his dismissal from parents at the school and to similar suggestions from the local branch of the National Union of

Teachers (NUT).

The campaign thus initiated lasted for eighteen months and led to Honeyford's eventual retirement, with compensation. During that time, Honeyford again published in *The Salisbury Review* and was defended by its editor, Roger Scruton, in *The Times*. Honeyford himself was subsequently invited to attend a seminar held at 10 Downing Street in October 1985 to discuss the long-term direction of the educational system and has since become a well-integrated member of the educational Right, a Conservative local councillor (elected in 1988) with an increasing number of publications to his name. More significantly, perhaps, in the context of the present study, Honeyford is also, at the time of writing, a member of the CPSESG.

Trials of Honeyford explored the background to the Honeyford affair and examined the motives of those who had charged Honeyford with 'racism'. The controversy surrounding Honeyford, Brown recalled, had been generated by his 'careless' and 'unfortunate' remarks concerning the deleterious effects of large Asian or black populations on the education of white children in a growing number of inner-city schools, in asserting both that the 'language problems' of non-whites held back the progress of white English children and that Asian and West Indian parents had shown no interest in coming to terms with the habits and attitudes demanded by an English education (Brown 1985: 30-2). In attempting to draw out some of the lessons and implications of the affair, *Trials of Honeyford* raised a number of problems in multicultural education.

The first concerns the question of whether Islamic (or other) schools observing the traditions and rules of cultures other than 'English' should necessarily be financed by the taxpayers of a host country out of the public purse. A second question concerns the extent to which a headmaster (or anyone) should 'claim or admit the superiority of this culture or that'. In this connection, the general lessons of the Honeyford affair were said to fall into two parts: those which could be derived from Honeyford's experience, and those which could be derived from his ideas. In the first place, it was argued:

> Training should be given to teachers in Urdu and other appropriate languages [and] proficiency in these languages should be rewarded. If there is a shortage of qualified teachers who speak Asian languages, this may be remedied in two ways. Either native speakers of Asian languages may become qualified teachers [or] already qualified teachers can learn the necessary languages and be thoroughly tested before they are paid for the extra skill.

Secondly, it was argued, the slogan 'no culture is superior to any other' would, were it to be taken seriously, make all education 'unthinkable'. That there should be a *hierarchy* of cultures and values was said to be 'fundamental' to education, precisely because education introduces children to cultures that are 'superior' to the ones they start off from (Brown 1985: 37):

> Cultural values are often less difficult to inculcate than moral ones: socializing the children of Pakistani immigrants in Bradford to accept the evolving patterns of English culture is not a more difficult task - in many ways, less difficult - than socializing the white children of Newham to accept a few standards of civilized behaviour.

'English, Our English'

In developing such 'cultural' themes of 'identity' and 'nation', the CPS published a series of pamphlets in 1987-8 on the teaching of English and history from which it is possible to get a good idea of the model curriculum of the cultural Right and the principles which underlie it. As Jones (1989) has recalled:

> As a national curriculum became an increasingly likely outcome of state policy, so the strategic objective of the Right became more focused: to ensure that what it called the 'consensus of the 1960s' played no part in formulating the courses of study and assessment targets integral to a national curriculum. The Right's attack thus centred around the issue of progressive influence, rather than simply the more radical extremities of curriculum development.

In 1987, *English, Our English* examined 'a new orthodoxy' in the teaching of English in schools in which teachers, boards of examiners and the school inspectorate (HMI) were said to have rejected the idea of English as a subject that requires the imparting of a particular body of knowledge. The teaching of English in schools, for John Marenbon, should pursue instead the two 'simple and well-defined' aims of 'teaching children to write and speak Standard English correctly and of initiating their acquaintance with the literary heritage of the language'. In this connection, the standard form of English was said be 'the language of English culture at its highest levels as it has developed over the last centuries: the language not just of literature, philosophy and scholarship but of government, science, commerce and industry'. Dialects of English, on the other hand, were said to reflect 'the much more limited range of functions for which they have traditionally been used: the exchanges of everyday life, mainly among those unrefined by education'. Besides learning the standard form, it was argued, students should also come to know the literary masterpieces of the culture; in this way, it was argued, children would acquire both that 'regard for literature [which] is itself a value' and the knowledge of a literary heritage which is an essential form of cultural understanding (Marenbon 1987).

A new orthodoxy was also the target of Alan Beattie's pamphlet on history teaching, *History in Peril* (Beattie 1987). The teaching of history, Beattie argued, had degenerated from a 'factually-based body of knowledge' to a 'method of inquiry-based learning' that rejects the possibility of establishing the facts of any event. Beattie's argument, according to Jones (1989), can be summarized as follows:

> Students are encouraged not to acquire a solid grounding of historical information, but to go off on a facile search for bias in the viewpoint of historians, to make anachronistic moral judgements about other times and to rely on empathy and imagination in re-creating the world of the past. In as much as this kind of history has a stable content, it is dominated by a mixture of events too recent to allow dispassionate and well-documented study, by histories outside the British story and by economic and social themes. British political history is no longer taught.

For Beattie, in particular, few (if any) of these changes were the result of considerations relevant to history, but had been generated mainly by ideological developments within educational institutions which had 'exceeded their authority' by 're-shaping what is taught as history in the pursuit of wider social ends'. The time had come for parents to 'redress the balance'. The government, for Beattie at least, should subject education to a rigorous regime of consumer choice, so that a 'healthier' kind of history could be restored (Beattie 1987).

History teaching in schools was a theme taken up in two further CPS pamphlets of 1987-8. The first set out to show how GCSE History syllabuses 'no longer teach pupils about our national heritage in an orderly fashion, if at all' because of 'a new philosophy which holds that, since nothing is ultimately knowable and records are inevitably biased, the evaluation of sources is more important than [the] learning of facts' (Deuchar 1987). Helen Kedourie's *Errors and Evils of the New History* (1988) examined the origins of the New History and argued that the teaching of history in terms of 'concepts, source evaluation and empathy' had produced a situation in which many pupils were leaving school unfamiliar with famous names and dates in English history: 'no sense of time and historical context are imparted to pupils' (Kedourie 1988).

In March 1988, Sheila Lawlor set out 'simple curricula' for the three core subjects (maths, English and science) of any national curriculum and warned the Government of the dangers of extending these curricula beyond the requirement that all schools should teach a simple minimum of content and technique. Beyond this, it was argued, headteachers should be given the freedom to decide what and how to teach, but should ensure that children leave school literate, numerate and with a grounding of knowledge (Lawlor 1988b). Oliver Letwin's *Aims of Schooling* (also 1988) contrasted 'the grandiose ambitions of educationalists over the last forty years with their sorry achievements'. The serious, practical aim of reform, to which all resources should be directed, should be to give every child 'a basic grounding which will stand him in good stead to face adult life, in a way that large numbers of today's school-leavers unfortunately cannot' (Letwin 1988).

'The Pied Pipers of Education'

In 1981, the Social Affairs Unit (SAU) published a collection of readings in which it was argued (Flew *et al* 1981) that:

> State schools are not giving value for money. They have lost sight of their central purpose which is to provide maximum learning at minimum cost. They do not monitor their efficiency. They attempt to conceal their enormous costs and poor results. Most important, they insist, against all evidence, that good results follow greater expenditure.

In common with other New Right groups (above), the publications of the SAU in the early 1980s were concerned, for the most part, with the structure and finance of state education (Flew *et al* 1981, Marsland 1981). In 1981, for example, Caroline Cox and John Marks called for the introduction of 'educational allowances' which parents could 'spend' in the school of their choice, whether in the state or independent sector:

> Such a change would give parents much more power and influence and would help to make schools more responsive to what parents want for their children and more adaptive to the changing needs of society.

Allowances, it was argued, would 'reinvigorate' state schools by enabling them to become self-governing and would involve parents more directly in educational decision-making. Allowances would also encourage diversity both within the state sector and among independent schools by allowing schools to specialize in subject areas; many groups, including some from ethnic minorities, would also 'welcome the opportunity to set up new schools'. Not least, it was argued (Cox and Marks 1981: 20):

Allowances would give parents real power, the power of exit - of saying 'no' - if they were dissatisfied. This would be far more effective than the existing system of control by elected local education authorities. Power would shift irreversibly to the people. If enough people once got their hands on educational allowances, it would be a brave government that tried to take them away again.

For Cox and Marks, in particular, the bulk of educational expenditure could be reallocated to effectively 'by-pass' local education authorities (LEAs), since the total estimated Rate Support Grant (RSG) paid by central government to LEAs was currently 'larger than the education budget'. A sum of money equivalent to the value of the RSG could therefore be given not to LEAs but directly to parents in the form of education allowances:

> The money would still come from central government but would be given direct to parents. If they chose to spend it on schools run by local authorities, well and good. If not, it would show their dissatisfaction with what local authority schools were offering.

The role of central government in education, it was suggested, would still be substantial: covering finance, the provision of services and the maintenance of standards. Allowances would, however, inevitably diminish the role of local education authorities. With many, or even most, schools becoming self-governing however, local authorities would be able to concentrate much more effectively on providing services which fell more into the category of 'public' rather than 'private' goods (Cox and Marks 1981: 22).

'Educated for Employment'

A second area of concern to the SAU in the early 1980s was the question of the relationship between schools and schooling, on the one hand, and 'the needs of industry/the enterprise culture', on the other (Anderson *et al* 1982, Brophy *et al* 1984). In 1981, for example, Dennis O'Keeffe argued that educational decision-makers had long been:

> sensitive to the demands of successful pupils - hence the huge numbers of children entering the arts and social sciences - but almost indifferent to what curriculum might be appropriate to an advanced industrial economy either from the point of view of industrialists and employers, or from that of the industrial working-class.

In seeking to explain why children truant, O'Keeffe argued that a significant factor might be the vocationally irrelevant curricula offered to working-class pupils who took (and whose parents took) a largely *instrumental* view of work (O'Keeffe 1981: 34):

> If large numbers of children are away from their lessons, the implication would seem to be that [the] curriculum on offer is at best less appealing than the alternative uses of time and at worst irrelevant and meaningless.... Like so much that is central to the analysis of education, truancy is a curricular issue. It is important, not least for the economics of the curriculum, to find out which lessons pupils truant from and why. It would be very surprising to find just one kind of content from which children recoil, or just one kind of presentation which they reject; but it is scarcely fanciful to imagine that they will not, *grosso modo*, stay for that which they perceive as useful and interesting and depart from that which they regard as irrelevant or incomprehensible.

'The Wayward Curriculum'

The content of the secondary school curriculum was of growing concern to the SAU after 1984. In 1986, the Unit published a collection of essays in which 23 teachers, curriculum experts, subject specialists and academics commented on the current state of the curriculum (O'Keeffe 1986). Their findings, written and presented especially for parents, were said to reveal 'cause for alarm not only for parents but for all who fund the state schools through their taxes and wish the future members of our society to be soundly prepared in school' (O'Keeffe 1981: 11):

> Bluntly, what if the curricular fare on offer to our secondary school children is at times actually counter-productive or even destructive - a 'wayward curriculum'? The intention of the scholars and contributors who have contributed to this collection is to help answer that question. Their views are not necessarily homogenous but all are uneasy about what is being taught in schools.

Contributors to *The Wayward Curriculum* expressed particular concern over the state of established subjects (mathematics, English, modern languages, classics, history and religious education), over 'unsuitable or dubious' newer subjects (peace studies, urban studies, political education, sociology, anti-racist education and women's studies) and over the institutional framework of the curriculum: its pseudo-scientific vocabulary, the hostility to exams, the use of mixed-ability groups, lack of specialist schools, misdirection of teachers and politicization of local authority education (O'Keeffe 1986: 14):

> The picture the authors paint of the school curriculum is one that will dismay many parents and taxpayers. Unfortunately, the state school system does not permit them to register that dismay by choosing the many schools which still offer a sensible curriculum and spurning the schools currently imposing a wayward curriculum. Until they are given that choice, the wayward curriculum will persist.

'Educational Achievement in Japan'

During the 1980s, then, the SAU expressed concern over both the values of schools and the content of state education. In 1988, the Unit published a study by psychologist Richard Lynn (1988) whose central purpose was:

> to present an account of the education system in Japan for the interest and, hopefully, for the benefit of educationists, social scientists and politicians in Britain, the United States and Continental Europe. In the West, educational standards have in recent decades become an increasing cause of public concern. In Japan, educational standards are exceptionally high, such that by adolescence average Japanese teenagers are some three years ahead of their counterparts in the West.

Educational Achievement in Japan set out to analyze how the high educational standards in Japan were achieved and what lessons the West might usefully learn from the Japanese system. For Lynn at least, there were four important principles to be learned - the first of which was said to be the 'important *negative* conclusion' that Japan's high educational standards had been achieved *without* greater financial resources than were available to schools in the West (Lynn 1988):

> The Japanese experience of high educational standards, secured at only moderate cost, confirms the conclusion that educational standards do not respond so well as has been hoped to increasing financial resources. Western governments should look in other directions for ways to increase educational standards.

The three remaining principles were said to be *positive*: namely, the provision of stronger incentives for school children in the West to undertake academic work; a substantial lengthening of the school year; and the significance of incentives for teachers to work efficiently (Lynn 1988: 144):

In Japan there are three powerful incentives for teacher efficiency, namely the detailed specification of the curriculum by the Ministry of Education, the competition between high schools for examination successes and the large numbers of private schools which are subject to the discipline of the market. All of these methods of rendering teachers more accountable to the public deserve consideration in the West.

'Full Circle'

Finally, in 1988, the SAU published a collection of essays in which 10 child psychologists and educationists considered three interrelated themes. First, what children are and what they need in their upbringing; second, how the behaviour of parents in their relations between each other and in mothers working affect children; third, the impact on parents and children of the fads of teachers, counsellors and 'experts' (Anderson 1988). Although *Full Circle?* was mainly concerned with the duties of parents in bringing up children in a post-permissive society, a number of contributors insisted that *schools* also had a role in teaching children law-abiding and sociable habits by restraint, teaching 'traditional' moral values and resisting the argument (from radical feminism) that 'traditional' gender distinctions between boys' and girls' subjects be abandoned. In particular, it was argued, traditional methods of teaching arithmetic (rote tables) should be restored; primary schools should 'get back to basics and ensure that children are numerate' (Anderson 1988).

Education and the New Right

Although the New Right has strongly supported reform of the state education system, its central strands do not indicate a 'unitary' model and it would be misleading to say that its spokesmen speak with a single voice. As Knight (1985: 228) argues, there has often been considerable disagreement over '*how* the currency of education, in the sense of curriculum and school-leaving certification, is to be restored'. The principal items on the educational agenda of the New Right, Knight argues, have been as follows:

- The restoration of the currency of educational credentials (the New Right has been keen to stem the inflationary tide of credentials/qualifications).

- The return to traditional values in education by the removal of curriculum 'clutter'.

- The raising of school standards, partly to be achieved by improving teacher quality, the removal of incompetent school staffs and the reform of the 16-plus examinations.

- The retrieval of education from its 'capture' by LEA bureaucracies, schools and teacher unions.

- The creation of real parental choice and participation in education; the creation of a 'market' in education to allow parents to choose the schools they want and escape from those they don't (FEVER's campaign for a school voucher).

- The reform of the school curriculum to give more emphasis to the requirements of industry.

Spokesmen for the New Right, Knight argues, belong to a 'loose nexus' of individuals and bodies who associate with one another on an *ad hoc* basis and who sometimes contribute to each other's journals but who *differ* on fundamental issues as do (for example) the 'liberals' of the IEA and the 'conservatives' of the Salisbury Group. Many and various institutions - the IEA, the ASI, the CPSESG, the SAU, the Conservative Philosophy Group (CPG), the Salisbury Group, the Freedom Association and FEVER - Knight argues, form 'an entire educational intelligentsia' which has:

> made appeal to the very large centre group in Britain who have strong views on law and order, morality, personal enterprise and responsibility, educational standards, discipline and national pride. Since the late 1960s an increasing number of intellectual and political figures have proposed setting off firmly in a 'new' direction, on a new programme of action to constitute a post-socialist society, a trumpet-call for the Good Society which would restore free choice, individualism and standards of excellence to their rightful place as central values in the life of the people.

The IEA, for Knight, has drawn attention to 'the perils of state monopoly in education, where the danger is that it will pursue objectives which are politically determined, removed from the wishes of the consumers who are forced to pay for it'. At the same time, he argues (Knight 1985: 231):

> The IEA has been less involved with the internal issues of educational standards, a debate carried forward fervently by the CPS, the SAU and the ASI. Whereas the

market economists of the IEA have argued for exits from state education where it is unacceptable ... it has been in the publications from the CPS Education Study Group [and the] Social Affairs Unit that the New Right's thrust to open out to teachers, parents and politicians the intellectual debate on standards within state education has been most effectively achieved. Unlike the CPS Education Study Group and the SAU, the Adam Smith Institute has made direct policy proposals to government. Its Omega Report, *Education Policy*, contains a series of initiatives which its authors ... offer as a route map of the future for the Conservative government. Indeed, the report suggests the largest and possibly most innovative policy programme ever devised, even though it is in part a somewhat derivative rehearsal of the argument as earlier formulated by other New Right authors.

At the same time, however, the various New Right groups organized to achieve drastic reductions in the state monopoly of education are not monolithic, nor do they all agree on the same priorities for reform (Knight 1985: 232). The tensions (contradictions) within conservative capitalism between traditionalists (communitarians) and individualists (free marketeers) over education reform/policy are explored in the final section of this chapter (below).

'Take Care, Mr Baker!'

The intention to produce a radical reform of Britain's education system was clearly expressed in the Conservative manifesto of 1987 (Tomlinson 1989):

Although there were some unintended leaks, the manifesto of 1987, which provided the 'mandate' for the 1988 Reform Act, was prepared in secret during the previous nine months under the general direction of the Prime Minister's Policy Unit. The aim was to make an irreversible change in the public education system, similar to that already achieved in other aspects of social and economic policy such as trade union legislation, the sale of council houses and the privatization of industry.

After the Conservative victory, the Department of Education and Science published a series of consultation documents in July and August, to which the Government sought responses within the following two months. Protests from teachers and others about the unreasonableness of requiring responses so swiftly (and at a time which coincided with the main holiday period) were in vain. In the event, the Government persisted with its schedule and the Secretary of State, Kenneth Baker, was able to introduce his Great Education Reform Bill (GERBIL) to Parliament on 20 November 1987.

In the event, some 18,000 replies expressing massive discontent with the Government's proposed reforms were received - advice which Mr Baker himself had invited but decided not to publish (Haviland 1988). Despite this unprecented opposition, the Bill itself contained few substantial changes that were not consistent with the views outlined in the consultation documents. During its passage through 370 hours of parliamentary debate, the Bill expanded its original 147 sections to 238; 113 concessions were made by the Government to the Bill as a whole. As far as the school aspects are concerned, however, most of these changes were at the margin. Thus the Act which finally became law in July 1988 contained all of the fundamental points which had been foreshadowed in the earlier consultation documents of July and August 1987 (Wilcox 1989).

The Education Reform Act

The ERA consists of 238 sections (exactly half of which are devoted to matters pertaining to schools) and 13 schedules. As far as schools are concerned, the major changes introduced by the Act are as follows: the introduction of a national curriculum and an associated programme of testing and assessment; an end to the artificial limits on parents' first choice of school; the right of schools to opt out of local authority control and receive direct funding from the central education ministry (DES); the establishment of city technology colleges (CTCs) and city colleges for the technology of the arts (CCTAs); the delegation of school budgets to the governors of secondary schools and larger primaries. As far as schools are concerned, then, the provisions of the ERA are in two main parts. The first of these has to do with the devolution of finance and management to school governing bodies, establishing a 'market' in education. Local Management of Schools (LMS) and Grant Maintained Schools (GMS) are the major thrusts of such a policy, together with the establishment of *per capita* funding, schools to operate at capacity and so on. The second part of the ERA saw the establishment of a national curriculum (for maintained and grant maintained schools only) consisting of three core subjects (mathematics, English and science) and seven foundation subjects (history, geography, technology, music, art, physical education and a modern foreign language) together with programmes of study and regular testing and assessment for 7, 11, 14 and 16 year-olds in all subjects.

For Tomlinson (1989: 186-7) at least, the Act contains elements of both old and new thinking which reflect the differences of ideology within the Conservative Party between free-marketeers and the more traditional centralizers:

The contradictions inherent in the legislation will be worked out during the 1990s and it is impossible to tell which element will gain the upper hand - that is to say, whether as we approach the twenty-first century the English and Welsh public education system will be highly centralized or largely privatized; or, as some fear as the worst option, there will be a privatized and successful middle-class sector supported by both public and private funds, alongside a remnant public sector 'educating' an underclass.

The tensions (contradictions) within conservative capitalism (the New Right) over education reform/policy in the 1980s are explored below. For the moment, however, our main concern is to trace the impact of the various groups whose proposals for educational reform have been reviewed in this chapter on the ERA itself.

'Useful, but exaggerated'

In a recent study of the Conservative 'revolution' in education in the 1980s, Jones (1989) argues that part of the explanation for its success - culminating in the ERA of 1988 - lies in the speed and creativity of New Right thinking between 1983 and 1987 in generating credible alternatives to an education system which was 'failing to respond enthusiastically to the demands of a new era':

> In 1984, the *Omega File* of the Adam Smith Institute had presented a blueprint for a reorganization based on market principles, with a supporting role for a national regulation of minimum standards. A similar approach was outlined in the proposals of the No Turning Back group of Conservative MPs in 1985 and in 1986 by the Hillgate Group of Roger Scruton and his co-thinkers. These different contributions, though varying in the stresses they placed on free market economics as against cultural continuity, formed a consensus on the right that was in agreement around the broad outlines of a radical policy.... Many of the measures contained in the 1986 Education Act - those relating to sex education, police influence and political neutrality - were the specific results of right-wing lobbying. The proposals of the ERA for local management of schools, open enrolment and opting out directly reflect the influence of the Hillgate Group and the Adam Smith Institute.

At the same time, however, it is important not to overstate the impact of any *particular* think-tank - or even of New Right groups generally - on policy itself. As far as the impact of particular groups is concerned, it is worth noting that several of the groups whose proposals have been reviewed in this chapter enjoy interlocking memberships, an observation which renders the question *which* think-tank was most obviously 'responsible' for suggesting the ideas which subsequently 'became' the ERA? both unhelpful and inappropriate.

As far as the impact of New Right think-tanks *generally* on the ERA is concerned, two further points are worth making. The first of these is Stuart Sexton's recent insistence that the part of the ERA (above) was in place long before Kenneth Baker became Secretary of State for Education in 1986 and during the time Sexton himself was Special Advisor:

> All of that *predates* the Hillgate Group's paper, the No Turning Back Group's paper and reports from the Adam Smith Institute and others. What *they* did was add their weight to proposals which had already been formulated. The first publication from the IEAEU [above] was ... simply an edited version of a longer, earlier, confidential document also by Sexton, which may be thought to have put together the ideas which eventually became enshrined in the ERA.... I do not think any of the think-tanks were *responsible* for the changes inherent in the ERA, but they all added valuable support to the concepts already formulated, often expressing them in slightly different terms.[1]

For Sexton at least, *all* of the think-tanks (IEAEU, ASI, CPSESG, SAU) played their part in creating a 'climate of acceptability' for the managerial/financial changes in the ERA:

> But they followed rather than led. I suppose my own [think-tank, the IEAEU] can claim to [have been] the more effective, but simply because the EU was really a continuation of the work begun as special advisor. I think the role and significance of think-tanks is useful, but exaggerated.[2]

The second point concerns the role of various other significant actors - notably, perhaps, officials at the DES and of Her Majesty's Inspectorate - in influencing the *second* part of the ERA (above). In its prescriptions regarding the national curriculum, HMI provided support for the bid by the DES to establish more central control over the curriculum. As Sexton himself argues, the second part of the ERA was:

> almost entirely the initiative of officials of the DES and of HMI. It was not prompted by Sexton or any of the think-tanks [but] was influenced largely by the well-entrenched establishment of the HMI, DES officials and DES quangos.[3]

Indeed, since the framing of the legislation, the worries and concerns of several New Right groups have become increasingly clear (below). Pamphlets from the CPS and the Hillgate Group have protested that, via the 'national curriculum', the ERA will simply reinforce *centralization* (Jones 1989):

> Far from enabling a great upsurge of consumer power, the Act, they fear, increases
> the influence of the state and, more importantly, of the educational establishment
> within it. The state will not have a minimal role; it will not limit itself to clearing
> aside what obstructs the operation of market principles, nor to securing a minimum
> level of educational grounding, beyond which diversity can flourish. It will be a lot
> more directive than that, and its policies, think the Right, will only entrench the
> orthodoxies of education, and raise again the dangers of producer control.

Underlying these arguments are profound differences within modern
Conservatism over the nature, purpose and direction of education reform/policy.
In the final part of this chapter, the tensions within the Conservative programme
for educational reform during the 1980s are - briefly - explored.

Traditionalists and Individualists

As we have seen in this chapter, Conservative educational reform/policy during
the 1980s was frequently dominated by the issue of *vouchers*. As we have also
seen, the political rejection of the Friedman/IEA education voucher in 1983 led
several New Right groups to suggest alternative proposals (designed to secure the
same economic benefits as the Friedman/IEA-type voucher, but without at the
same time incurring its political costs) between the two General Elections of 1983
and 1987. Arguably, the provisions contained in the ERA (1988) for financial
delegation, open enrolment and opting out have now successfully engineered the
circumstances in which Britain's education system can be so adapted as to make
a future transition to vouchers politically feasible without undue disruption
(Maclure 1988: 42-3).

At the same time, however, it is important to recognize that the voucher
continues to *divide* conservatives, some of whom would reject the basic
underlying premise on which the scheme is based - namely, that education can
or should be treated as a 'market'. It is also worth recalling that some
conservatives have consistently argued against the voucher on both practical and
philosophical grounds. In the mid-1970s, for example, Vernon Bogdanor (1976:
124-5) argued that:

> The basic premise behind the voucher scheme is that the market mechanism is the
> best means to secure freedom of choice for parents. It is this premise that
> immediately arouses suspicion: for although Conservatives believe, of course, in the

vital role of the market economy, they have never worshipped the market with the dogmatic ferocity of the nineteenth-century Liberal Party or the contemporary Institute of Economic Affairs. The Cobdenite elevation of the market to the level of an ideology has little to do with true Conservatism, which distrusts all ideologies and general statements of political principle, whether those of Socialism or those of nineteenth-century liberalism. In particular, Conservatives have always recognized that it is wrong to identify freedom with the market *per se*. After all, the twentieth century has seen restrictions on the operation of markets in Britain as in other Western democracies but the result of these restrictions is that most people in these countries feel more (not less) free and more (not less) secure.

In fact, it is unrealistic to suppose that the market mechanism can be directly applied to education, since it is not possible, in the short run, to expand 'good' schools and to close down 'bad' schools. For school buildings are a commodity for which the supply is inelastic, and cannot be made, in the short run, to respond in changes in demand. Unfortunately ... *there must be a physical constraint in the degree of choice possible, under any system of educational administration or finance.* At the same time, the voucher scheme could lead to the disadvantages of schools in areas of deprivation becoming cumulative as fewer and fewer parents wish to send their children to these schools. Instead of paying extra attention to areas of deprivation, the voucher policy would shift resources to more favoured schools. Good schools would be able to raise their fees so as to exclude able children from poor backgrounds, thus accentuating the wastage of talent amongst these children. There would be a system of educational apartheid with pre-1870 Poor Law provision for those not already from favoured backgrounds. *Anything militating more strongly against a true Conservative philosophy it is difficult to imagine.*

The Conservative Party, as Hoover and Plant (1989) suggest, has *always* contained both traditionalists and individualists: 'those who believe in using authoritative institutions to secure social and economic ends, and those who have preferred to see the operation of the market wherever and whenever possible' (see also Greenleaf 1983). In this connection, it is worth recalling that Sir Keith Joseph's education team in 1981-82 consisted of Conservative Educationalists (CEs) representative of the two major schools of right-wing educational thought, namely the *centralizers* (paternalist-right) and the *decentralizers* (market-right). As Knight (1990: 161) has argued:

It is important to note this division, because... although [Sir Keith] Joseph's team was united in its broad support for raising educational standards [it] displayed less agreement over precise schemes to improve the mechanics of parental choice. Significantly, each grouping was distinguished by its varying degrees of support for, and opposition to, the education voucher.

The exclusion of the voucher plan from the Conservative manifesto of 1983 was, in fact, 'a major triumph for the centralizers over the decentralizers'. The feasibility of vouchers, as Knight also recalls, was discussed in 1983 by the Conservative Group on Education established by Sir Geoffrey Howe in preparation for the 1983 manifesto and chaired by the 'unashamedly centralist' Lord Beloff (Knight 1990: 160). The Beloff Group's report considered proposals to strengthen moral and religious teaching in schools - as well as a more vocational slant to the curriculum. It also, however:

> rejected the idea of education vouchers as the great majority of the Group were not convinced that the voucher scheme was the best method of increasing parental choice and thereby improving standards, and because its cost would be hard to justify to a highly sceptical public at a time of stretched resources. Here may be found both the reason for the exclusion of vouchers from the Party's 1983 manifesto and Sir Keith's subsequent rejection of the voucher idea [in] 1983. Lord Beloff did not publicly disclose his opposition to [the voucher] until February 1983. His Group's report advised that more thought and public discussion were essential, and that only when outstanding questions had been settled and when there was evidence of a public demand should a pilot scheme be attempted, particularly since it would have to be preceded by legislation.

All of which appears to confirm the view of one of the principal advocates of the voucher that its 1983 abandonment was essentially political (Seldon 1986) though 'even he fails to examine in any detail the impact of the deliberations of the Beloff policy group' (Knight 1990: 161).

A further interpretation of the political rejection of the voucher in 1983 is given by Lord Joseph's biographer (Halcrow 1989):

> Why did Keith Joseph resist the 'intellectual attractions' of the voucher? Basically, the reason he gave was that it would cause an enormous row, between the political parties and within the Conservative Party; Edward Heath had promised to lead a crusade against vouchers; the bitterness could be enough to counterbalance the benefits; the scheme would have to be imposed on unwilling local authorities and on unwilling teachers.

The voucher lobby itself, however, also felt this to be an incomplete explanation for Sir Keith's decision and has long suspected that Joseph was, in the end, 'reluctant' to apply market forces to parental power in education. For Halcrow (1989: 187 and xi) at least:

> A clue may be found in the One Nation pamphlet *The Responsible Society*, for which Joseph had been partly responsible as a young MP back in March 1959. The

pamphlet set out an early form of the philosophy which has become associated with Thatcherism; but it recognised more limitations than the Thatcherites would recognize. It approved of the notion that the individual should pay for his health care and for the education of his children [but also] included this caveat:

> We could not, however, support the right that this implies for persons or parents to neglect their own or their families' health or education. Such neglect would be as much a wrong as positive ill-treatment.

There are different kinds of neglect. There was a part of Joseph which was always suspicious of whether parents knew what was best for their children. At the Department of Education, he retained much of the character of the *paternalistic* Tory.

Here we come to one of the paradoxes of Keith Joseph's career. He tends not to enjoy being told that the power of free-market forces (which are the dynamic of the new Conservatism) can have a *radical* effect. As a Thatcherite minister he was involved in a revolution, yet a part of him was wedded to the *status quo*. It was the honourable conflict between the revolutionary and the traditionalist sides of his nature that made his efforts, as Secretary of State for Education, to reform Britain's schools such an interesting operation.

For Christopher Knight, the 'Joseph years' (1981-6) marked a period of deep unease within the Conservative Party over the best strategy deliver 'better education for all'. Significantly, however, both 'the economic evangelical, Sir Keith Joseph' and 'the preservationist, Lord Beloff' had questioned whether a combination of parent power and the market offered the best way forward (Knight 1990: 180).

Given the death of the voucher scheme in 1983, however, the ERA of 1988 seeks to challenge the interest-group status of teachers in other ways by introducing market surrogates (Hoover and Plant 1989: 175). Yet, the paradox here is that the resort to *political* means of achieving this ambition has increased the powers of central government in ways that a voucher scheme would never have done:

> Several mechanisms have been introduced to strengthen the role of parents on governing bodies of schools, and to ensure that there is an annual meeting for each school at which teachers and parents would meet to discuss the work of the school. On the whole this idea runs rather counter to the general ways to which free-market capitalists believe accountability should go.

For Hoover and Plant, in particular, individualist conservatives (free marketeers) are typically 'sceptical about the capacity of democratic procedures to make interest groups accountable to those whom they are supposed to serve: only a market relationship will do this properly in their view'. In addition to these attempts to increase parent power, however, the ERA introduced measures which will curtail the powers of LEAs, but increase those of central government (Hoover and Plant 1989: 175):

> Schools are to be given the capacity to opt out of the control of local education authorities after a democratic decision by parents and staff and to be directly funded by the Department of Education and Science, the central education ministry. While this is presented as a way of enabling schools to escape from what is considered to be the malign influence of Labour-controlled local education authorities, it does, nevertheless, increase the power of central government, as does the proposal to introduce a national curriculum.

As Chitty (1989: 215) has argued, 'a key point of disagreement among those members of the New Right specializing in educational matters and one which reflects essential differences between the conservative and liberal wings of the movement concerns the desirability or otherwise of a centrally-imposed national curriculum'. As long ago as 1975, he recalls, Dr Rhodes Boyson was arguing, from a neo-conservative standpoint, for a nationally-enforced curriculum which would have the support of parents (Boyson 1975: 141):

> The malaise in schools in Britain has followed from a breakdown in accepted curriculum and traditional values. There was little concern about either political control or parental choice so long as there was an 'understood' curriculum which was followed by every school. Schools may have differed in efficiency but their common values or curriculum were broadly acceptable. The present disillusionment of parents arises from their resentment that their children's education now depends upon the lottery of the school to which they are directed. Standards decline because both measurement and comparison are impossible when aims and curriculum become widely divergent. These problems can be solved only by making schools again accountable to some authority outside them. The necessary sanction is either a nationally-enforced curriculum or parental choice or a combination of both.

The Hillgate Group, for example, argued in 1986 that a national curriculum was essential but recognised the danger in using the 'coercive apparatus of the state' to impose it. The curriculum should have a core (reading, writing and arithmetic) and a settled range of proven subjects; above all, however, it should seek to uphold the values of a *traditional* education (Hillgate Group 1986: 7):

> The tradition we have inherited is, we believe, a good one. Foreign languages, mathematics, science, history and literature are of lasting value to the person who

learns them. Such subjects involve a testable and coveted body of knowledge which it is the duty of any educational system to pass on from generation to generation, and which can broaden the mind and the experience of anyone who has the good fortune to be initiated into it.

Increasingly, in the late 1980s, the New Right involved itself in curricular wars. For several reasons, its chosen battlefields were the teaching of English and of history: 'The kinds of understanding of culture prevalent on the Right led it towards these areas, and it was there that its political project could most easily take hold, in developing themes of identity and nation' (Jones 1989).

As we saw earlier, these themes were taken up in a series of pamphlets issued by the CPS in 1987-88, at which point several New Right groups were broadly speaking in agreement that, with the exception of a minimum of content and technique to be laid down centrally, the *market*, and not the state should determine the content of any national curriculum - at least in the short run. Thus it was that competing and conflicting elements within the New Right converged around the broad outlines of educational reform/policy - even though several of their publications varied in the emphasis they placed on free-market economics *'as against* cultural continuity' (Jones 1989).

For Hoover and Plant (1989: 176), education provides a fascinating example of the tensions (contradictions) within conservative capitalism (the New Right) between traditionalists (communitarians) and individualists (free marketeers):

> Traditionalists saw the voucher scheme as too libertarian and not securing communitarian values which, in their view, a state system together with a national curriculum would. Free marketeers, on the other hand, preferred the voucher as the only realistic way in which actual control could be exercised over producer groups - namely, through the cash-market mechanism. It remains to be seen whether the attempt to increase parent power through political as opposed to economic means will be as useless as free-market critics would tend to assume. For the free marketeer the only effective form of accountability is through economic exchange. Traditionally, the left has considered democratic accountability as the replacement for the market forum. In the case of education, the failure to introduce a voucher scheme has required the endorsement of what many will regard as a much less effective means of accountability.

These tensions (contradictions) notwithstanding, the New Right also has a confused and divided attitude towards vocational studies (Chitty 1989). As Jones (1989) argues:

> Conservatism in education, as elsewhere, is three-headed, rather than double-faced.

The point can be made in this way: the tendency of free-market thought, supported in practice by [the cultural Right] is to insist that the future of the British economy is dependent almost entirely upon free enterprise and privatization: economic planning of any sort would play little part. It is from this perspective that the Adam Smith Institute approaches education. In this attitude free-market thinkers and traditionalists stand at some distance from a third important aspect of Conservatism, that could roughly be described as a modernizing tendency not because it is the only current which wishes to achieve economic regeneration and modernizing change in education, but because more deliberately than any other it seeks to *intervene* in many areas of social life with the prime and specific intention of achieving them. This does not mean that it wishes to return to an economic and political strategy of corporatism: it is intent, rather, on creating an 'enterprise economy' and on reducing union influence, and thus borrows much from the free-market programme. It does, however, intend that the *pace and the content of change should be shaped by state intervention*. In education, this entails the belief that the content of the curriculum is far too important to be left to the individual school.

Both free marketeers and the cultural Right may see the role of the state as essentially negative, in putting down all those forces, bureaucratic or insurgent, which, for Roger Scruton, 'threaten the freedom and trouble the life of the ordinary citizen' (Jones 1989):

The modernizing tendency, however, has a more *positive* conception of the state's powers. Strong government action is needed - particularly in an area like education - to correct historic weaknesses and set down the clear outlines of a path along which the system should go.

As Secretary of State for Education, it was Sir Keith Joseph who permitted - then observed with increasing interest - the first direct vocational inroads to be made on the school system, through the Manpower Services Commission-funded Technical and Vocational Education Initiative (TVEI). Joseph, as Jones (1989: 17) recalls:

saw Britain as a country let down by its intelligentsia, which had shunned the disciplines of productivity and competition to cultivate softer areas of interest. Education was implicated in this long process of betrayal. One of the tasks of Conservative policy was to liberate it from its intellectual captors: to saturate it with respect for enterprise; to shake teachers and administrators out of their old practices; to accept no longer the low standards which disabled the country in international competition.

During his period as Secretary of State, Joseph was often persuaded by arguments of the kind set out in Correlli Barnett's *The Audit of War* (1986) which linked the decline in Britain's economic power with its failure to adapt sufficiently its education system to the modern industrial world. Perhaps not surprisingly, then, the instrument of educational renewal chosen by Joseph between 1981 and 1986 was not so much the 'blind, uncoordinated wisdom of the market' - nor even the 'unruly and hazardous enterprise of promoting a grassroots movement for educational change' - but the central apparatus of the state (Jones 1989: 17-18).

In 1986, Sir Keith's educational 'utilitarianism' was condemned in *The Salisbury Review* as 'likely to be destructive of humane sensibility' and as 'seeking to produce a population ready only to fulfil technological functions' (O'Hear 1986). Moreover, when Sir Keith's successor, Kenneth Baker, introduced a national curriculum as part of his Great Education Reform Bill (GERBIL) of 1987, the conflict between the cultural Right (whose emphasis on curricular continuity is supported in practice by free-market groups like the ASI) and the modernizing tendency (which regards the grammar school tradition as part of the problem with, rather than the solution to, Britain's education system) appears to have intensified. As Jones (1989) argues:

> There remain important tensions at the heart of the Conservative policy which explain why Baker, the minister who had made a reality of so much of the Right's programme, was still so widely distrusted by it. In the vision of radical Conservatives, the school system would be almost entirely shaped by the play of parental choice. The pressures of the market place would hold in check the excesses of reform, while necessitating a continual benign product innovation in the curriculum. To this extent, the educational market would regulate itself.

For Baker himself, however, this programme was insufficient and 'threatened to produce the kind of unregulated system that, with its substantial pockets of blatant under-achievement, would bring the whole programme of reform into disrepute'. Moreover, the imperatives of international economic competition required that a strong central hand should take hold of education and shake it into sensing new priorities and the need for higher standards. For this task, the market was regarded as too weak an instrument and the curricular ideas of the New Right too antiquated to be of use (Jones 1989):

> Instead Baker, like Joseph before him, looked to a different source of support. He returned to a section of the educational establishment, and sought their help in devising the programmes of study and the targets of assessment that were essential to the national curriculum. Nowhere else could he have found a detailed concern with what a 'modernized' education system entails. The Right regarded this as a betrayal. The very experts whose influence they had set out to curtail were now

being invited through the front door of the DES to devise a curriculum for all state students! The simple proposals of the Right were being magicked into a system of learning and assessment that repeated the detested catch-phrases of the 1960s about an 'activity-based, student-centred' curriculum.

Not surprisingly, perhaps, the Deputy Director of the CPS warned in 1988 of the danger that the sharp edge of reform/policy would be blunted by Baker's reliance upon the functionaries of the *ancien regime* (Lawlor 1988b). For the New Right, then, the passing of the ERA is not the summit of its achievement, but one more stage along the way; the struggle is not over, and powerful enemies remain (Jones 1989).

Notes

1.   Correspondence.
2.   Correspondence.
3.   Correspondence.

6 Health

Introduction

The purpose of this chapter is twofold. A first aim is to examine how the four New Right think-tanks (IEA, ASI, CPS and SAU) have addressed health-care issues, given the ideological differences between these groups discussed in Chapters 1-4 (above). A second aim is to seek to trace the impact of such groups on health policy in the late 1980s, following the Government's decision - announced by the then Prime Minister, Margaret Thatcher, in January 1988 - to establish a Review to consider the future of the National Health Service (NHS). The 'Prime Minister's Review' of the NHS lasted a full twelve months, and ended in January 1989 with the publication of the White Paper, *Working for Patients* (HMSO 1989). Legislation embodying this White Paper and a second White Paper on Community Care was introduced to Parliament in November 1989 (Paton 1990). The final part of this chapter assesses the role of the four think-tanks in either contributing, or failing to contribute, significantly to this process.

'Health Through Choice'

The National Health Service, as Green (1987: 176) argues, has been severely criticized by New Right neo-liberals. In the early 1960s, the leading critic of the NHS among neo-liberals was Dennis Lees, whose penetrating essay *Health Through Choice* was first published by the IEA in 1961. At that time, as Ralph (now Lord) Harris has recalled, Lees was 'the *first* British economist to subject the NHS to systematic analysis as a monopoly supplier of hospital and medical services for which the consumer paid a zero or purely nominal direct price' (Harris 1965: 11).

The NHS, Lees argued, was only one of several ways in which medical care could be organized and financed; nor was the NHS *necessarily* the most appropriate. The fundamental issue, for Lees, was:

> whether the supply of medical services should be based on the principle of consumers' sovereignty or be made the subject of collective provision: whether,

that is to say, the institutions responsible for providing medical care should charge for their services and vary that supply in accordance with consumer choice or whether services should be supplied free, with costs met from taxation and supply regulated by administrative decision.

For Lees at least, the supply of goods and services, including medical care, should, as far as possible, be based on personal preferences. The major task of public policy was therefore 'to devise the set of institutional arrangements that would achieve this end most effectively' (Lees 1961: 14).

Individuals, Lees argued, express their preferences for goods and services in two main ways: 'by spending money in the market and by casting votes at the polls'. Generally, Lees argued, it would be agreed that, of the two, the market was the superior means of registering those preferences. In rejecting the claim that medicine has characteristics that differentiate it sharply from other goods in the market, Lees insisted that medical care is (for the most part) a personal consumption good and was thus 'a highly dubious candidate for collective provision' (Lees 1961: 21).

The problem with the NHS, for Lees, was that medical care had been brought under public control at a time when various industries had been nationalized as 'a practical expression of the belief current between the 1930s and the 1950s that administration is everything and large-scale organizations are more efficient than small'. Since 1948, he argued, *political* decisions had increasingly replaced the personal choices of consumers. Expenditure on the NHS, for Lees, was considered not on its merits but 'weighed instead against other items of public outlay as part of policies to deal with rising prices and expenditure'. Far from being extravagant, expenditure on the NHS had been '*less* than consumers would probably have chosen to spend in a free market'. Spending on hospital building programmes, in particular, had been 'deplorable'.

For all practical purposes, Lees argued, the NHS was a complete *monopoly*. Private expenditure on health care, he calculated, was 'perhaps 5% of the total'. The most serious weakness of the NHS, however, was its 'absence of built-in forces making for improvements in quality and efficiency'. Within the NHS, Lees argued, the insistence on a single standard of service for all had eliminated the internal forces making for improvement that would be generated by emulation between diverse standards. In addition, he argued, medical care should be open to experiment and innovation; at present, however, it was closed. Under the monolithic structure of the NHS, he claimed, no new ideas could be introduced without the prior approval of the Minister of Health, which in practice usually meant that of 'some hard-pressed government official'.

If the concentration of power in ministerial hands was inimical to medical progress, however, it was also said to possess other dangers - not least, perhaps, for the medical profession itself. The NHS, for Lees, was a complete *monopsonist* as 'virtually the sole purchaser of the services of doctors and dentists'. As a result, the NHS had created discontented professions, not least in matters of remuneration. Successive Ministers of Health, Lees argued, had:

> used their extraordinary power to exploit doctors and dentists in the interests of greater financial stability. That power would be better abolished. In most other countries, including those with state schemes, doctors and dentists earn their incomes from fees, freely agreed with their patients.

The fundamental weaknesses of the NHS, Lees argued, were 'the dominance of political decisions, an absence of built-in forces making for improvement and the removal of the test of the market'. These defects, he argued, endangered the *quality* of medical care and could be eliminated only by far-reaching reform:

> A monolithic structure financed by taxation is ill-suited to a service in which the personal element is so strong, in which rapid advances in knowledge require flexibility and freedom to experiment, and for which consumer demand can be expected to increase with growing prosperity. While from the point of view of the general health of the community [the] NHS has not in any obvious way failed, it has given rise to problems that a more market-oriented system would have avoided, and those problems are increasing in number and complexity, On the longer view, the most acute danger of [the] NHS is that it will prevent the emergence of more effective methods of medical care.

Reform, Lees argued, should be based on six principles. First, it should aim to diminish the role of political decisions and enlarge the influence of consumer choice. The aim should be to confine ministerial responsibility to ensuring that minimum standards were maintained and, when necessary, providing subsidies. Secondly, governments should 'move away from taxation and free services and towards private insurance and fees' by allowing tax concessions to those who could provide for themselves and giving direct assistance to the 'dwindling minority who cannot' (Lees 1961: 61).

Thirdly, Lees argued, the control of hospital services should be dispersed by transferring ownership of hospitals from central government to local authorities and private institutions. Fourthly, he argued, professional incomes should be determined by markets, not ministers. Fees should thus be freely settled between doctors (or dentists) and patients, who could reclaim part of the cost from public funds. Fifthly, Lees argued, pricing should be reintroduced in the drugs market by requiring patients to pay a percentage of the cost of each prescription, with special provision for costly life-saving drugs or those on low incomes. Finally, the capacity of medical and dental schools should be released from state control by funding student costs by loans instead of grants. Reform, Lees argued, should proceed cautiously, but should move towards 'the creation of a medical system that holds more promise than the NHS appears to do' (Lees 1961).

'After the NHS'?

By the early 1970s, the IEA's neo-liberal critique of the NHS was being led by Arthur Seldon. For Seidon at least, *only* the NHS - a 'mass, make-believe, macro-artifact' - teaches the 'myth' that the best health care can be preserved or restored 'free for all' (Seldon 1977: 83). In practice, however, Seldon argues, the NHS:

> does not do what it preaches: it has to ration kidney machines, for example, and so condemns some patients to death. (And it is a bit of a fraud as a supposedly comprehensive 'National' 'Health' Service. It is both too all-embracing, since it comprises private benefits as well as public goods, and not all-embracing enough, since it does not supply all the services required for good health - the right food and other requisites).

In the real world, Seldon argues, there are both unavoidable and accepted risks to health and treating ill-health uses resources. The costs of health care, for Seldon, can mostly be covered by individuals taking out private (or social) insurance. The poor can also be enabled to insure by a reverse income tax (Chapter 7) or by 'having their premiums paid on a sliding scale' by government, as happens in Australia. Catastrophic health risks such as major surgery or crippling diseases, for Seldon, can be paid for collectively from the proceeds of general taxation, as war damage was from 1939 to 1945 (Seldon 1977: 84).

Most Western industrialised countries have mixed systems of health-care, consisting of social and private, compulsory and voluntary, insurance. The result, for Seldon at least, is that these countries channel more resources per head to medical care than Britain does: In Europe, North America and Australasia, he argues, 6.5 to 8% of GNP goes to medical care. In Britain, the figure is much lower at 'barely 5.5%'. The higher figure, for Seldon, indicates the advantages of diversifying sources of finance. More importantly perhaps, it reflects the preferences of those who pay (Seldon 1977: 84):

> This is the reply to defenders of the British system, which relies mainly on one source, who say that resources, even if less in Britain, are used more efficiently than in other countries. The reply is that, whatever the relative efficiency of the British state system, which is debatable, it does not allow people to pay in the ways they prefer. It is imposed on the people by politicians, officials and 'experts' who claim they know better. They have not been able to escape from it because all the political parties have supported it.

For Seldon, in particular, this is precisely why we in Britain (and 'only we' among Western industrialized countries) have a 'National Health Service'. The reason asserted for making people pay by taxes for health care, Seldon argues, has been (and is) that 'it removes the price barrier, so that everyone can have the treatment he needs without worrying about paying'. For Seldon (1977: 84-5), however:

> The real, main motive for replacing prices by taxes in 1946, and for persisting with taxes despite the social and economic changes in the intervening thirty years, has nothing to do with medical care as a public good. Nor is the motive basically the desire to deal with poverty ... The central motive for maintaining state medicine in the face of economic change has been the anxiety of impatient reformers who want to establish instant equality; they dislike the reverse income tax because they think paying for medical care is 'obscene', and they cannot wait for incomes to be equalized as social mobility spreads the opportunity to learn and to earn.

Seldon, in particular, has attacked this tendency to look upon price as a 'barrier'. In the UK, he notes, the desire to remove the 'barrier' standing between the citizen and medical services has led to the removal of price itself - the abolition, in other words, of 'rationing by the purse' (Seldon 1977: 85).

For Seldon, however, price is simply a reflection of the interplay between the forces of supply and demand and 'normally varies inversely with supply and directly with demand'. Price is also, for Seldon, a symptom of *scarcity*. As far as the health care situation in the UK is concerned, Seldon argues that the removal of the symptom (price) has emphatically *not* destroyed its root cause (scarcity). The abolition of price has indeed removed the 'barrier' from people with incomes too low to pay for medical care. For Seldon, however, the abolition of price has also produced other, but malign, unintended consequences.

In the first place, he argues, the abolition of price has removed or distorted the other functions or effects of price in measuring or disciplining demand and in rationing or generating supply (Seldon 1968: 22-3):

> It has depressed the supply of funds available for medical care and inflated the demand for, or strained, human and material resources. It has created an unreal world in which resources that are scarce and should be husbanded have been made to appear plentiful because they are supplied 'free'. Removal of price, moreover, has not abolished rationing but changed its form from financial to administrative: that is, appointment systems, waiting-lists, queueing, political wire-pulling, which can be more arbitrary than pricing.

The abolition of price, for Seldon, makes politicians important and creates jobs for bureaucrats. Yet the problem of rationing remains. For Seldon, in particular, where there is no price to apportion supply between the various demands, there must be rationing by other means. In the NHS, Seldon asserts, medical care is rationed above all by *time*. The principle 'first come, first served' sounds fair. In practice, however, 'it favours the fleet of foot, the loud in voice' (Seldon 1977: 85):

> People and patients who are rich in time receive more or better medical care than those who are poor in time. The more individuals can wait and queue, the more attention or the better treatment they receive.

For Seldon at least, the other rationing devices, which are 'no *less* arbitrary' than price, used to allocate time within the NHS include, for example:

- *Influence*: If you know your doctor or hospital official personally, you will receive better treatment from the NHS than if you don't.

- *Literacy*: Middle-class people who 'speak the same language' as doctors do better under the NHS than the working-class.

- *Cunning*: Those of any class who know how to 'work the system' receive better treatment from the NHS than those who resignedly accept it.

- *Political Status*: This ensures earlier treatment for Ministers from the NHS than for the tax-payers whom they are supposed to serve.

The irony of rationing in the NHS, for Seldon, is that these differences are 'even *more* objectionable than differences in income, which at least to some degree reflect differences in value to the community', because differences in influence or bully-power are more difficult to reduce or remove (Seldon 1977: 86):

> Favouritism is more widespread in the National Health Service than we like to admit, as it is in other 'free' systems in Russia, Hungary, Poland and Bulgaria. The NHS has not abolished inequality: it has driven inequality underground and made it more difficult to correct.

If the abolition of price has been undesirable, however, it has also, for Seldon, been simply unnecessary. The removal of price, he argues, is emphatically not the only, or even the best, way to give those on low incomes access to medical care. Most people on low incomes, for Seldon, 'could have been given access to medical care not by removing price but by *enabling* them to pay it' (Seldon 1968: 23):

> In the UK, estimates of the population living below, at, or minimally above the poverty line vary mostly from 10 to 20 per cent. Some are mentally or physically incapacitated by age, illness or disability to the point at which they require personal care or services in kind, but most could be enabled by patient teaching, advice and guidance to learn independence, judgement and discrimination by giving them purchasing power to enable them to insure for insurable medical services.

For Seldon, in particular, only a small minority of UK citizens have inadequate earnings out of which to pay or insure for medical services. To the 80% (or more) of the population whose incomes are adequate for insurance, he argues, a further 10% (or more) could be made financially able to insure. Indeed, one of the functions of *government* in creating an environment in which the most effective and desirable forms of health care can emerge is to supply the purchasing power that would enable *all* citizens, not only the wealthy, to pay for services. The only exceptions, for Seldon at least, should be 'the incapacitated who need care in kind' (Seldon 1968: 23-4).

For Seldon, however, the strongest argument against the NHS is that it prevents people from channelling the resources to medical care that they would otherwise do. Evidence from abroad suggests that tax financing 'reduces the funds for salaries, equipment and buildings for health centres and hospitals' (Seldon 1977: 86). In Britain, on the other hand:

> There is almost no discussion ... of the central reason why doctors emigrate and patients wait, surgeons lament inadequate equipment, research languishes, casualty departments are closed, wards are short of nurses. The central reason is that, since people and patients do not pay directly by fees but indirectly by taxes, the decisions are made by the politicians, guided and advised by officials, who can impose their

notions of the good and the bad. And the 'good' notion for thirty years has been that price stands in the way of equality of access and shall therefore be banned *even if the resources channelled to medical care are less than they would otherwise be.* That is the truth that no amount of repeated assertion that 'the National Health Service is the envy of the world' can suppress.

For Seldon at least, the choice that has to be made is between 'the planned, tidy, tax-financed NHS' with less resources and 'a *priced* system with more resources, organized and financed by diverse methods' (Seldon 1977: 86):

> In all, a much more refined financing mechanism is required than taxation, both to minimize the deterrent effect to patients of fees or insurance costs and to use price as a reminder to them and to doctors and nurses that medical care uses scarce resources that could be applied elsewhere.

Seldon does not advocate a wholly unfettered market in health care, but prefers the mixed systems of voluntary and compulsory, state and private insurance of the kind that have gradually developed in the United States and in Australia:

> The main triumph of the mixed systems overseas is that they maximize the resources available for medical care, which the NHS does not. More accurately, they approach nearer to the *optimum* amount, in the sense that they enable people to say how much they want to spend on medical care at the expense of all the other goods and services they could have. These mixed systems create no false hopes and no myths. They show what the vast range of medical services cost, and they allow people to pay in the ways they prefer. They have created no Nirvana or mirage of 'the best medical care for everyone' which we in Britain have been misled into thinking was not only possible but what the NHS was giving us in our everyday lives, but which it has not given, does not give, and cannot ever give.

Seldon's preferred scheme is to issue a health voucher to each person to ease the transition from taxation to charging. This would cover not fees (as in education), but the cost or part of the cost of insurance premiums. Topping up the voucher out of pocket would provide additional finance for health care (Seldon 1977: 90). This would ensure everyone was covered and provide for each person to once again acquire the skills needed to exercise choice. Against the demand-side argument that the NHS ensures that the poor receive adequate provision, then, New Right neo-liberals have argued that this can be achieved in more than one way. Subsidies or vouchers, it is argued, can protect the poor whilst enhancing their ability to direct their own affairs by 'increasing the power of the patient *vis-à-vis* professionals and administrators' (Green 1987: 179).

'Everyone a Private Patient'

By the mid-1980s, the IEA's health portfolio had become the responsibility of David Green. For Green (1990: viii) at least:

> The fundamental defect of the NHS is that it restricts individual choice. Choice of doctor is limited, the patient's ability to participate in choosing a method of treatment is curtailed and it is impossible to opt for a higher standard of amenities. The NHS was established in the belief that it would offer free, equal and comprehensive care, but the NHS is not free: we all pay for it. It is not equal: social skills make a great difference to the quality and quantity of service rendered. And it is not comprehensive: no-one has a right to treatment. It is a rationing system in which patients get what the medical decision-makers consider appropriate. The promise of free care is a gross deception. There is no escape from cost-consciousness. We face a choice between, on the one hand, the cost-conscious paternalism of the medical and political authorities, and on the other, cost-conscious personal choice. Effective consumer choice is not possible if someone else has paid: it can only be facilitated by consumer payment.

For Green, as for IEA authors generally, the attempt to finance and supply medical care for all through the NHS has produced two fundamental problems: namely, endemic under-funding and inadequate competition. The NHS, he argues, has a serious *structural* 'flaw' because it has severed the link between supply and demand. For as long as health services are supplied free at the point of use and funded, for the most part, from the proceeds of general taxation, governments will always find themselves confronting 'not priced demand but *unpriced* expectations, uninhibited by contemplation of the other goods and services, like housing and education, which might have been enjoyed instead' (Green 1988: 1).

In addition, Green argues, there is no urgency or emergency about much health care. The risks involved in drug-taking or surgery must be weighed against benefits and cost in time and money will also be a factor as decisions are made about which treatment, if any, is advisable (Green 1988: 2). In this sense, Green argues, much of what we think of as health care:

> is not very different from other consumer goods which we consume, or refrain from consuming, because of the cost or personal preference. Certainly there is no finite quantum of 'need' which governments can measure.

For Green, as for IEA authors generally, the NHS has also impeded competition. The majority of people have only so much disposable income out of which to pay or insure for medical services. Yet, because most are forced to pay for the 'monopolistic' NHS, individuals and families are typically unable to choose alternative forms of health care provision - even if this is what they themselves would actually prefer.

This absence of competition, for Green, is undesirable in two further respects: first, because it encourages bad service and, secondly, because it discourages innovation and diversity. For Green, on the other hand, there is virtue in diversity and merit in variety. For Green at least, a competitive market in health care would allow many ideas to be 'tried out' at once, creating growing room for human ingenuity, so that if one answer does not work well there will always be something to compare it with, and alternatives to which consumers can turn for better service. The present NHS, precisely because it is a 'monopoly', both denies people access to alternative sources of supply and conceals from them 'the information required to form rational judgements about the quality of service they now receive'.

For Green, however, 'perhaps the most damaging effect of the NHS promise of free health care' is that it has undermined individuals' and families' capacity for self-direction and spread a 'child-like dependency' on the state (Green 1988: 5):

> Personal payment cannot be escaped, but we can choose whether the payment takes the form of a tax or a freely-paid price. Paying a price is a disposal of income, whereas a tax is a *deduction* from income which takes away personal responsibility for deciding how much money will go into health care and curtails personal responsibility for selecting the best arrangements for the supply of medical services.

Dependency, for Green, also has wider, if less tangible, social consequences. In particular, he argues, the welfare state ethic has steadily undermined Britain's cultural inheritance, the foundation stone of which is said to have been a spirit of self-direction and economic independence. Dependency, Green argues, undermines the chief foundation of a free society, namely:

> the willingness of people freely to restrain their own exercise of freedom so that others may also enjoy it. As J.S. Mill clearly foresaw, by promising to provide for every important want, governments diminish opportunities for people to acquire the 'moral, intellectual and active' skills needed for self-rule.

In May 1988, shortly after Margaret Thatcher's announcement of her government's intention to establish a Review into the future of the NHS, Green offered an analysis of the structural flaws in the NHS and of how they could be remedied (Green 1988). In common with most IEA authors (above), Green insisted that central government must continue to play a major role in maintaining access for the poor and in 'ensuring that competition is not artificially obstructed by providers'. The necessity of government intervention of *some* sort did not, however, mean that the functions of government in relation to health care should remain exactly as they were. In this connection, Green argued (1988: xii-xiii) that:

> It is common to identify three main roles that government can perform. It may *regulate* production by laying down rules; it may *finance* production by subsidizing either prices or incomes (cash transfers); or it may directly *produce* goods or services. A fourth could be added, *publishing* information to assist consumers in making choices. For 40 years, governments have both *financed* and *produced* services through the NHS, and I will argue that this all-embracing therapy has had inescapable side effects that now call for a radical remedy.

The solution to the problems of endemic underfunding and inadequate competition within the NHS, for Green, lay in 'private, but government-assisted' insurance:

> If we truly want each citizen to enjoy guaranteed access to a well-defined set of essential health-care services, regardless of their ability to pay, then this objective could be more effectively accomplished if each person had a *contract of insurance*, setting out his or her entitlements.

Of the six main approaches available for reforming and improving the NHS, Green argued, private insurance had shown itself to be 'the most promising way of putting consumers in the driving seat' (Green 1988: 70).

How, though, could Britain move from the NHS to an insurance-funded system? For Green at least, the problem here was that:

> We cannot get to a situation in which everyone capable of independent choice pays their own way in one move. Some intermediate steps are necessary. The underlying principle I will follow is that the NHS should continue to rely on taxation, but that people who are dissatisfied should not be forced to pay for the NHS if they are not happy with the service they are receiving. No system will ever be responsive to consumers if producers receive payment whether or not their work is satisfactory. It follows that if consumers are dissatisfied they must be free to go to an alternative and to retrieve all or part of the taxes they have already paid.

The NHS, for Green, should remain essentially intact, but pilot projects for restructuring health services should be attempted 'in one or more regions'. Those dissatisfied with the NHS, on the other hand, should be free to 'escape' by accepting instead an 'age-weighted' voucher, representing the taxes they had paid towards the NHS. In such cases, Green suggested, two conditions would apply. Those wishing to 'opt out' would relinquish their claim to free NHS services, and should be compelled to take out private insurance to the value of the voucher or more:

> There is always a danger that people will underestimate the risk of catastrophic illness and therefore underinsure. The expectation that government or private charity will pay for treatment may encourage this tendency still further. For this reason it is permissible for government to require that all insurance policies should include coverage against catastrophic illness.

Those opting out of the NHS could turn either to private sector or to NHS hospitals for treatment and 'would not be confined to using only private hospitals'. If, however, they chose to use NHS services, they would be required to pay as private patients. Separate vouchers would be available for hospital care (excluding long-stay provision for the elderly, the mentally and physically handicapped and the mentally ill) and primary care (covering the cost of GP services only, and excluding the cost of drugs).

The poor, Green argued, should also receive vouchers to buy a 'civilized minimum' of health care services (Green 1988: 82). The poor, after all, were:

> supposed to enjoy the same rights of access to medical care as everyone else, but in the first place, access depends partly on social skills, and the poor disproportionately lack these skills. If, however, the government delineated a package of health-care services which it considered to be the civilised *minimum*, put a price on this package, and gave the poor sufficient money in the form of a voucher to buy it, the poor would be better off. They would have a clear *entitlement* to a well-defined set of services which was bought-and-paid-for and enforceable at law.

Those deciding to opt out of the NHS would take their vouchers not to insurance companies, but to other buyer groups, *health purchase unions* (HPUs), which would 'obtain the best deal for their members from insurers'. Most people, it was envisaged, would obtain cover through their employer or through a private association. Eventually, it was argued, statutory HPUs could be established in all regions; because it would take time for these groups to develop suitable expertise, however, it was suggested that (initially at least) the Government should establish only four HPUs - one each for England, Wales, Scotland and Northern Ireland (Green 1988: 88). Insurance companies would be free to recruit individual subscribers, but would not receive voucher payments unless the individual subscribed to an HPU. This, Green acknowledged, was a 'coercive' measure, but was 'justified by the technical difficulties involved in making a competitive market in health insurance work to the advantage of all'.

'Omega Health Policy'

For Madsen Pirie (1988a: 236), the NHS presents, in theory at least, a difficult case for exponents of 'micropolitics' to work on (Chapter 2, above):

> The National Health Service is generally regarded as the most sensitive area in which to attempt reform. A widely held attitude esteems the security it brings, and opposes any move which might jeopardize it.

For Pirie at least, a number of obstacles make any departure from the *status quo* which is the NHS difficult to establish (Pirie 1988a: 236):

> There are large interest groups who, when their influence and empires appear to be threatened, will resist change. Professional groups, trade unions, and civil servants are obvious examples. Not only do these groups exert influence on politicians as powerful concentrated pressure groups ... they also derive influence from their supposed professional expertise. For example, a health minister would hesitate before advocating any policy ... condemned by the British Medical Association. But although the *medical* expertise of the BMA is unquestioned, it is not always qualified to comment on the economic and political implications of new proposals in health policy.

Politicians, for the ASI, are 'activists, anxious to intervene, legislate, regulate and generally be seen to be doing something about present problems'. For the ASI, on the other hand, it is often impossible to improve things through political action; in many cases, the 'unplanned' activity of millions of individuals brings about a better overall result than the well-intended but insensitive efforts of politicians to plan the whole of any given activity (Butler *et al* 1985: 289). A further problem, for these authors, is that:

> The most sophisticated arguments and most carefully devised plans for change may founder on the simple feeling that what is proposed is not fair. Among the British

people at large there is no conclusion, however illogical, more likely to lead to thumbs down than the elliptical statement that something is unfair. In the social services particularly, people's feelings can be worked upon easily - to the detriment of sound policy analysis.

For the ASI, however, the NHS is also typical of its class. It offers a standardized service and is characterized by its lack of attention to consumer requirements. Its long waiting-lists 'bear witness to its inability to match supply to demand'. The NHS, it is argued, is unable to exercise control over its costs. Indeed, for many areas, it has no idea what they are (Pirie 1988a: 236).

For the ASI at least, there is also an in-built tendency for services controlled by politicians to be subject to persistent expansion, simply because of the 'vote motive' (Butler *et al* 1985: 292). As voters, people may vote for programmes which, as taxpayers, they are not prepared to pay for:

> This expansionary tendency in all public services naturally imposes budgetary problems on any government that is unwilling to raise taxes. But if the government tries to control or regulate the work of the medical profession, it soon runs into difficulty because of the monolithic nature of the service. It becomes involved in the creation of an elaborate system of bureaucratic controls. Throughout the history of the NHS, there has been an inverse ratio between the number of administrators and the number of hospital beds actually available for the public.

The 'politicization' of health care, for the ASI, has also had the (inevitable) consequence of giving the poor a second-class service (Butler *et al* 1985: 290):

> Middle-class individuals, who know how to manipulate the system, do well from it. They can complain to get better attention, they can use their influence with politicians and others to jump the queues, they are more able to find out what benefits are on offer ... poorer people do not do so well: they have little political influence to ensure that the available services are designed for them; less knowledge of the benefits on offer; and very little power to complain effectively about inadequate or low quality services.

For the ASI, however, the needs of the poor are the *only* arguable target for the services of a welfare state. 'The rich do not need state welfare: the middle and working classes - if they were not penalty taxed - could provide for their own. It is only the poor and handicapped who need public welfare. If it can be shown that it does not help them in the best way, the present welfare state has lost its *raison d'être*' (Butler *et al* 1985: 290).

In 1983, the ASI proposed a number of reforms to the NHS, ranging from minor improvements to major reorganizations of structure and financing and covering many areas, 'including management structures, service delivery structures, pricing and payment policies and financial organization in general' (Butler *et al* 1985). Specifically, the Omega proposals for health and personal social services included the extensive use of private contractors in performing a wide range of ancillary services and functions currently being performed 'expensively' by NHS personnel. The following ancillary services were said to be 'candidates for potential savings, given modern equipment and efficient management and manpower use' (Butler *et al* 1985: 296):

> catering; portering; domestic services and housekeeping; administrative and personnel functions; estate management; linen and laundry; security; building and plant maintenance; architects, surveyors and other professional services; general and specialist cleaning; pest control; and engineering, plumbing and electrical services.

Contracting-out these services, for the ASI, would achieve huge savings for the NHS, which should remain within the hospital or the other units that made them and not (for example) result in reduced financial allocations from the centre. If such savings were not retained, there would be no incentive to experiment or make changes. Health authorities, hospitals and other units should therefore invite tenders for particular functions. This would oblige the units concerned to thoroughly appraise their needs and how they were currently being provided; competitive tendering would reveal to the units concerned if and how the current structures could be improved upon by outside experts (Butler *et al* 1985: 298).

There was also said to be a strong need for 'auditing controls and internal pricing' within the NHS. Auditing and cost control, for the ASI, were skills that could be 'bought in' from outside. There was a case here for establishing such a contract, at least temporarily, in every NHS unit. A leading firm of chartered accountants, it was suggested, could also be commissioned to undertake an external audit of at least three state hospitals (a teaching hospital, a large urban general hospital and a smaller rural hospital), perhaps at the same time auditing two or three similar private hospitals (Butler *et al* 1985: 298-9):

> Depending on the findings, it may then be possible to sub-contract the management of three general hospitals in different areas to private management firms for a two-year experimental period while the results are assessed.

The NHS's capital assets, for the ASI, could also be used more efficiently. Local units should therefore be given the power to sell or lease all unused or under-used assets to private health care firms, thus 'increasing the total provision of health care by opening wards and other facilities that are presently unused or under-used'. The income generated from rents or sales could then be used 'to improve existing facilities for the benefit of all patients and the provision of yet further accommodation for those presently on the waiting-lists'.

To give free services to everyone, irrespective of income, was said to be a waste of public money. Finite resources were often spent on people able to pay their own way. Charging, especially for non-essential hotel services, was therefore a reasonable way of asking the better off to take up a greater part of the health care burden. At the very least, it was argued, charges to cover 'hotel' accommodation in hospitals 'strongly suggest themselves' as potential candidates for charging. There was also, for the ASI, a strong case for charging those who could afford it 'the full cost of family planning services' and eventually to contract out these services completely. Charging, for the ASI, could also be introduced for non-essential ambulance journeys, non-essential drugs (such as mild tranquilizers and appetite suppressants) and visits to GPs. Once this first step had been accepted, the next sensible step would be to extend pricing more deeply into medical care, and to begin charging for a number of minor medical services (Butler *et al* 1985: 301).

At the same time, it was argued, individuals designated as genuine welfare cases should not be required to pay in full for health or other services; current recipients of social security payments could be issued with a health credit card, or *medicard*, which could be used to pay any charges levied. This principle, for the ASI, would allow economic pricing to be maintained but exempt genuinely deserving cases from the cost. It would also 'help to reduce the present injustice whereby wealthy people who happen to be young or old are subsidized by people far less well-off than themselves' (Butler *et al* 1985: 300). In particular, it was argued:

> The medicard idea, under which genuinely poor people receive free health care while those who are better off pay at least some ... of the cost of routine services, therefore brings a twofold benefit. It allows some basic pricing system within the NHS that is not there at present and so improves allocative efficiency; it ensures that resources are increasingly diverted to those who genuinely need them. And it gives even the poorest ... a chance to purchase services from the private sector, through their 'credit card' system, thus reducing the strain on the NHS and increasing the choice available to the public.

New ideas were also said to be required to encourage better-off individuals to withdraw their demands from the NHS and 'allow the resources thus freed to be used on people who really need them'. In this connection, Pirie (1988a: 237) argues that:

The question arises as to whether a scheme can be devised which, like those suggested for schools and universities, might re-route the funding within the system so as to give effect to consumer preferences. If this can be achieved, it will gradually succeed in individuating what has hitherto been a uniform, unresponsive output. The answer is that such a scheme can indeed be devised. The state may be large, but so is human creativity. Armed with a valid method to direct it, there are few problems so big that they cannot be brought down by it.

For the ASI at least, the first step of such a scheme should be to 'augment the total funding finding its way into health care, not by increasing its allocation from the taxpayer, but by encouraging those who can afford it to add their own resources'. Other advanced countries, after all, manage to achieve a higher level of spending on health as a fraction of GDP because people 'spend more personally, and perceive benefits to themselves and their families' (Pirie 1988a: 237).

For Pirie at least, measures to encourage and accelerate the growth of private medicine were already in place, and more could be put into effect:

> Tax incentives can provide the means of encouragement, reducing the cost of private insurance to large numbers who cannot quite afford it at present. This has the advantage of simultaneously increasing the total spending on health, even while it reduces the demand on the National Health Service. The NHS would be in a far worse position without the 9% already in private medicine or the 400,000 items of elective surgery performed privately.... None of this need bring major hostility from interest groups, since no significant ones are threatened. Even the general public which depends on the NHS does not oppose the spread of private medicine. One of its effects will be after all to relieve the burden of demand on the state system.

'Health Management Units'

For the ASI, however, the most obvious avenue for improvement in the NHS was said to be its absence of any intermediate facilities between general practitioners and hospitals. For Pirie (1988a: 237) at least:

> It is overwhelmingly a two-tier system. If the doctors' prescriptions do not cure the patient, they are sent on to hospitals. The private sector and health systems overseas have a range of facilities between the two, featuring such things as group diagnostic facilities and out-patient clinics. Since much of the treatment which is given expensively in hospitals could be performed more efficiently outside them,

and since treatment would be more local and more consumer-friendly than large-scale institutions can provide, there is an opening for possible reform if the interest groups can be assuaged.

One answer, the ASI argued in 1985, could be a reorganization of the NHS to include Health Maintenance Organizations (HMOs) which offer both primary and hospital care *en bloc* in return for 'a subscription from a company to cover the health costs of their employees and sometimes also of their dependents' (Butler *et al* 1985: 303). HMOs work in the United States and elsewhere to provide total health cover and include doctors, clinics, specialists, diagnostic facilities, and hospitals. As Pirie (1988a: 238) notes:

All work within the HMO to provide whatever health-care is appropriate. They will usually receive a fee on behalf of each patient, making it in their interest to keep their customers healthy in cost-effective ways. They have the range of intermediate facilities so absent from the NHS and have to attract and keep patients who have the choice of going to other HMOs instead.

For the ASI, in particular, a successful health-care system must have the interests of patients, doctors and insurers moving in the same direction at the same time (Butler *et al* 1985: 303):

The HMO does this by making sure that it is in the interest of all three to have treatment done immediately, cheaply and properly. The doctor, because he is sharing in the profits of the HMO, is keen to see that the expenditure is not excessive but appropriate, since otherwise the profits of the HMO will suffer. On the other hand he does not wish to do his job badly, because it will be much more expensive to correct mistakes afterwards and he might even be sued. He aims to get the patient well and out of hospital at the earliest appropriate moment, in order to prevent the costs of the hospital side of the HMO from rising.

In 1983-84, the ASI argued that the establishment of HMOs in the UK could be straightforward if organized initially around larger firms:

The schemes could be extended to the general public through a subscription scheme. However, there is presently no basis for any arrangement of this type and its establishment would take much effort to encourage. There may be a case for extending tax rebates to HMOs, and for allowing state reimbursement of HMO subscriptions for the less well-off population through the 'medicard' scheme.

The HMO arrangement, for the ASI, was an attractive solution to the problem of containing medical costs while providing greater consumer choice and high standards of care:

> It is most likely to spring up in an atmosphere where private insurance is widespread - and therefore the principles of subscription medicine and private practitioners are common - than from the bedrock of socialized medicine ... the optimal strategy would be to encourage and help grow the existing elements of universal medical insurance and then to let HMOs or other beneficial systems develop out of it.

In 1988, the ASI argued that (as a possible next step in this optimal strategy for reform) HMOs should be formally introduced. Regional and District Health Authorities, it was argued, should be replaced by newly created and independent *Health Management Units* (HMUs). These would be funded from taxation and provide total health cover for patients. GPs would sign up with an HMU, taking their patients in with them. Patients dissatisfied with an HMU could always leave to join another, by signing with a GP registered with another HMU. GPs would no longer be paid by a combination of capitation fees, basic salary and special allowances, but would be paid by their HMU for work done, with fees for each consultation or item of treatment (Butler and Pirie 1988a, 1988b).

When patients were sent for treatment by hospitals or specialists, their HMU would select an appropriate course of treatment and would have an incentive to choose a cost-effective supply from the alternatives available; each hospital would have to know the cost of its activities and perform them efficiently. For Pirie (1988a: 238) at least:

> The system which these changes produced would induce competitive pressures into the system, bringing the benefits of efficiencies and innovative techniques. It would enable management at various levels to be more flexible and to take independent decisions. The doctors and their patients would have a choice of between HMUs and HMUs would choose between the services of different hospitals for their patients.

HMU, for the ASI, could be financed by an annual allocation for each patient and would have to provide health care for that sum, up to standards determined nationally. If a patient left an HMU to join another, their annual allocation would move with them to their new HMU. As in education, money would 'follow' the choices made (Pirie 1988a: 239):

> There could be refinements to make this system work. HMUs would not be able to refuse patients, except for a limit on their total size. Even then they would have to establish waiting lists. The annual allocation could vary with the category of

patient, or even the geographical area of residence, to reflect the different health care costs.

This system, for the ASI, would not incur the odium which would greet an attempt to replace the NHS. Instead, it was argued, the new system would both retain and improve it:

> Patients see their doctors as before, and it is still free at the point of consumption. They receive hospital and specialist services and these are still free. The change is that an internal market has been created in which there are variations and choices, in which there are incentives for efficiency and competition, and in which the resources of the state are redirected as a result of those decisions.

The result, for the ASI, would be to set in motion a sequence of events which would gradually 'individuate' the service to conform to the various needs and preferences of consumers:

> It would still be a public sector supply, still a National Health Service, but pressures and forces within it would be working to produce different results. HMUs which satisfied consumers would receive more funds and others would be encouraged to do the same. Cost-effective HMUs would be able to offer greater rewards to their participants than inefficient ones, so talent would find new opportunities. The example of the National Health Service indicates the range of problems to which these principles can be applied. Once political markets have creative solutions applied to redirect their forces, major reforms can be achieved. The NHS is almost the limiting case; if the methods work there, they can perhaps work anywhere.

'Healthy Competition'

In November 1980, the Centre for Policy Studies (CPS) issued a collection of readings in which it was argued (Seldon 1980a: 5) that:

> The NHS has done the health of the people a 'disservice', because it has prevented the development of more spontaneous, organic, local, voluntary and sensitive medical services that would have grown up as incomes rose and medical science and technology advanced. If it were not for the politically-controlled NHS, we should have seen new forms of medical organization and financing that better reflected consumer preferences, requirements and circumstances. These lost opportunities of better medical care are the disservice the NHS has done the people

of Britain.

In the mid-1980s, the CPS published *NHS: The Road to Recovery* which made the following recommendations (Elwell 1986):

- The gathering together of all health-care under the roofs of the 190 or so District Health Authorities (DHAs).
- A correspondingly reduced role for Regional Health Authorities (RHAs).
- More freedom for patients to choose and change their GP and the payment of fees for visits.
- The setting up by all NHS hospitals of associations of fund-raising friends.
- Charging for insurable 'hotel' hospital services.
- Encouragement of private health insurance schemes.
- The appointment of a Secretary of State for Health, of Cabinet rank.

In 1987, a further pamphlet proposed some practical steps to improve the performance of the NHS. In particular, *Healthy Competition* identified a number of areas (such as community care, hospital building, surgery and primary care) where the introduction of more vigorous competition could 'improve the performance of the NHS, whose top-heavy direct labour organizations should be made to compete with tenders from the private sector' (Peet 1987).

In November 1987, these points were debated at a conference sponsored by the CPS and whose panellists included managers of DHAs. In early 1988, the Centre called a Review of the NHS to consider such options as the establishment of the NHS as a separate Trust; more extensive use of joint ventures with the private sector; more extensive use of charging; introducing a system of health credits and the setting-up of a real national health insurance scheme, for some conditions and treatments at least (Letwin and Redwood 1988).

Managed Health Care

In February 1988, the CPS published the first of two 'Health Policy Reviews' co-written by its Director of Studies, David Willetts, and Dr Michael Goldsmith, a member of the Executive Committee of the Conservative Medical Society and a Research Fellow at the CPS. The first of these proposed an HMO-type of organization but, unlike the privately funded American version, one funded by tax revenues. The Government, it was suggested, should set up new tax-funded financing facilities - or *Managed Health Care Organizations* (MHCOs). These would then become the main purchaser and distributor of health-care, by combining the financing functions of Districts (DHAs) and Family Practitioner Committees (FPCs).

MHCOs, it was argued, would 'contract out' the provision of services like FPCs, but manage their utilization and delivery like HMOs. MHCOs would be created by 'taking existing DHAs and combining them with those parts of FPCs which fall within their borders'. MHCOs would then 'contract with doctors and other providers in the same way as HMOs' - with primary care services being supplied to the MHCO on the American Independent Practice (IPA) model. This implied a form of fee-for-service payment to GPs, but with considerable control and the use of tighter performance-linked contracts to enhance the standard of primary care. Consultant and other hospital doctors would be employed either on contracts by their local MHCO or directly by community hospitals, subject to peer review and utilization control taking place.

MHCOs, it was argued, should also contract both with newly-formed, community-run NHS hospitals and with private hospitals, which should 'compete with the newly-formed community hospitals to provide services to the MHCOs'. An extensive *internal market* would then develop, with MHCOs purchasing care from both NHS and private hospitals. Community nursing services and other aspects of community care would be provided by MHCOs by direct employment or contracting out services in an arrangement like that of the IPA. Patients would be free to change their MHCO if they wished, with government funding 'following' patients to the MHCO of their choice. Private managers would also be free to 'set up their own MHCOs and compete for publicly funded patients'. Patients could top up their tax-funded health-care and use their own funds to buy extra services, notably hotel facilities like single rooms, bathrooms, personal phones and a wide choice of meals and would pay for medical extras such as cosmetic surgery. For Goldsmith and Willetts, however:

> medical services beyond this, such as choice of consultant or hospital provider, would probably not be available from an MHCO.... Consumers who still want a consultant of their choice would be free to contract directly with him, paying with their own money or through private medical insurance. Finally, competition alone is not enough to raise quality. There is a strong case for a consumer-oriented inspectorate of health care. This would work in much the same way as the government inspectorates of education and the constabulary. It should be staffed by professional and lay members and be required to carry out assessment of any establishment which offered NHS care.

The precise size of MHCOs was nowhere definitely stated in the proposal. America's experience with HMOs, however, suggested that it was necessary to have 'approximately 100,000 patients within an HMO to even out the risks'. District-sized MHCOs, then, were suggested as appropriate for the UK. For Goldsmith and Willetts, however, MHCOs could be smaller than existing DHAs to 'increase the chance that people in most parts of the country would have a real choice of MHCO' (Goldsmith and Willetts 1988a: 5, 15).

A second Review by Goldsmith and Willetts in 1988 explored ways of topping up public finance with spending from private sources, in the hope of generating more spending on health without raising more in taxes. In this connection, tax relief for those wishing to take out private insurance was found to be unsatisfactory. For Goldsmith and Willetts, however, the NHS could (and should) sell more services to private patients: for example, by expanding the provision of paybeds and amenity paybeds. Companies should also be encouraged to spend more on health for their employees (Goldsmith and Willetts 1988b).

Finally, in 1988, the CPS published John Redwood's *In Sickness and in Health*, which recommended that the NHS Management Board be strengthened; that RHAs be abolished and Districts report directly to the Board; and that partnership ventures between the public and private sectors be encouraged. Extra resources, Redwood argued, would become available by expanding privately-financed care via a contracting-out insurance scheme. Money should also move with the patient and reflect the actual cost of treatment. The prime objective of reform should be to achieve high quality patient care. In particular, the reduction of waiting-times by better management information systems should be at the top of the Government's agenda. New revenues/savings, Redwood argued, could be generated via property renewal and disposal, additional resources from private sector providers of hotel services and administrative savings (Redwood 1988).

'A Diet of Reason'

Alone among the four think-tanks examined in this study, the Social Affairs Unit (SAU) has taken no part in the debate into the future of the NHS. Nor was the Unit involved in the Prime Minister's Review of the NHS which resulted in the 1989 White Paper, *Working for Patients*. Instead, the SAU has sought to address questions to do with the role of health pressure groups, as well as issues in public health and preventive medicine. As Anderson has recalled, the publication of a report by the British Committee on the Medical Aspects of Food Policy (COMA) Commission (1984) stimulated a widespread public debate about the eating and drinking habits of the population. A significant feature of this debate, Anderson argues, was that it produced an entire 'food lobby' claiming to have conclusive proof that the British people:

> all eat too much meat, fat, sugar and salt, and not enough fibre; that many of them are dangerously fat and that their eating habits cause major killing illnesses such as heart disease.

The group therefore urged a radical change in national diet to reduce the risk of such diseases - to be achieved by the state funding propaganda on healthy eating or banning the production and advertising of foods the group decreed to be unhealthy. In 1986, the Unit published a collection of readings (Anderson 1986) whose authors and contributors rejected this position and who argued that the evidence relating diet to health was emphatically:

> not conclusive. Indeed, much of what is presented to the public even in supposedly official reports such as that of the National Advisory Council on Nutrition Education or by quasi-official bodies such as the Health Education Council, is not strictly scientific. There is no single clear, simple message about fat, salt, sugar and fibre or even about body weight agreed and packaged by scientists and ready for popular dissemination. There is no guarantee that if we change our diet to avoid allegedly unhealthy foods that all, even many of us will enjoy better health, let alone live longer. Indeed, some changes might even make some people less healthy.

A particular concern of the SAU, then, has been the statistical use (and abuse) of science/social science/epidemiology. As noted earlier, however, the SAU has published nothing to date on the NHS issue as such, preferring instead to leave this to other groups (IEA, ASI and CPS).

'The Prime Minister's Review'

As Calum Paton (1990: 119) has recalled, the 'Prime Minister's Review' of the NHS, announced in January 1988, was so-called because the Prime Minister herself (Mrs Thatcher) announced a fundamental review into the future of the NHS in response to questions on *Panorama* - unknown in advance by Ministers, civil servants or even the Conservative Party:

Growing concern, expressed especially in 1985 and again towards the end of 1987, about under-funding of the National Health Service was occasioned by alleged crises in large teaching hospitals, in London and Birmingham especially. The Government felt increasingly on the defensive about the politics and financing of the National Health Service. Eventually, the Prime Minister decided to try to move on to the offensive and announced the fundamental review into the future of the National Health Service at the beginning of 1988.

The Review process, Paton argues, continued a trend in the Conservative administration of by-passing traditional policy-making bodies or investigatory mechanisms such as Royal Commissions:

> Instead of Departmental officials from the policy divisions of the Department of Health as well as the Permanent Secretary and others at the top of the office constituting the key personnel in the Review, informal deliberations constituted the key sessions of the process. These were dominated in the early stages by the Prime Minister herself and dominated throughout by more informal advisers such as those in the Number 10 Policy Unit, former members of that Unit [below] and members of 'think-tanks' - the Centre for Policy Studies in particular, but also the Adam Smith Institute (and in the early days the Institute of Economic Affairs Health Unit, before its prescriptions for dismembering the NHS's public financing system ran aground on an eventual pragmatism).

The Government had initially resisted an inquiry into the future of the NHS, but 'ultimately felt compelled by public pressure to act' (Green 1990: 1-2):

> The year of public debate that followed was dominated by discussion of alternative methods of funding, including an earmarked health tax, national insurance with or without an entitlement to contract out, and private insurance by means of vouchers or tax reliefs.

Private inquiries into the funding of the NHS were established, the most important of which was the Institute of Health Service Management's Working Party on *Alternative Delivery and Funding of the NHS* (IHSM 1988).

An 'Internal Market'

In the end, the Prime Minister's Review (above), in an attempt to maintain public financing yet escape the allegedly 'bureaucratic' system of planned provision, adopted the core ideas of provider markets within the NHS, a broader version of the *internal market* concept suggested by Professor Alain Enthoven (1985) as a means of solving the problems faced by large teaching hospitals who were losing money under the Resource Allocation Working Party (RAWP) formula. By the time of the Review, the concept of an internal market had already gained currency (Green 1990: 2):

> The idea had first been put forward in 1985 by ... Enthoven and had attracted little hostile criticism and some support, which for a government anxious to appease worried backbenchers made it politically feasible. Pressure for an internal market was reinforced by the new managers who were increasingly chafing at the bit. They were on short-term contracts and part of their pay was performance-linked, yet many felt they were not masters of their own destiny and called for greater managerial decentralization and more flexibility, particularly in the remuneration of staff and the determination of capital expenditure. In addition, by 1988 the NHS had successfully put out to tender cleaning, catering and laundry services and in the process managers had acquired skills in the selection and employment of private contractors. Increasingly, it was thought that the same methods could be applied to clinical services.

'A Missed Opportunity'

The possibility of a radical solution to the NHS had been produced in 1982, when the Government's own 'Think-Tank', the Central Policy Review Staff (CPRS), submitted a paper to the cabinet on *Public Expenditure in the Longer Term*. This paper appeared to have the blessing of the then Chancellor, Sir Geoffrey Howe, who attached notes to the paper. Among the CPRS proposals for cutting public expenditure - and hence the role and agenda of government - were the introduction of private health insurance (with the option of a minimum private insurance for everyone), charges for visits to GPs and higher prescription charges. However, these proposals, which would have set a clear agenda for the reduction of public expenditure and the role of government, caused a massive outcry and, during the 1983 General Election campaign, Thatcher stated that the NHS was 'safe' in Conservative hands (Hoover and Plant 1989: 163-5 and 173).

For David Green, the internal market was an obvious compromise for a government 'constrained by this earlier pledge', but which nonetheless believed in the value of competition (Green 1990: 7). At the same time, he argues, there is more than one kind of competition and the model which the Government has in mind is very restricted:

It can be called a *defence-industry* procurement model of competition, in which relatively few suppliers submit tenders to provide goods or services stipulated by a Government agency. This produces results which are very different from a *consumer sovereignty* model of competition in which the paying customer can choose from among a range of suppliers thus signalling their approval or disapproval of the service offered.

For Green at least, the Government's NHS reforms have been 'a missed opportunity'. The White Paper proposals, he argues, were designed to eliminate some of the inefficiencies which have been the hallmark of the NHS since its inception, yet the White Paper itself is fatally flawed (Green 1990: 3):

> Above all, the proposals were flawed in that no effort was made to overcome the perennial difficulty of any system of rationing, namely that public expectations will always exceed the Government's ability to raise taxes to pay for the services demanded.

For Green at least, the White Paper proposals do not tackle the fundamental defects of the NHS - namely, its '40-year record of under-funding' and 'poor record of responsiveness to consumers'. These problems, he argues, can be remedied *only* by changing the way the NHS is financed (Green 1990: 13):

> The fact is that consumer *choice* is only possible with consumer *payment*. Perhaps the greatest irony of all is that the vast majority of people are paying in taxation the full cost of the services they receive. Yet because they have surrendered up their buying power by handing over taxes to the Government, they have also surrendered their ability to choose. The White Paper provides no answer. The best solution is a fully-fledged competitive market in which consumer choice would be based not on a Government promise but on that personal power to inflict economic pain on unsatisfactory producers which consumer payment alone can bring.

'An Eventual Pragmatism'

For Green, in particular, the Government's inquiry was 'a sorry affair' from the outset. In the end, it lasted a year, but each step was conducted in a rush and amidst much concern to maintain secrecy (Green 1990: 2):

> Moreover, from the outset, its focus was very narrow. This was because Mrs Thatcher decided that to appear to be opposed to the NHS was to commit political suicide and, in any event, she felt constrained by her earlier pledge that the NHS

was safe in Tory hands. Consequently, the only proposals that were taken seriously were those based on continued funding of health care from taxation and delivery (largely) free at the time of use.

As Calum Paton recalls, the first stage of the review saw much pamphleteering by New Right think-tanks such as the IEA Health Unit, the ASI and the CPS (Paton 1990: 120):

> Apart from a brief investigation in 1981-82 of alternative systems of financing for health care, this was the first time since the introduction of the National Health Service in 1948 that radical alternatives to a National Health Service model of funding health care were being seriously considered in Britain. John Moore, the Secretary of State from 1987 to 1988 was keen on examining alternative systems of financing: principally, various health insurance models ranging from National Health Insurance (publicly funded in the main) through to various alternatives in the realm of private insurance; vouchers to individuals earmarked for health care and significant tax relief for private insurance.

In the end, Moore personally chose the option of a 'financing' initiative - allowing individuals to contract out of the NHS on the analogy of contracting out of state pensions - a policy with which Strachan Heppel, the Deputy Secretary in the Department of Health and Social Security heading the administration of the Review, was also identified. Such options, however, according to Paton, were:

> anathema to the Treasury (as they meant 'unnecessary' tax relief to those already with private insurance and, more importantly, the loss of direct revenue on a large scale) and politically very risky. Even Mrs Thatcher felt she could not move against the NHS, and her personal advisers felt that the radical policy agenda for the third term of office was already taking its toll on government energy and taxing public patience.

Given the unpopularity of radical moves away from a tax-funded NHS, Paton argues, there was difficulty in designing proposals compatible with a radical NHS review but 'within the bounds of political pragmatism' (Paton 1990: 121). In the end, it was Mrs Thatcher herself who opposed the reforms in the funding of the NHS which had been 'boldly contemplated' by John Moore (Green, 1990: 6). As Paton (1990: 121-2) recalls:

> The Prime Minister's dissatisfaction with Moore's radical yet 'impractical' proposals on the *financing* side yet absence of ideas concerning the *provision* of health care (on the supply-side) led to his dismissal in July 1988 from the

Department of Health half of his job (and later complete dismissal in 1989). The Department was now split into two departments, Health and Social Security. Moore's poor performance in dealing with his critics, in particular in Parliament, had not helped his case.

Phase Two of the Review was marked by consolidation by the new Secretary of State for Health, Kenneth Clarke, formerly Minister of State in the Department from 1982-85. Clarke, a supporter of the National Health Service when set against many of his more sceptical Conservative colleagues, was thought likely to go further down the road of efficient 'public management' as represented by the Griffiths Inquiry [1983] with which he (rather than the Secretary of State at the time, Norman Fowler) had been particularly identified. Thus it was likely that existing initiatives for better management of public money, such as resource management, and measures such as clinical audit would be continued and 'beefed up'. It was further thought that, as well as forcing doctors to take responsibility for speciality and departmental budgets, Clarke might seek to put NHS clinicians on short-term contracts in return for higher salaries.

However, the Review entered Phase Three when the Prime Minister's dissatisfaction with the lack of a radical agenda led to the adoption of radical ideas on the 'supply-side' of health care. The concept of provider markets, a broader version of ... Enthoven's concept of the internal market was the linchpin of the Review. Other less radical components of the Review included further moves to medical audit and the control of Family Practitioner services. Furthermore the move to a corporate management model ... was enhanced, as the NHS Supervisory Board (now wholly defunct) and the NHS Management Board were replaced with (respectively) an NHS Policy Board composed primarily of Ministers and businessmen, and an NHS Executive, to be responsible for [the] implementation of ministerial strategy.

Reforming the NHS

If the SAU took no part in the Government's NHS Review, and the IEA's prescriptions for dismembering the NHS's public financing system soon ran aground on an eventual pragmatism, however, the CPS and the ASI - together with members of the Number 10 Policy Unit and former members of the PU, such as its former head John Redwood and ex-health and social policy member David Willetts - continued to dominate the key sessions of the Review. Of these two, however, the CPS appears to have been the more significant 'player' during the Review. It remains for us to say *why* this was so.

In this connection, it is worth recalling that the Centre was instrumental in suggesting that there should be a Review in the first place (Letwin and Redwood

1988). Before announcing the Review in January 1988, Mrs Thatcher herself sought advice (in late 1987) from a number of political intimates - some of whom went on to produce pamphlets for the CPS considered during the NHS Review (Goldsmith and Willetts 1988a, Redwood 1988). A second point to note is that the ASI had urged a reorganization of the NHS - involving the replacement of Districts *and Regions* with independent HMUs (Butler and Pirie, 1988a). Mrs Thatcher, however, made it clear during the Review that reorganization of the NHS was not on the Government's agenda. Certain aspects of the ASI's reform package, then, also appear to have run aground on an eventual (administrative) pragmatism.

The institutional significance of the CPS notwithstanding, a final point concerns the role of certain key individuals before, during and even after the Review. As we have seen, among those whose advice Mrs Thatcher sought in late 1987 were John Redwood and David Willetts. Of these, the suggestion here is that the latter was particularly significant; himself a former Treasury official, Willetts had formerly advised Mrs Thatcher on health issues before taking up his present post at the CPS in January 1987, was involved in the Review, and 'kept in touch with' both John Moore (Health Secretary when the Review was announced) and later with his successor, Kenneth Clarke.[1] And significantly, perhaps, it was Willetts who - shortly after the publication of *Working for Patients* - produced a proselytizing 'account of the Government's proposals for the future of the NHS' in a pamphlet for the Conservative Political Centre (Willetts 1989).

Conclusion: Working for Patients?

The argument of this chapter has been that the Centre for Policy Studies (CPS) was the most significant and influential New Right 'think-tank' involved in the 'Prime Minister's Review' of the NHS. The ASI had some earlier (and later) influence in arguing for HMUs i.e. HMO-type providers whereby GPs would have to square referrals with contracting purchasers. As Paton has argued, however:

> The 'internal market' came directly from Enthoven; the 'purchaser/provider' split and contracting from general inputs/elucidation of the logic; and GP budgets as an idea 'floating around' - not least from Professor Alan Maynard at York.[2]

For the IEA's David Green, however, despite occasional references to consumer choice and money following patients, the reformed NHS will remain 'a producer dominated monopoly which ekes out service to patients at the discretion of the authorities' (1990: viii). In particular, he argues, the Government's approach to competition is based on separating the financing or purchasing of health care from its provision. In essence, this is extending to clinical services the principle of contracting already applied to ancillary services such as cleaning, catering and laundry (Green 1990: 7-8):

> The White Paper contains two versions of the theme. In one version, the District Health Authority [DHA] becomes the purchasing agency and no longer manages hospitals directly. In the second, GPs are at the centre. Instead of paying DHAs to provide services, the Government assigns GPs a budget for a range of hospital services, and they become responsible for getting the best deal for their patients from either NHS or private hospitals.

The Government claims its proposals will increase consumer choice because money will 'follow the patient'. For Green, however this claim is implausible because, while money will technically follow patients, the patient will *not* determine where the money will go. Instead, he argues, the patients will be 'assigned to a treatment centre according to local contractual arrangements, not according to their personal preferences' (Green 1990: 8):

> After the reforms, the Treasury will finance health care much as it does now and District Health Authorities will become purchasing agencies, entering into contracts with either public or private hospitals. Hospitals will become independent of the district management and a number will become self-governing hospital trusts.

The Government's proposals, for Green, will remove some of the more manifest perversities in the NHS structure, but they will not increase consumer choice:

> For instance, at present two health authorities may receive the same funding even though one is more efficient than the other and treats more patients. This is partly why an authority can have empty beds and unused operating theatres as well as large waiting-lists. Henceforward, hospitals will be paid according to the number of patients they treat, but District Health Authorities will still be cash limited and hospitals will only be able to increase output if the DHA will pay, with the result that they could still have empty beds side by side with waiting-lists.

At present, Green argues, GPs are not cash limited, but if they become budget holders, as the Government proposes, they will face such limits for the first time (Green 1990: 9-10):

Currently, GPs have the freedom to choose the best hospital for their patients and, if there is a waiting-list locally, the good GP will refer patients elsewhere. But, under the new scheme, hospital referrals will have to be paid for out the GP's own cash-limited allocation. If the end of the financial year is approaching and funding is a bit tight, the GP will have an incentive to make patients wait so that they will not become a charge on his budget. This may save money but it will not give GPs an incentive to serve consumers. A comparison with American HMOs reveals the chief weakness of the Government's proposal. HMOs have been able to deliver cost-effective health care because providers are required to remain within a fixed budget, but it is also recognized that HMOs have an incentive to under-serve patients. The chief protection against bad service is the consumer's ability to escape from an unsatisfactory HMO to an alternative, such as a preferred provider organization, another HMO with a different practice style, or a fee-for-service insurer. HMOs that find themselves losing customers must respond to consumers' revealed preferences or go out of business.

For Green at least, it is this power to reveal preferences by exercising choice that gives the consumer power, but 'the NHS offers no such effective way of signalling displeasure or registering disapproval - nor will it do so after the latest reforms have been implemented' (Green 1990: 10). For the time being at least, the Government has determined to continue to finance health care from taxation. For Green (1990: 12-13), however:

> this strategy makes sense only if limiting total national spending is set above all else - including consumer responsiveness, the introduction of new technology, the enhancement of cost-effectiveness, and the promotion of higher quality care. So long as the Government determines how much the nation can afford to spend on health, the NHS will remain, above all, a device for rationing access to medical services.

Because the NHS attempts to make all health-care available free, however, it cannot meet all the demands made upon it. The irony here is that - despite the formal equality of the NHS - the poor are not well-served (Green 1990: 12):

> The NHS gives people what the medical authorities consider to be good for them, not what they would choose for themselves in the light of the cost and their personal preferences. Abolishing prices helps the relatively well-off more than it helps the poor. If the poor or the frail elderly were protected by giving them purchasing power instead of services in kind, they [could] insist on a more responsive service from producers.

For Green at least, a voucher scheme would offer the poor a real guarantee, as it would be based on a contract of insurance, not a political pledge (Green 1990: 11-12):

> The real challenge is to define the 'civilized' or 'decent' standard of care to which everyone should have access and to determine how to make this available by means of enforceable contracts of insurance. So long as the minimum is morally acceptable, then the majority of the population that is not poor can be left free to choose the arrangements they prefer. To provide the poor with access to the civilized minimum, but no more, would be a perfectly reasonable policy, but after 40 years of pretending that 'comprehensive' health care was being provided equally for all, the British Government found public opinion ill-prepared for any such departure. It decided to duck the issue but the end result is that NHS rationing will continue to create waiting-lists, lead to the outright denial of treatment to many patients and suppress personal choice.

More seriously still, Green argues, the poor and vulnerable will be the 'chief losers' of the Government's NHS reforms (Green 1990: 12).

Notes

1.   Interview.
2.   Correspondence.

7 The Dilemma of Dependency

Introduction

The purpose of this chapter is twofold. A first aim is to explore the sense in which the issue of welfare-dependency (below) plays differently as between individualist (free-market) and traditionalist (communitarian) conservatives and so constitutes something of an ideological dilemma for conservative capitalism (the New Right). A second aim is to examine the response of the four New Right think-tanks (IEA, ASI, CPS and SAU) to precisely this issue/dilemma, given the ideological differences between these groups discussed in Chapters 1-4 (above).

The New Right's ideological dilemma over dependency can be stated in the following way. Individualist (free-market) conservatives, as we saw in Chapter 1 (above), typically reject conceptions of social justice as a basis for public policy on the grounds that a consensus over issues such as need or desert is simply unavailable (because unobtainable). For Hayek (1976) and the 'Austrian' school, in particular, such claims are inherently *subjective*. 'The market is best suited to accommodating this reality since it allows for individual valuations of the worth of each person's claims and efforts; the state, on the other hand, cannot secure social justice precisely because of this diversity of moral valuations' (Hoover and Plant 1989: 73).

The dependency argument, on the other hand, assumes something which runs counter to this: namely, that there is indeed a desirable set of values relating to human character that define individual virtue in a capitalist society. Moreover, the suggestion from the American Enterprise Institute (1987) and others who accept this analysis is that public policy on welfare should reflect precisely these moral valuations. As Hoover and Plant (1989: 73-4) argue, the tensions between individualist (free-market) and traditionalist (communitarian) versions of conservatism pose an ideological dilemma for conservative capitalism (the New Right) on the question of dependency:

> In order to avoid incoherence, conservatives must be able to explain how it is that one set of values concerned with individual virtue can be the concern of the state, while another, relating to the proper level of resources for an individual, cannot be.

A further dimension to this argument, for Hoover and Plant, concerns the capacity of the state:

The state is presented by Hayek and Friedman as lacking the capacity to involve itself with distributive questions because of the complex, fragmented, dispersed and largely tacit knowledge that is required. The market is thought to be the institution that responds most efficiently to this aspect of the human condition. For Friedman, the state's only role with respect to welfare would be to provide subsistence resources through a 'negative income tax'.

'Workfare/Learnfare-type' policies (below), on the other hand, assume that the state has a role in seeking to develop individual virtues in welfare recipients. As Hoover and Plant (1989: 74) argue:

A state which gears its policies to the maintenance of certain virtues will be a long way from the limited government prefigured by Adam Smith and his individualist conservative followers. It is not a path that would attract the advocates of a neutral stance regarding economic behaviour as well as social and personal behaviour understood in a wider context.

Dependency theory, for Hoover and Plant, 'leads straight to traditionalist paternalism and the idea that 'Victorian values' can form the basis of state policy, a reversal of *laissez-faire* in the most sensitive areas of human conduct'. A further problem with the dependency argument, they argue, is that of hypocrisy (Hoover and Plant 1989: 74):

While the poor are to be regulated to induce moral behaviour by the terms of dependency theory, the rich are given licence to be indulgent by the terms of free enterprise and *laissez-faire*. There remains the criticism that dependency-based policies amount to the class-based imposition of values upon the poor that are merely a pretence on the part of the rich - the central criticism of the Victorian moral order.

A second aim of this chapter is to examine the response of the four New Right think-tanks (IEA, ASI, CPS and SAU) to precisely this issue/dilemma, given the ideological differences between these groups discussed in Chapters 1-4 (above). That the Centre for Policy Studies (CPS) should have been the first of these groups to introduce the arguments of American dependency theorists into Britain (in 1987) should surprise no-one, given the Centre's editorial interest in (because ideological commitment to) restoring 'Victorian values' (Himmelfarb 1987). What is perhaps more surprising - and presumably therefore more significant - is that the IEA's Health and Welfare Unit and the Adam Smith Institute (ASI) have since moved in this direction, with the result that a degree of convergence seems now to have taken place between four otherwise ideologically diverse

'New Right' groups (below). In this connection, two further questions arise: namely, to what extent does their decision to embrace this 'moral' agenda on welfare reform/policy imply an ideological shift on the part of the IEA and the ASI; and, secondly, to the extent that this can be inferred from some recent IEA/ASI publications, why might this shift have occurred? These and other questions are considered in more detail in the pages that follow.

'The Long Debate on Poverty'

For the IEA's David Green (below), a particular target of New Right neo-liberals has been the version of history which taught that nineteenth-century capitalism made the lives of the workers worse than they had been in the eighteenth century (Green 1987: 166-7):

> It had previously been taught by historians like Macaulay and economists like Alfred Marshall that the Industrial Revolution had improved the conditions of the great mass of the population. But from the late nineteenth century socialist historians like the Webbs, the Hammonds and G.D.H. Cole contended that conditions had worsened compared with the previous century. In the 1960s and 1970s this doctrine continued to be propounded by academics such as E.P. Thompson and Eric Hobsbawm. This 'immiserisation' thesis was criticized in the 1920s and 1930s by historians like John Clapham and Dorothy George, and a little later by T.S. Ashton, but neverthess it continued to be the dominant orthodoxy during the post-war years.

In the 1950s, F.A. Hayek, W.H. Hutt and others reopened the debate, arguing that living standards had undeniably improved during the nineteenth century. 'According to Hayek, the new urban proletariat would not have come into being at all without the additional wealth industrialization made possible. A smaller population would have continued to exist in a rural setting at a lower standard of life' (Green 1987: 167).

In 1974, the Institute of Economic Affairs (IEA) published a more recent survey of the evidence, the general conclusion of which was that industrialization brought growing prosperity to all and narrowed the gap between the wealthiest and the poorest citizens (Hartwell *et al* 1974). 'Poverty is not the product of capitalism, in this view: on the contrary, the free-market principles which brought about industrialization also produced the prosperity which made it possible to eradicate extreme poverty for good' (Green 1987: 167).

New Right neo-liberals, Green argues, have also been severe critics of the modern welfare state. 'Social security systems in all Western nations have been under criticism. In recent years Britain's arrangements have been particularly heavily criticized by commentators from all points of the political spectrum' (Green 1987: 167). For the neo-*liberal* New Right, in particular, the activities of government 'are so wasteful and misdirected that we would be better off with much less of it' (Bosanquet 1983: 136). The following sections examine this argument in more detail as it applies to social security reform/policy.

For Nick Bosanquet (1983: 136), the New Right's neo-liberal case against existing social security arrangements has developed over the years and has changed in its emphasis (below). The argument, however, is an old one going back to the early 1960s (Friedman 1962). For Bosanquet at least, the early version of this neo-liberal argument can be summarized as follows:

- Social security is misleadingly labelled an 'insurance scheme'. In fact it is nothing of the sort because individual benefits are not related to individual contributions.
- Social security is an unnecessary interference with freedom. Individuals can be left to decide what amount of security they want for the future.
- There might be a problem, in that some people may decide not to save for their old age but to rely instead on welfare payments. This difficulty could be overcome by making it compulsory to purchase annuities.
- The social security system is paid for by a regressive tax which is particularly hard on those who enter the labour force early and have a short life expectancy. It provides for an arbitrary and unnecessary redistribution in favour of the better off.

For David Green (1987: 169), the neo-liberal approach to the reform of social security has been as follows. 'Natural rights theorists, including anarchists like Rothbard and minimal staters like Nozick, dislike the welfare state in its entirety. They would have no national minimum maintained by government. All assistance to the poor would be voluntary'. Such full-blooded voluntarism has not, however, been the mainstream neo-liberal view. Instead, as we shall see below, more pragmatic New Right neo-liberals like Friedman, Hayek and IEA authors have advocated a continued role for government in the maintenance of a national minimum income (Green 1987: 169).

Negative Income Tax

For Friedman at least, Western capitalism has greatly reduced the extent of extreme - or absolute - poverty. Poverty, however, he argues, 'is in part a *relative* matter, and even in these countries, there are clearly many people living under conditions that the rest of us label as poverty' (Friedman 1962: 190). In small communities, Friedman argues, public pressure can usually suffice to relieve poverty through private charity. In the large, impersonal communities that have increasingly come to dominate American society, however, it is much more difficult for it to do so (Friedman 1962: 191).

If one accepts, as Friedman does, this line of reasoning as justifying action by the state to relieve poverty - to set, as it were, a 'floor' under the standard of life of every person in the community - the question arises as to *how* this might be done. In this connection, Friedman argues that:

> Two things seem clear. First, if the objective is to alleviate poverty, we should have a program directed at helping the poor. There is every reason to help the poor man who happens to be a farmer, not because he is a farmer but because he is poor. The program, that is, should be designed to help people as people not as members of particular occupational groups or age groups or wage-rate groups or labour organizations or industries.... Second, so far as possible the program should, while operating through the market, [neither] distort the market [nor] impede its functioning.

For Friedman at least, most existing welfare programmes should never have been enacted. Indeed, he argues, had they not been, many of those who now depend on them 'would have become self-reliant individuals instead of wards of the state' (Friedman and Friedman 1980: 150):

> In the short run, that might have appeared cruel for some, leaving them no option to low-paying, unattractive work. But in the long run it would have been far more humane. However, given that the welfare programs exist, they cannot simply be abolished overnight. We need some way to ease the transition from where we are to where we would like to be, of providing assistance to people now dependent on welfare while at the same time encouraging an orderly transfer of people from welfare rolls to payrolls.

For Friedman, in particular, a transitional programme to 'enhance individual responsibility, end the present division of the nation into two classes, reduce both government spending and the present massive bureaucracy, and at the same time assure a safety net for every person in the country' should be enacted at the earliest available political opportunity (Friedman and Friedman 1980: 150):

> The program has two essential components: first, reform the present welfare system

by replacing the ragbag of specific programs with a single comprehensive program of income supplements in cash - a *negative income tax* linked to the positive income tax: second, unwind Social Security while meeting present commitments and gradually requiring people to make their own arrangements for their own retirement.

This comprehensive reform, for Friedman, would succeed in doing more efficiently and humanely what the present welfare state does inefficiently and inhumanely. 'It would provide an assured minimum to all persons in need regardless of the reasons for their need, while doing as little harm as possible to their character, their independence or their incentive to better their own condition' (Friedman and Friedman 1980: 150).

As Bosanquet (1983: 144) argues, negative income tax (NIT) has been the most widely-canvassed neo-liberal alternative to social security. As with the education voucher, he argues, the basic idea of NIT is simple:

> The scheme sets a break-even level of income. A household with an income below that break-even level will get all or some of the difference between its actual income and the break-even level. A household with an income above that level will pay tax in the normal way. The payment is made to those who qualify because their incomes are low rather than on grounds of being sick, unemployed or retired.

In addition to Friedman, NIT has also been consistently advocated, through various authors, by the Institute of Economic Affairs. While IEA authors differ over the question of how much redistribution is desirable (Clark 1977, Seldon 1981b), there has been agreement on the basic proposition that most of the welfare state could be replaced by a negative (or reverse) income tax scheme (Bosanquet 1983: 82).

At the same time, however, it is worth noting that the reverse income tax (RIT) suggested by Colin Clark (1977) is different to Friedman's negative income tax scheme. 'RIT payments would be made only in particular circumstances such as unemployment, sickness or regular low earnings.... The scheme seems to be to replace the social security system with something very like the supplementary benefits scheme under another name. At the same time, health and education would move towards private provision. In effect this is a form of welfare payment rather than a negative income tax. In practice it would turn out to be rather like the supplementary benefit system but with lower rates of payment' (Bosanquet 1983: 82 and 144-5).

As we have seen, Friedman has consistently advocated NIT to integrate the tax and benefit systems. A similar plan for implementation in Britain has been proposed by Patrick Minford (1984). Minford's scheme has two aims. 'To help the poor achieve an above-subsistence living standard without damaging incentives and to privatize provision for health, education and pensions whilst ensuring that the poor spend adequately on these services' (Green 1987: 169). For the poor in work, Minford envisages two poverty lines. The first is a subsistence income for each family. This is to be a 'true minimum' and must therefore 'exclude all items not necessary for survival'. The second is a poverty threshold, 'defined in relation to social views of the income *above* which help would not willingly be given by society'. This is also the income tax threshold. Minford's NIT thus has two aims. It never allows incomes to fall below a subsistence level and for incomes below the level of the poverty/income tax threshold a supplement of 70% of the difference between actual income and the threshold is paid (Green 1987: 169).

A similarly technocratic/economistic approach to reform can be found in Hermione Parker's (1982) IEA study of the 'moral hazard' of social benefits, the central finding of which is that present social policies 'have had perverse economic effects by weakening or destroying incentives to work'. A 'rational system of income distribution', Parker asserts, should rest instead on 'objective criteria such as assumed basic needs and taxable capacity, which in turn could be calculated using scales derived from family budgets' (Parker 1982: 104):

> Such budgets, taking account of minimum nutritional and other needs as well as spending patterns, already form the basis of social aid scales in the United States, Germany and elsewhere. The same standards should apply to allowances against income tax.

Alternatively, for Parker, the tax and benefit systems could be integrated, either through a system of tax credits or through a negative income tax:

> The position in Britain today [is that] some people receive state benefits when they already have sufficient resources of their own, or pay less in tax than they might reasonably be expected to pay. Others go without. Almost everybody feels cheated. And because the system is so complex and inaccessible, constructive and effective criticism is difficult. Where it can be shown that the existing tax/benefit structure is likely to have such effects, it would be better to change that structure quickly rather than waste time arguing about the exact number of people affected. The only logical alternatives are to accept a continuing increase in the so-called 'natural rate of unemployment' or to introduce direction of labour. The problems ... will not be remedied by *ad hoc* or patchwork solutions. The present system requires radical reform by the consistent application of objectively defined criteria. One option would be a complete integration of social security and taxation either through a system of tax credits or through a negative income tax. Radical reform within the existing system ... is another possibility. But either way the twin problems of income distribution and incentives to work should be the responsibility of a single

government department.

As we shall now see, this long-standing and characteristically 'Friedmanite' (because economistic) agenda on welfare from IEA authors has also been embraced - until recently, that is - by the Adam Smith Institute (ASI).

'Omega Social Security Policy'

The ASI's 'Omega Report' on social security and pensions policy proceeds from a recognition that the UK's existing social security system is 'the largest single government programme and in 1984-5 will account for about 29% of public expenditure' (Butler *et al* 1985: 313). For the ASI, however:

> Despite ... massive expenditure - and other forms of support such as concessionary bus and rail fares, regional and industrial subsidies, subsidized state housing, rate support grants and free education - poverty, however defined, still exists. Our benefit levels are among the lowest in Western Europe. A significant proportion of those entitled to claim them fail to do so. And yet, at the same time, billions of pounds are paid out to people who could not, under any criteria, be said to be in need.

The reasons for this failure, for the ASI, lay in the very nature of a system said to be characterized by comprehensive complexity, on the one hand, and lack of choice, innovation and discrimination, on the other. Specifically, the drawbacks of the present system were said to be as follows:

- *Complexity*: A substantial number of benefits is available. These can be grouped into 3 main categories: contributory, non-contributory and means-tested benefits.

- *Confused Goals*: The system lacks any single, defined set of objectives. National insurance contributions are said to be simply another form of taxation (and a peculiarly regressive one at that).

- *Political manipulation*: New benefits have also developed in response to the activities of political pressure groups who have found it more profitable to pursue the narrow interests of readily-identifiable sections of society than to seek to restructure the system to defeat poverty as a whole. Groups with no such identity, on the other hand, tend to lose out.

- *Lack of Understanding*: Many do not claim benefits to which they are entitled. It may be that some don't know what they are entitled to; others may be deterred by the difficulty of making a claim; still others may be poorly advised by DHSS staff or find the forms and booklets designed to explain the system impossible to understand.

- *Administration*: The system requires a large administration. Over 85,000 people are employed to organize and distribute benefits. The system is costly and leads to substantial duplication. Those who qualify for more than one benefit, for instance, may have to undergo more than one assessment of their means by different groups of officials.

- *Lack of Innovation*: The system inhibits competition and innovation. Because benefits are provided under a unitary system and payment for them is obligatory for taxpayers, there is virtually no opportunity to develop private provision over large areas of social welfare.

- *Lack of Discrimination*: Benefits paid equally to rich and poor alike cannot be generous enough to those in need. The present system hurts the poor by squandering resources on those who do not really need them.

For the Omega authors at least, radical change was long overdue and should rest on the following four principles:

- Help should only go to those in need of it.
- Help should be given, as far as possible, in the form of financial support to enable recipients to maintain a basic standard of living and to exercise individual choice over how the benefit should be spent.
- There should be an incentive towards taking work, however poorly paid, and towards improved earnings.
- Circumstances capable of being provided for by insurance should be covered by properly funded, privately funded and compulsory insurance, with the state paying the premiums of those unable to provide for themselves.

On the first of these, the simplest way to ensure that those (and only those) in genuine need would receive assistance was said to be to fix a *minimum income* level per person (or different minima for different categories of people or for different geographical areas) and 'pay everyone with incomes below that the necessary amount to bring them up to the level' (Butler *et al* 1985: 315):

In a sense, this is what supplementary benefit payments seek to do. Unfortunately, however, so many other separate benefits, both flat-rate and means-tested, are superimposed on top that it is at best a very imperfect weapon in the fight to eliminate poverty. It is our view that all these benefits should be replaced by a single system combining the payment of income tax and the distribution of benefit based on a single assessment of need or ability to pay. In broad terms, such a system would assess an individual's or a family's needs and make payments to them if they were below the determined level or deduct taxes from them if they were above.

The purpose of reform, for the ASI, must be to ensure that no-one should fall below an agreed standard of living:

> Any minimum income guarantee [should] therefore... take into account local and even seasonal variations in housing, food, transport and so on. To set the appropriate figures and keep them updated would probably be the work of an independent panel. Revisions would reflect changes (upward or downward) in the costs of the commodities ... thought essential to provide a minimum standard of living, rather than general movements in prices or incomes, and from time to time new 'essentials' would enter the equation and outmoded items drop out.

Above the level of zero earnings, benefits would still be paid, but their size would be gradually reduced. 'This would mean that there was always an incentive for individuals to seek employment, or better-paid employment, although nobody would fall below the minimum living standard' (Butler *et al* 1985: 316).

Taxation, for the ASI, should be rationalized. 'A number of unified tax and benefit schemes have been suggested in the past, from modest ones covering limited measures of income support to fully-fledged systems of negative income tax [to] incorporate virtually all social security support. It is the latter comprehensive approach that we are proposing'. Instead of collecting income from those above the poverty line in national insurance contributions at 9% and income tax at 30%, the ASI proposed a single income tax structure (Butler *et al* 1985: 316):

> Increasing the basic rate of income tax to 40% would produce roughly the same income as is currently produced from employees. Those with higher incomes would be a little worse off, most would be very little affected, but those on lower incomes would gain.... We also suggest the abolition of the employers' element of the national insurance contribution which is not in fact an insurance contribution in any meaningful sense, but merely a tax on jobs and an administrative headache for the very people - small businesses - that are most likely to generate new jobs if given the opportunity and incentive.

Unifying the various systems of assessing need, it was argued, would pose no (or at least no insurmountable) administrative problems:

> At present the annual tax return provides for the taxpayer claiming tax relief for... reasons such as dependent relatives, the need for a housekeeper or blindness. We see no difficulty in expanding it to include all the equivalent information required to assess need. For the vast majority of people, one such assessment per year would be sufficient, since the size of their families, the scope of their responsibilities and the nature of their handicaps will not change. For most of the rest, changes would be unlikely to be frequent (birth, death or serious accident being the likeliest). While there would undoubtedly be some extra cost to the Inland Revenue in collecting and processing this additional information, it would be more than compensated for by the substantial reduction in work undertaken by the DHSS and (if housing benefits are incorporated into the scheme) the local authorities.

Given these two changes, there would also be no administrative difficulty in issuing a new form of tax code. 'Those, the big majority, with incomes above the level of the guaranteed income and incentive threshold would pay tax at the appropriate rate or rates. Those with incomes below the [GI & I] level would receive benefit, again at an established rate' (Butler *et al* 1985: 317).

To successfully implement this apparently simple scheme (which would also allow considerable savings in administration) was not, however, without its difficulties. For the ASI (Butler *et al* 1985: 317), in particular:

> The most difficult, and the most costly, problem to solve is the provision of some incentive to people in receipt of benefit to take work if it is available or to increase their pay if they are already working.

In this connection, a sliding scale provision would be needed in the detailed arrangements at the margin to create some incentive in favour of taking up employment or working towards higher wages (Butler *et al* 1985: 315). In particular, it was argued:

> Removing the barrier created by the threshold at which national insurance contributions become due might well lead to increased employment and higher wages among part-time employees. Eliminating the poverty and unemployment traps would provide enough encouragement to persuade many people to improve their position. Such effects are impossible to quantify but they are bound to have a beneficial effect on costs and on attitudes. All in all, we are confident that the changes we have put forward would eliminate poverty much more effectively and ... at lower cost than the present system which is failing to do so. And it would provide an encouragement, sadly lacking in the present system, for people to

improve their lot.

As we shall now see, this characteristically 'Friedmanite' agenda on welfare reform/policy is by no means representative of the New Right as a whole and has since become increasingly uncommon among New Right think-tanks in particular.

'Politically Impossible ...?'

In the first place, Friedmanite negative income tax (NIT) has been rejected across the political spectrum as an unworkable proposal. Bosanquet (1983: 144), for example, has argued that:

> The critical problem [with NIT] is that of the size of the negative payment. On a generous scheme the break-even level of income might be set at the level of supplementary benefit rate. If households are not [to be] worse off than under the present system the break-even level would be about 40% of average earnings. The marginal tax rate required to finance this payment together with other government spending would be about 55%.... Thus a generous negative income tax system would require very high rates of tax above the break-even level. It would also have effects on labour market incentives. These would be serious both for people who were getting the negative payment and for those who were paying the heavier tax rates. It would be possible to set a break-even level [below] the current supplementary benefit level [or] to cover only part of the gap between actual and break-even income. Thus if the tax rate were 33% claimants might only get one-third of the difference between their income and the break-even level. But this would produce a much lower level of payment for many people than does the current system.

As Milton and Rose Friedman (1980: 155) recall, no fewer than three American Presidents (Nixon, Ford and Carter) have considered or recommended a programme including elements of a negative income tax:

> In each case political pressures ... led them to offer the program as an addition to... existing programs, rather than as a substitute for them. In each case the subsidy rate was so high that the program gave little if any incentive to recipients to earn income. These misshapen programs would have made the whole system worse, not better. Despite our having been the first to propose a negative income tax as a replacement for our present welfare system, one of us [Milton Friedman] testified before Congress *against* the version that President Nixon offered as the Family Assistance

Plan.

The political obstacles to an acceptable negative income tax, for the Friedmans, are of two related kinds. 'The more obvious is the existence of vested interests in present programs: the recipients of benefits, state and local officials who regard themselves as benefiting from the programs and, above all, [the] bureaucracy that administers them. The less obvious obstacle is the conflict among the objectives that advocates of welfare reform, including existing vested interests, seek to achieve' (Friedman and Friedman 1980: 155).

In 1978, Friedmanite approaches to the alleviation of poverty were rejected by another New Right neo-liberal, Martin Anderson, a researcher at the Hoover Institution and former policy adviser to President Reagan. For Anderson at least, *all* radical welfare reform schemes had three basic elements that were politically sensitive to a high degree (Anderson 1978: 135):

> The first is the basic benefit level provided, for example, to a family of four on welfare. The second is the degree to which [it] affects the incentive of a person on welfare to find work or to earn more. The third is the additional cost to the taxpayers.... To become a political reality the plan must provide a decent level of support to those on welfare, it must contain strong incentives to work and it must have a reasonable cost. *And it must do all three at the same time.*

No such radical plan, however, could be devised. 'There is no way to achieve all the politically necessary conditions for radical welfare reform at the same time' (Anderson 1978: 142). To overcome this dilemma, Anderson enunciated seven principles which should underpin welfare reform:

- Payment should be made according to need only. Welfare programmes must conform with public opinion as it is. For Anderson at least, American public opinion wants real need to be met by government aid, but does not like welfare payments to be made to all and sundry.
- Efforts to detect fraud should be increased.
- Governments should establish and enforce a fair, clear work requirement. It is here that Anderson is most at odds with Friedman and Minford [see earlier], both of whom advocate an 'incentives' approach to the 'unemployment trap'. Financial work incentives, Anderson argued, do not achieve their goal. To work effectively, intolerably low basic welfare payments would be necessary. High marginal tax rates among welfare beneficiaries are also inevitable without lowering payments too far. The error in the financial incentives approach, for Anderson, is that it seeks to 'persuade' people to work but does not *require* them to do so. The principle

should be that 'a person gets welfare only if he or she qualifies for it by the fact of being incapable of self-support'. If they don't qualify, 'they have no right to welfare'. If a person can earn part of what they need, they have an *obligation* to work to that extent [see later].

- Inappropriate beneficiaries should be removed from the rolls. Two prime candidates, for Anderson, are workers on strike and 'college students who queue up for food stamps'.
- Many welfare recipients are one-parent families. Absent parents, for Anderson, should be *required* to contribute to the support of their offspring [see later].
- The efficiency and effectiveness of welfare administration should be improved.
- More responsibility for welfare should be shifted from the federal government to state and local governments and to private institutions. Generally speaking, Anderson argues, the more decentralized the administration the better.

Indeed, Friedman himself has since argued that a negative income tax is not possible 'so long as it is not politically feasible to reduce ... payments to many persons who now receive high benefits from multiple current programs' (Friedman and Friedman 1980: 157). As Nick Bosanquet argued in 1983: 'He [Friedman] hopes that what is not politically feasible today may become politically feasible tomorrow, but it seems unlikely that a programme which would involve such major reductions in benefit levels would find much favour' (Bosanquet 1983: 144).

'The Welfare Challenge'

In March 1987, a conference was held at the Institute of Civil Engineers in London entitled 'The Welfare Challenge'. Sponsored by the Centre for Policy Studies (CPS) and addressed by visiting speakers from the Manhattan Institute of Policy Studies, this was the *first* attempt to introduce into Britain the arguments of the American dependency theorists Glenn Loury, Lawrence Mead, Charles Murray and Richard Nathan (CPS 1987). Introducing proceedings, and setting out an agenda for discussion, the Centre's then Director of Studies, David Willetts, argued (CPS 1987: 2-3) that:

One of the reasons why the arguments about social policy have become rather sterile in this country is that the left and the right have actually shared a rather blinkered vision, preoccupied with two questions: firstly, costs; and secondly, a largely technocratic agenda of reform of the tax and benefit system - negative income tax, tax credits, social dividends and various other recipes for tax/benefit integration.

For Willetts at least, a striking feature of the American debate on welfare reform/policy was that (CPS 1987: 3):

> the agenda in America 15 years ago was measured like this, with big experiments with income tax. Both Presidents Nixon and Carter attempted to legislate such schemes, but you will no longer find a single distinguished American social policy expert who has such an agenda. I find it very depressing that we, here in England, have not moved beyond the preoccupations underlying the Heath government's attempts to introduce tax credits in the early 1970s.

For Willetts at least, there appeared to be two main flaws in the argument that all Britain's problems in this area could be solved by tax/benefit integration:

> If you think of that classic kinked line which you always see on every graph showing the poverty trap where, as people's earnings from work rise so their net earnings hardly move at all, and then suddenly it takes off. There have always been two ways of dealing with that problem: one is to simply drive a straight line through the whole system, at a lower rate than 100% at the bottom [of the] scale, but [at] a higher rate than 40% further up the scale. The problem with all these programmes for increasing the net pay of people on low earnings is that they extend the tax/benefit mess further up the scale and then increase the marginal rate of taxation [and] benefit withdrawal precisely where most work is concentrated. You can then simply try to cut benefits at the bottom of the scale. We have achieved some success in improving the operation of the labour market there, but we have again some chastening lessons from America. Benefits for a single unemployed man are virtually non-existent: nevertheless, [America has] a very resistant problem of unemployment in the inner cities. While I do not want to throw the Patrick Minford agenda [see earlier] out of the window ... I do not think we should pretend [it will] solve all the problems of unemployment in Lambeth.

What, though, did the Centre's four American guests stand for if they were not preoccupied with the cost of the welfare state nor with this 'technocratic' agenda for reform? In this connection, Willetts argued (CPS 1987: 5) that:

> It seems to me they are concerned with the values by which poor people live, the patterns of behaviour which may be keeping them trapped in the underclass (as it is called in America). They are concerned with dependency on welfare, they are

concerned with the collapse of civic life in the great American cities, and that, I
think, is a set of real world problems which we need to address here.

The Americans who, twenty years before, had introduced a set of 'Great Society'
programmes, were now 'preoccupied with the fact that after two decades of high
social spending, the problems in America's inner cities are, if anything, *worse*
than ... before' (CPS 1987: 5-6).

A New Consensus?

During the 1980s, a number of American social policy analysts 'began to identify
what they saw as flaws in existing welfare programmes' (Green 1992). The
dependency theorists Lawrence Mead (1986) and Charles Murray (1984) argue
that, while economic growth is a necessary condition for improving the position
of the poor, it is not a sufficient one. Dependency theory can be summarized as
follows (Hoover and Plant 1989: 70):

> Poverty is not just a matter of the possession of resources, it is also a question of the
> cultural attitudes and dispositions of many poor people. Under the welfare state, the
> poor have grown increasingly reliant upon the state and lost their sense of initiative.
> The work ethic has been weakened. Many poor people have lost their sense of
> obligation to their family and to the wider community.

Some poverty, then, can be attributed to lack of income, but a distinction should
be drawn between poverty due to insufficient cash and poverty due to a person's
unacceptable or inappropriate *behaviour*. The pursuit of welfare policies based
on the image of the beneficiary as a 'victim' was, in the view of critics like
Murray, not only failing to remedy poverty, but causing it to increase. 'Cash
transfers paid without regard to the self-damaging behaviour of some (but not all)
welfare recipients fail to solve the problems of the dependent poor. Indeed, such
payments reinforce dependency and encourage more people to fall into the same
trap' (Green 1992: 9).

In 1987, similar arguments appeared in Britain in speeches by the then
Secretary of State for Social Services, John Moore, and in 'The Welfare
Challenge', a symposium sponsored by the CPS and addressed by Murray, Mead
and Richard Nathan, all of whom are in the forefront of the dependency
movement in the United States. In August that year, the CPS issued a pamphlet
on 'Victorian values', values seen by 'Thatcherite' conservatives as centring on
the qualities of self-sufficiency and independence (Chapter 3).

Finally in 1987, the American Enterprise Institute published a report produced by a working group assembled under the chairmanship of Michael Novak which included participants from all points of the political spectrum and which its authors regard as the statement of 'a generally agreed perspective on dependency' (Green 1992, Hoover and Plant 1989). The report begins by summarizing the authors' approach to poverty and welfare issues (AEI 1987: xi):

- A good society is judged by how well it cares for its most vulnerable members.

- No person should be involuntarily poor without others coming to his or her assistance.

- No able adult should be allowed voluntarily to take from the common good without also contributing to it.

- Low income and behavioural dependency are two quite different problems and require different remedies.

The report goes on to say that the distinction between two types of welfare dependency - 'objective' dependency on the public purse and 'behavioural' dependency - is an important key to poverty and welfare reform/policy in the years ahead (AEI 1987: xiv):

> Because this distinction has not always been taken into account, some observers have come to see existing welfare policy as toxic; they believe that it is damaging the very poor it intends to help. Even if welfare policy has not *caused* the widespread behavioural dependency that has now become so highly visible, at the very least existing public policies have done little to remedy the situation.

Welfare's separation of clients from the world of work is said to have led to an abandonment of the values essential to work and to family life. 'Existing welfare policies may encourage the break-up of families by making the cost of separation easier to bear, by not requiring the fathers of illegitimate children to support their upkeep and by mitigating the costs of promiscuity and fecklessness' (Hoover and Plant 1989: 71).

A substantial minority of the poor, the report argues, 'suffers from something more than the low income familiar in family memory to most Americans', - namely 'behavioural dependency'. The latter, the authors argue (AEI 1987: 5):

> is more like an inability to cope. Many of the poor need order in their surroundings and in their lives; they need the intellectual and moral skills that enable them to

escape from poverty and to live as full and independent citizens. Low income is comparatively easy to remedy; to overcome behavioural dependency requires a much more human, complex and difficult engagement.

It is argued that successful behaviour to stay out of poverty is not mysterious and includes completing education; getting married and staying married; and staying employed, even if at a wage and under conditions below one's ultimate aims. Those who do these three traditional things may experience periods in poverty but are quite unlikely to stay involuntarily poor. By no means foolproof, these are the methods that have worked, and are still working, for millions (AEI 1987: 5).

Money income alone, the report argues, does not define poverty. The *character* and disposition of many poor people is also important. 'The most disturbing element among a fraction of the contemporary poor is an inability to seize opportunity even when it is available, and while others around them are seizing it. Some may have work skills in the normal sense, but find it difficult to be regular, prompt and in a sustained way attentive to their work. Their need is less for job training than for meaning and order in their lives' (AEI 1987: 11). Escape from poverty, the authors maintain, is in part a matter of attaining 'personal control and independence so as to respond to changing circumstances' (AEI 1987: 13).

For Hoover and Plant (1989: 72) have pointed out, this emphasis on the role of character, motivation and self-control as central to poverty is far from new:

It was a central feature of the approach of the Charity Organization Society [COS] in Britain in the nineteenth century as well as the 'settlement houses' in the United States. In this view, resource provision had to be discriminating and discretionary in order to encourage the development of personal habits conducive to survival in a competitive society.

At this point, it is worth noting that this historical allusion raises several important issues. The first is that the COS's emphasis on the *character* of the poor as a central aspect of poverty is mirrored in 'The New Consensus'. Second, the COS were clear that character as an aspect of poverty cannot be addressed by the state, for two reasons: namely, that the state and its bureaucracies are too indiscriminate and because of the rule of law. 'It was not possible to devise general rules to govern poor relief if attention had to be paid to the moral character of poor people' (Plant 1988: 3). Thirdly, the COS had clear views about social work - namely, that it had to be judgemental. 'It had to pay attention to individual character and devise in an individualized way paths out of poverty helped, of course, by charitable provision' (Plant 1988: 3).

It is not clear, however, that 'The New Consensus' adequately addresses these issues. The rule of law in the work (say) of Hayek is linked to the idea that it does not serve particular purposes, yet the whole philosophy of 'The New Consensus' is that public policy in this field should be concerned with character and motivation. Secondly, there is astonishingly little about social work, which the COS saw as fundamental. 'As the report notes in one of its few references to social work, modern social work has as one of its basic professional values a non-judgemental approach to the client' (Plant 1988: 3). In short, what are the implications for the practice of social work of reintroducing the idea of character and the need to develop qualities of self-sufficiency and self-reliance, and how is the profession to be changed to meet these?

The main emphasis of 'The New Consensus' concerns families and children. In this connection, central importance is attached to the role of the father in maintaining the cohesion of the family unit. The authors argue that acceptable behaviour in family life is of crucial importance (AEI 1987: 17):

> Recent rises in family break-ups and out-of-wedlock births have pushed increasing numbers of Americans below the poverty line. Children born out of wedlock face a higher probability of low birth-weight and greater health risks than children of married parents. Children in single-parent homes on average perform less well in school and are more likely to drop out from school than children in intact homes. Society bears the costs of such disparities and, in this way, personal decisions end up being the concerns of public policy.

As Hoover and Plant (1989: 72) argue, the aim here is to encourage men to have a greater sense of responsibility towards their offspring and to provide role models for them in order to break the generational cycle of dependency and deprivation. The point is made graphically by the conservative commentator George Gilder (1982: 51):

> In the welfare culture money becomes not something earned by men through hard work, but a right conferred on women by the state. Protest and complaint replace diligence and discipline as the sources of pay. Boys grow up seeking support from women, while they find manhood in the macho circles of the street and the bar or in the irresponsible fathering of random children.

This assessment, as Hoover and Plant (1989: 72) point out, fits into a broader conservative critique of feminism that lays part of the blame for the 'feminization' of poverty on attitudinal shifts about 'traditional' gender roles.

'Beyond Entitlement'

In dealing with 'behavioural dependency', the authors of 'The New Consensus' and, on the British side, Conservative spokesmen such as Michael Heseltine (1987) suggest that part of the solution is to require welfare recipients to engage in paid work or further training as a condition of obtaining benefits. The AEI report, for example, argues that '*all* able recipients should be enrolled in work, or duration limited education, or short-term training programs in return for collecting welfare benefits' and makes the following recommendations:

- Young mothers should be required to complete education and prepare themselves for future employment.

- Older mothers with previous experience of the labour market should be expected to find work in the private sector or as a last resort to accept an assignment in the public sector.

- Those involved in work programmes, both staff and trainee, should regard every job, even if part-time and low-wage, as an obligation to society, as the key to future work experience and as an occasion of self-development.

- A minimal emphasis should be on public service jobs; the overriding emphasis should be on personal responsibility to find work in the private sector. Jobs in government should be accepted reluctantly and only in areas so depressed that insufficient jobs of any kind are available.

Public policy, it is argued, establishes a 'moral' climate as well as an economic one. 'Thus an effort to require work by recipients is worthwhile if it establishes throughout society the essential notion that an individual's benefits are conditioned upon the meeting of social obligations'. In this way, it is argued, the poor will be treated with the same dignity and respect as other citizens (AEI 1987: 113).

In this connection, 'The New Consensus' argues that clear and fair sanctions should be imposed on able recipients of benefits who fail to work without good cause, such as a serious physical or mental disability. Sanctions, it is argued, signal the core values of a free society and act as a guide to self-development (AEI 1987: 114). A welfare policy without clear incentives and sanctions, on the other hand, promotes:

> disorientation about values and thus does injustice to those it would help. Sanctions
> may be constructed positively or negatively ... offering incentives in the form of

rewards or denying benefits unless obligations are met. The underlying principle is that the welfare system must be infused with a sense of obligation in order to build a sense of reciprocal bonds among the members of the civic community.

The community, it is argued, can best help the needy by including them in its own productive activities. 'Accordingly, care must be taken not to allow welfare programs to be governed by misdirected compassion, in which benefits are offered without reciprocity' (AEI 1987: 114). This, it is argued, undermines the humanity of recipients and treats them with less dignity than other citizens.

As Hoover and Plant (1989: 72) argue, 'workfare' programmes of this kind reinstate the nineteenth-century notion of requiring work in exchange for welfare:

> A variation of this approach known as 'learnfare' makes the continuance of benefits conditional on dependent school-age clients remaining enrolled in classes. Against the charge that this demonstrates a lack of compassion, the defence is that inducing a condition of dependency is not a compassionate act either. Workfare may be harsh in the short run, but it can break the cycle of despair.

There is also (as we have seen) the philosophical argument that, if benefits are conferred without reciprocity - that is without discharging a concomitant obligation - then this will undermine the basic dignity of welfare recipients and set them apart from the citizenry generally (Hoover and Plant 1989: 72-3). This last point, for Hoover and Plant, goes to the heart of Lawrence Mead's argument in *Beyond Entitlement* (Mead 1986) that the rights guaranteed in a democratic society imply:

> a corresponding obligation to live in terms of the dominant values within which [those] rights are granted. After all, the very existence of rights depends upon that society and its values; why should not obligations equally require a recognition of social values? Since democracy rests upon the capacity to make choices, and rights are accorded to protect this capacity, why should public policy on welfare undermine the very capacities on which democratic citizenship depends?

'Why Work ...?'

As we have seen, the argument that the state should 'establish and enforce a clear, fair work requirement' is not new, at least in the United States (Anderson 1978). In Britain, various New Right authors argue that the Beveridge Report also recommended a work test (Green 1987, Howell 1991). Willetts, in particular, has argued that the Report contains 'rather authoritative views about the role of the state in providing welfare, a view that it is entitled to require certain sorts of behaviour in return from recipients of benefit [which has since] degenerated into a much more permissive attitude to the payment of benefit' and quotes Beveridge with approval (CPS 1987: 12):

> Men and women in receipt of unemployment benefit cannot be allowed to hold out indefinitely for work of the type to which they are used or in their present place of residence if there is work they could do available at the standard wage for that work. Men and women who have been unemployed for a certain period should be required as a condition of continued benefit to attend a work or training centre.... The period after which attendance should be required need not be the same at all times and for all persons. It might be extended in times of high unemployment and reduced in times of good employment; six months for adults would perhaps be a reasonable average period of benefit without conditions.... But for young persons who have not yet the habit of continuous work the period should be shorter; for boys and girls there should ideally be no unconditional benefit at all; their enforced abstention from work should be made an occasion of further training.

For some Conservatives, notably Ralph Howell (see later), the 'why work?' syndrome in the 1970s was so severe that Britain should move openly towards direction of labour (Parker 1982). As we shall see below, however, the dependency argument on which such policies rest is highly problematic for conservatives and poses something of an ideological dilemma for conservative capitalism (the New Right).

'From Cradle to Grave'

As we saw in Chapter 4 (above), the Social Affairs Unit (SAU) has shown a persistent editorial interest in the 'culture of poverty' and in the 'Moral Aspects of Social Problems' and has published a number of studies to this effect. In 1985, for example, the Unit issued a series entitled 'Taking Thought for the Poor', in which three theologians and one non-religious philosopher analyzed what contemporary society's response to the poor should be, stressing the common point that those who would help the poor have an obligation to eschew emotive and ideological rhetoric and 'take *thought* for the poor' (Flew 1985, Hexham 1985, Sacks 1985, Sadowsky 1985).

A more recent study from the SAU, published in 1989, cites with approval the Swiss way of welfare in which locally-based workers - acting as social workers and sources of social security - work with claimants to draw up individual contracts specifying what the claimant and the social worker will do to restore the client to independence as soon as possible. The authors also press for the abandonment of national rates of relief and for the localization of welfare, together with much stricter liability to maintain laws (Segalman and Marsland 1989).

In 1991, the Unit's Director, Digby Anderson, sought to revive the idea of 'secondary poverty'. Examining some recent studies of low-income families, Anderson claimed that these contain evidence of incompetent budgeting, improvidence, lack of persistence and male 'irresponsibility' with regard to income distribution within the family. For those living, as it were, 'on the edge', he argues that 'domestic incompetence can push them over into lasting misery and a tangle of debt and prolonged welfare dependency' (Anderson 1991: 5). Again, the emphasis here is on the 'culture of poverty' and the role of 'non-state' institutions (families, charities, neighbourhoods and so on) in helping the poor to avoid 'welfare-dependency' and so escape from poverty (see Chapter 4).

'Liberty, Poverty and the Underclass'

That the Centre for Policy Studies should have been the first of the four New Right think-tanks (IEA, ASI, CPS and SAU) examined in this study to introduce the dependency argument into Britain (above) should surprise no-one, given its editorial interest in (because ideological commitment to) restoring 'Victorian values' (see Chapter 3). It was predictable too that the SAU should have adopted this agenda, given the Unit's long-standing interest in the moral aspects of social problems (see Chapter 4). What is perhaps more surprising - and presumably therefore more significant - is that the IEA and the ASI have now moved in a similar direction, with the result that a certain convergence seems to have taken place between four otherwise ideologically diverse 'New Right' groups (Chapters 1-4, above).

In May 1990, for example, the IEA's Health and Welfare Unit published Charles Murray's 'Underclass', an article which first appeared in *The Sunday Times Magazine* in November 1989 and which argues (Murray 1990: 4) that:

> Britain has a growing population of working-aged, healthy people who live in a different world from other Britons, who are raising their children to live in it and whose values are now contaminating the life of entire neighbourhoods.

The term 'underclass', for Murray, refers not to the degree of poverty but to a type of poverty and is defined by undesirable behaviour such as drug-taking, crime, illegitimacy, the failure to hold down a job, truancy from school and casual violence. In focusing on three indicators (crime, dropping out of the labour force and illegitimacy), Murray concludes that:

> Britain [has] an underclass, still largely out of sight and still smaller than the one in the United States. But it is growing rapidly. Within the next decade, it will probably become as large (proportionately) as the United States' underclass. It could easily become larger.

Also in 1990, the IEA Health and Welfare Unit published Michael Novak's authoritative re-statement of the ideals of classical-liberal tradition, *Morality, Capitalism and Democracy*, which argues that today's free societies have evolved from a rich philosophical tradition with three interlocking elements (Novak 1990: vi):

* An economic system based on competition under law to channel self-interest into the service of others and to promote human creativity as the key to ending poverty.

* A political system, emphasizing constitutional checks and balances to protect ordered rights and to avoid the abuses of power.

* A moral and cultural system, inspired by Greece and Rome, by Judaism and Christianity, by Renaissance and modern humanism - in short, a pluralistic, open, tolerant, but vital and dynamic ethos.

Democratic capitalism, for Novak, is emphatically not morally stunted. 'On the contrary, it challenges the still-predominantly collectivist status quo, not only with an alternative political and economic theory but also with a moral vision which is more than a match for any rival' (Novak 1990: vii).

The urgent question of the present time, for Novak, is 'how to liberate, and not make servile, the able-bodied poor'. In this connection, Novak draws a contrast between two different 'mental constructions' concerning how to help the poor. The first of these, he argues (Novak 1990: 33):

> projects a large set of clients, now marginalized, to whom goods must be delivered to bring them up to a level of relative equality with others. In the other mental construction, the social task consists of so arranging an abundance of opportunities that the poor can become the agents of their own development, personal and economic, and gain power over an even broader array of personal decisions in their own lives. One construction focuses on giving to the poor. The other construction

focuses on multiplying opportunities among the poor, so that the poor can rise as far as their talents take them. It goes without saying that I believe the second to be more humane, more Christian and more promising than the first.

In this connection, he argues, policies designed to stimulate the appropriation of personal responsibility by every citizen without exception - and thus especially to liberate the poor - should be designed to elicit their innate capacities and to bring these to fruition: 'Social assistance, given generously, ought to operate under the strict criterion of personal liberty; namely, that it generates in all a sense of responsibility, both to their own possibilities and to one another' (Novak 1990: 33).

An important aim of public policy, for Novak, is to enable the poor to achieve independence. The task of giving assistance, however, is said to be paradoxical in the case of 'large numbers of able-bodied persons who could be independent but [who] for one reason or another are not' (Novak 1990: 31). Clearly, he writes:

> such persons do need assistance; yet assistance badly given may increase, rather than alleviate, their dependency. If our aim is to help such persons to appropriate their own liberty, we would falsify that purpose were we inadvertently to ensnare them in perpetual dependency. How to move such persons from dependency to independence is not always clear or, even when clear, easy to accomplish. Nonetheless, if our self-proclaimed aim is liberty [this] is the transition necessary to accomplish.

Without it, Novak argues, there can be no real civic community: 'only a nation half-free, half-servile; half free-standing and independent, half-mired in dependency' (Novak 1990: 31-2).

In a paper published by the Policy Studies Institute in 1992, the IEA's David Green (1992: 5) argued that:

> The difficulty with much contemporary debate about social welfare is that, of the two main schools of thought, one believes that a remedy can be discovered primarily within the political sphere and that moral considerations are inappropriate; whilst the other urges a remedy based on the application of economic principles to welfare policy - in practice adjusting benefit recipients' incentives at the margin.

A central claim of Green's paper is that 'neither approach will succeed without a concern to improve our understanding of the varied ways in which a moral community of free persons can be founded and maintained' (Green 1992: 11). Instead, he argues, public policy on welfare should acknowledge that:

> There is an important difference between low income and behavioural poverty and in recent years there has been an increase in the numbers of people in Britain dependent on welfare ... as a result of their own values and behaviour. This development has been reinforced by the materialistic focus of welfare policy on money transfers alone and will not be overcome unless we develop an alternative welfare strategy.

For Green at least, British public policy should develop a new approach designed to restore the 'dependent' poor to 'independent' citizenship (Green 1992).

'An Enabling Welfare State'?

Also in 1992, the IEA Health and Welfare Unit published a study by Dr John Gray entitled *The Moral Foundations of Market Institutions* (see Chapter 8). Gray's essay, as we shall now see, contains three sets of comments that have a direct bearing on certain issues which have been raised in this chapter. The first concerns a favourite policy measure of latter-day neo-liberals, namely negative income tax (see earlier).

Here, John Gray's first point is that the indeterminacy that afflicts discourse about (his theory of) basic needs is but an instance of the pervasive indeterminacy that haunts moral and political discourse. This, for Gray, is not a defect of (his) theory, but rather a fact of life. Thus, the favourite policy measures of latter-day neo-liberals - negative income tax and voucher schemes, for example (Gray 1992: 68):

> confront precisely the same indeterminacies. What should be the size of a school voucher, and how (and by what) is this to be determined? What level of income is to be specified as the minimum in a negative income tax scheme, and how can such a specification avoid invoking contestable value-judgements about the level of subsistence? Or, to turn to the functions of the so-called minimum state, to what level of police protection are citizens entitled, and by what formula is this to be decided?

For Gray at least, it is clear that classical liberal principles and proposals are beset by all of the indeterminacies that would seem to afflict (his) own. A second point, for Gray, has to do with the incentive and epistemic objections to targeting welfare benefits, and the correspondingly good arguments for universal provision (see Gray 1991). In this connection, Gray argues, targeting policies in welfare face:

grave epistemic problems in assessing needs that are often variable, and whose measurement is disputable. In respect of the favoured neo-liberal measure of the negative income tax, how would it cope with the fluctuating monies of seasonal and part-time workers? What would be the unit of assessment - individual or household? If household, how could that be defined?

These epistemic difficulties notwithstanding, Gray argues, the negative income tax, with its usual marginal tax rate of around 70 per cent, would generate huge disincentives and create a deep poverty trap: 'It is hard to see why this absurd measure (with its inevitable consequence of a further large socialization of income) has gained the support of so many neo-liberals' (Gray 1992: 70).

Gray's second set of comments concerns the issue of discretion versus entitlement in welfare benefits. In this connection, he notes that neo-liberals have shown a fondness for discretion in welfare policy that is 'strange', given their concern for the limitation of power over the lives of individuals. For Gray, in particular, the model of discretionary allocation by governmental authority such as that practised in Switzerland (above) should be objectionable to liberals for several reasons, the most important of which is that it concentrates power over individuals' lives to a wholly objectionable extent (Gray 1992: 70):

> Because the authority exercised is discretionary, it cannot conform to any ideal of the rule of law which in other areas liberals claim to cherish. In practice... benefits will be allocated at the discretion of welfare professionals whose decisions will... be animated by questionable orthodoxies and ephemeral fads.

In addition, Gray argues, 'because in reality the discretionary authority is bound to be subject to budgetary constraints, the integrity of that authority as the guardian of the recipients' interests and needs will inevitably be compromised'.

Thirdly, Gray entertains the possibility of Britain's having a labour policy 'preferably on Swedish lines' - as an element in (his) enabling welfare state, the intention of which would be to promote the autonomy of members of the 'underclass' by restoring them to independence in a market economy (see Gray 1991). In Britain, he argues (Gray 1992: 65):

> policy on unemployment is one of the worst imaginable, with stagnant pools of the long-term unemployed eking out their lives on low benefits, without having in most cases any real prospect of genuine re-skilling. Policy-makers in Britain could with profit study labour policy in Sweden, where very generous assistance in re-skilling is given, but has attached to it an obligation to accept employment in the areas for which the person has been retrained. One consequence of this - neglected by American and British neo-liberal and neo-conservative theorists who argue that

welfare institutions always generate dependency - is that Sweden... has no underclass, or only a very small one, of the multi-generationally unemployed.

Similarly, in Britain, having a job 'is for most people a basic need, since for most people involuntary long-term unemployment deals a severe blow to self-esteem' (Gray 1992: 65). In this connection, Gray argues that:

> A welfare benefit to re-skilling, whenever this is feasible, together with the complimentary obligations, is for this reason one element in the matrix of welfare policies that promote autonomy.

'Why Not Work ...?'

The Swedish 'employment principle' is also considered in a 1991 report from the Adam Smith Institute (ASI), by the Conservative MP Ralph Howell (see earlier). Unlike the 'cash assistance principle' of Britain's welfare state, Howell argues that Sweden bases its labour market policy on an attempt to secure the availability of jobs or vocational training for the unemployed, rather than (as Britain does) passively providing isolated cash benefits. The most profound difference between the two systems, however, is to be found in the way the young unemployed are treated. In this connection, he argues (Howell 1991: 14):

> An important and distinct feature of the Swedish system is that *no cash benefits* are made available to anyone under the age of 20 unless they accept work or take up an assigned training slot: much as Beveridge recommended for Britain.

For Howell, in particular, there is a wide consensus of opinion in Britain that people drawing unemployment benefit should give something back to the community in return for the help which it gives them (Howell 1991: 19-20):

> Beneficiaries, even those in the US who live under *workfare programmes* which require precisely that, also recognize this principle as being fair. Thus a workfare programme ... may not be found so shocking in the UK either. Nevertheless, a simple 'work for benefits' programme would meet a great deal of political opposition in the UK since imposing new conditions on a welfare benefit is almost as controversial as scrapping one.

A politically feasible approach, for Howell, must go beyond the workfare principle and provide real jobs, at realistic wages well above the basic unemployment benefit rate. Relief work as a last resort against youth unemployment, as in Sweden, might also be a practicable programme for Britain and would 'prevent many school leavers from being sucked into the welfare culture, as Beveridge feared'. Specifically, Howell argues (1991: 22) that:

> Instead of receiving unemployment benefits only on condition that they remain idle, people would be expected and required to contribute something back to the community through useful work that would pay realistic wages - wages much higher than current unemployment benefit levels. It may be that the idea of 'workfare' worries people. Many presume that it means a 'work for benefits' scheme in which unemployed people are compulsorily drafted into some unpleasant and pointless make-work programme in return for their existing social benefits. But because we are talking about providing work for wages much higher than present unemployment benefit rates, and because as a result it could be introduced as a voluntary scheme, the proposal is much more sensitive and workable than such critics imagine.

A View From the Left

Recent IEA/ASI publications, then, both acknowledge the existence of an 'underclass' in Britain and invoke the notion of 'dependency' (see earlier). At the same time, the dependency argument itself raises a number of problems, two of which are mentioned here. The first of these is a counter-argument based on Plant's (1988) commentary on 'The New Consensus on Family and Welfare' and is that:

> Dependency is part of the human condition. We are dependent in our early life, in old age, on society generally as a framework of co-operation, and on the economy. Clearly, the classical liberal economists saw modern economies as a vast framework of mutual interdependence. While I may not depend on the altruism of the butcher for my Sunday dinner, as Adam Smith rightly saw, I still depend on him for my being able to get it.

The issue, then, is not the abolition of dependency, but what are good and bad *forms* of dependence. Moreover, as Plant suggests, a good deal of the New Right writing on dependency is not about the 'abolition' of dependency, but about *transferring* dependency from the state to the family. Charles Murray, for example, argues in his book *Losing Ground* (Murray 1984: 228) that his policy (to cut all state benefits to the young able-bodied, on the grounds that he sees no way of establishing a safety-net without also generating damaging and even perverse incentives) would effectively:

> leave the working-aged person with no recourse whatsoever except the job market, family members, friends and public or privately funded local services.... Sons and daughters who fail to find work would continue to live with parents or relatives or friends until they do. Teenaged mothers would have to rely on support from their parents or the father of the child and perhaps work as well. People laid off from work would have to use their savings or borrowings from others to make do until the next job is found.

As Plant argues, this is emphatically not about eliminating or reducing dependency, but about redistributing it from the state to families. In addition, there is the point that shifting the burden of poverty onto families in this way is frequently to put such costs onto the very groups who are frequently least able to bear them (Plant 1988: 4). Indeed, critics of the introduction of the Social Fund have argued that a reduction in dependence on the 'benefits culture' has led to 'an *increase* in dependence on local authority social services departments and private forms of assistance such as families, charities and loan sharks' (Lister 1989: 114). Here, it is worth noting that - having already felt the impact of the cutbacks in clothing grants in 1980 and the 1986 single payments cuts - charities expressed deep anxiety over the (predictable) implications of the Fund for them when it was first introduced (Morley 1988, Pugh 1987).

A second issue, for Plant, concerns the notion of behavioural dependency which is frequently invoked in 'The New Consensus' (see earlier). The issue here goes back to J.S. Mill's argument, rehearsed in his *Principles of Political Economy*, that:

> in all cases of helping, there are two sets of consequences to be considered; the consequences of the assistance itself and the consequences of relying on the assistance. The former are generally beneficial, but the latter, for the most part, injurious; so much so, in many cases, as greatly to outweigh the value of the benefit.

The argument here is that, once people plan to rely on the help of others, a sense of dependency will arise. 'That is to say dependency is an *intentional* idea. The poor plan their lives on the assumption that aid will be forthcoming, rather than that in some sense that they are dependent in a functional or unintended sense' (Plant 1988: 5). However, there are difficulties with this argument.

The first is that part of the thrust of 'The New Consensus' is that the poor lack the skills and competence to plan their lives and to foresee the consequences of their actions. If this is so, however, it is not clear what remains of the idea of *intentional* dependency, given that this assumes the poor *plan* their behaviour in the long term on the basis of state aid. Secondly, as Plant (1988: 5) suggests:

> there is ... substantial evidence that insofar as welfare policies do have an effect on behaviour it is those with a strong insurance element, while social assistance schemes seem to have little effect. Similar evidence seems to hold for the experiments in negative income tax, in which the overall evidence seems to suggest that where the scheme was tried labour supply did reduce by about 5 per cent, but among the poorest groups labour participation sometimes increased. It is difficult to draw definitive conclusions about intentional dependency on the basis of such evidence.

Indeed, in Britain, it is arguable that the middle class is, if anything, *more* intentionally dependent on state subsidy in the fields of pensions, mortgage tax subsidies and use of the NHS (LeGrand 1982), yet this is not seen as a pathological form of dependency. This evidence, for Plant (1988: 5-6) at least:

> suggest[s] we have not got the basis for large-scale judgements about intentional dependency. Of course, the 'New Consensus' authors might argue that despite some of their language they are not talking about intentional dependency. However, if they are not this sits very badly with their assumption that the poor should be treated as being responsible for their behaviour.

'Why Not Workfare ...?'

Even if it is thought that welfare creates dependency and a lack of self-esteem, however, it is not clear that 'workfare' offers the best solution to this. If jobs are to be provided - or at least funded - by the state, then it is arguable that these are not like jobs acquired in the normal labour market, but forms of 'make-work' for those who would otherwise be unemployed. It is not clear that this will enhance independence and if it does not, then the fact of dependency - if indeed it is a fact - is simply being transferred (again, not eliminated) from the Department of Social Security to whichever government ministries were involved in securing employment which the economy proper cannot generate (Plant 1988, 1992).

Secondly, given the New Right's concerns about public expenditure, it is not clear where the rationale for such a system could come from in terms of neo-liberal political economy, since a workfare system with the state as employer of last resort will presumably cost more than unemployment benefit, for two reasons. The first is that if genuine work is being done, then the rates of return to labour are likely to be higher than the current level of unemployment benefit.

Secondly, the work itself will have to be organized, and this will involve either government organizing it directly, or funding others to do so. Either way, it is likely to be more expensive than paying unemployment benefit through an existing bureaucratic system (Plant 1992: 135).

It could, of course, be objected by neo-liberals that the state should not distort the labour market in this way. Yet, if it is thought that the state should *not* be the employer of last resort, a third objection would then apply. This is that if there is no prospect of a return to full employment in Britain (subject to NAIRU) and there will *not* be jobs for trained people to do, then workfare is a deception, in the sense of imposing on the poorest in society an obligation from which many of them will not be able to benefit. If the state is not going to be the employer of last resort, then 'workfare' against a background of persistently high unemployment is a deeply unjust policy in respect of the poor and unemployed (Plant 1988, 1992).

A further issue is how inclusive the scheme should be. If, for example, it is thought that the workfare/learnfare principle must be extended to female-headed households (as 'The New Consensus on Family and Welfare' intimates), then further problems are seen to arise in terms of the ideology of the New Right. The first would be the traditionalist objection that public policy should prefer women not to go out to work and earn income, but to stay at home and look after the children, especially if the latter are of preschool age (Burrows 1988). Secondly, however, if workfare or learnfare is going to include, say, single parents, it is likely that public expenditure would increase, in one of two ways.

The first of these is that the state will have to provide child day-care facilities, or fund others to do so. Alternatively, the state could supply single parents with vouchers to buy child-care privately. The objection here, of course, would be that both are expensive in terms of public expenditure, and that - *pace* Charles Murray - both create incentives for family breakdown. If, on the other hand, the state neither funds nor provides adequate child-care facilities, the additional cost will again fall on the very families who - *pace* Professor Plant - are frequently least able to bear them, namely female heads of poorer families.

There is also, however, a deeper philosophical issue at stake here. Workfare, as we have seen, attaches *conditions* to welfare rights for the able-bodied, since it requires them to discharge concomitant obligations in return for welfare. However, as Plant (1992: 136) argues:

> we do not make civil and political rights contingent on leading a virtuous life, except in the limited sense of criminals losing the right to vote.

Workfare/learnfare programmes, on the other hand, establish a clear link between welfare rights and leading a virtuous life, that is living in accordance with the dominant conceptions of autonomy, self-reliance and independence. The difficulty with this is that if, as Plant and Gray (1992) agree, there is no clear categorical difference between welfare rights and civil and political rights, then it is unclear on what kind of principle the former should be made 'conditional' on virtue being shown when civil and political rights are not. Is Gray's willingness to entertain a conditional basis for welfare rights perhaps symptomatic of an assumption that welfare rights are not, in fact, genuine rights at all?

If so, it is surely incumbent on Gray and others who advocate workfare or learnfare to say why this assumption is valid if, as Gray (1992: 59) concedes, there are no cogent philosophical reasons for seeing a categorical distinction between civil and political rights (which are unconditional) and welfare rights (which the authors of 'The New Consensus' and others want to make conditional). As Plant (1988: 6) argues:

> This issue is extremely complex [but] one of the central arguments for the difference is that civil and political rights do not imply resources, whereas social and welfare rights do. However, this is just not so. If we believe that we have a right to the protection of civil rights such as a right to privacy and security, then this protection is going to cost money and the amount of money spent protecting such rights will be a matter of political judgement and negotiation just as much as the resources to protect welfare rights. These sums will also increase: before the invention of computers, there was no need for a Data Protection Act with all the costs on institutions which this implies. The defence of a right to personal security also increases with inventions, social mobility of criminals, etc. The distinction between the two sorts of rights cannot be drawn in this way. However, if it cannot, then it is not clear why welfare rights should be regarded as conditional, and civil rights not.

The argument would then come back to 'dependency', that granting unconditional rights to social assistance creates dependency, whereas unconditional civil rights does not. As we have seen, however, there are several reasons to doubt the 'dependency' argument.

An Ideological Dilemma?

As Hoover and Plant (1989: 73) argue, the conservative-capitalist critique of dependency 'picks up on the resentment that working people feel towards those who receive public benefits'. At the same time, however:

It is worth noting that the tensions between individualist and traditionalist versions of conservatism pose a dilemma on the question of dependency. Individualist conservatives reject conceptions of social justice as a basis for public policy because there is no consensus possible about issues such as merit, desert, or need. Such claims are inherently subjective. The market is best suited to accommodating this reality since it allows for individual variations of the worth of each person's claims and efforts. The state, on the other hand, cannot secure social justice, precisely because of this diversity of moral valuations.

The dependency argument, however, assumes something which runs counter to this: that there is indeed a desirable set of values relating to human character that define individual virtue in a capitalist society. As we have seen, the suggestion from the authors of 'The New Consensus on Family and Welfare' and others who accept this analysis is that public policy on welfare should be based on precisely these moral valuations. As Hoover and Plant (1989: 73-4) argue:

> In order to avoid incoherence, conservatives must be able to explain how it is that one set of values concerned with individual virtue can be the concern of the state, while another, relating to the proper level of resources for an individual cannot be. Conservative capitalists who accept dependency theory ... seem to imply that we have some kind of insight into what forms moral dispositions when it comes to welfare, but that such knowledge of moral concerns is totally unavailable to democratic governments as they address issues of redistribution, need and desert more generally.

A further dimension to the argument, for Hoover and Plant, has to do with the capacity of the state:

> The state is presented by Hayek and Friedman as lacking the capacity to involve itself with distributive questions because of the complex, fragmented, dispersed and largely tacit knowledge that is required. The market is thought to be the institution that responds most efficiently to this aspect of the human condition. For Friedman, the state's only role with respect to welfare would be to provide subsistence resources through a 'negative income tax'. Yet the workfare/learnfare policies [see earlier] assume that the state has a role in seeking to develop individual virtues in welfare recipients. Certainly a state which gears its policies to the maintenance of certain virtues will be a long way from the limited government prefigured by Adam Smith and his individualist conservative followers. It is not a path that would attract the advocates of a neutral stance regarding economic behaviour as well as social and personal behaviour understood in a wider context.

Workfare, as Lawrence Mead argues, affects neither the *scale* of government intervention to help the poor, nor the *principle* that the poor should be helped, but affects only the *character* of the assistance to be given (CPS 1987: 68):

> There should be reciprocity; we should demand something in return. That is a different thing from cutting back the extent of assistance or pretending the market-place should govern. There is a difference between workfare as a policy for enhancing certain values and a policy of simply denying assistance. This is a different *kind* of conservatism; this is *big government* conservatism rather than small government.

The philosophical-policy dilemma here is this. The liberal New Right has always emphasized government *failure* and *incompetence*. Again, rarely has government tried to undertake policies which 'seek to change the motivation of a substantial number of citizens' (Plant 1988: 8). Indeed, it was for precisely this reason that the COS strategy fell into disuse: 'They believed that character is all, but it became clear that the government cannot alter character, and yet poor relief in a modern society has to be the ultimate responsibility of the state while at the same time the state cannot address the moral character of its citizens' (Plant 1988: 8).

Dependency theory, for Hoover and Plant, 'leads straight to traditionalist paternalism and the idea that "Victorian values" can form the basis of state policy, a reversal of *laissez-faire* in the most sensitive areas of human conduct':

> There is as well the problem of hypocrisy. While the poor are to be regulated to induce moral behaviour by the terms of dependency theory, the rich are to be given licence to be indulgent by the terms of free enterprise and *laissez-faire*. There remains the criticism that dependency based policies amount to a class-based imposition of values upon the poor that are merely a pretence on the part of the rich - the central criticism of the Victorian moral order.

An Ideological Shift?

A second aim of this chapter has been to examine the response of the four New Right think-tanks (IEA, ASI, CPS and SAU) examined in this study to the issue of dependency, given the ideological differences between these groups discussed in Chapters 1-4 (above). Recent IEA/ASI publications, as we have seen, both acknowledge the existence of an underclass in Britain and invoke the notion of dependency. To the extent that the IEA and the ASI are now pursuing a moral - as opposed to an economistic - agenda in welfare reform/policy, this would seem to imply that a certain convergence has now occurred between four otherwise ideologically diverse groups (Chapters 1-4, above). It remains for us to say a little about why this 'shift' might have occurred.

In this connection, we have already noted David Green's (1992) objection that the application of *economic* principles to welfare policy - in practice adjusting benefit recipients' incentives at the margin - will not succeed without a concern 'to improve our understanding of the varied ways in which a *moral community* of free persons can be founded and maintained'. In a similar vein, David Willetts argued in 1987 that, for perhaps rather too long, much of the argument in social policy had been about the claims of economics (CPS 1987: 164):

> Economics is the Queen of the social sciences, but is it the Empress of the social sciences? Economists believe, by definition, that they can explain any pattern of behaviour. It is what economics stands for in principle. Any behaviour is maximizing something and economists can then go out and find out what is being maximized.

A more interesting argument, however, concerns 'whether there is any independent or autonomous area of explanation which does not ultimately collapse into economic explanation' (CPS 1987: 164). This is a theme to which I return in the next chapter.

8 Beyond the New Right?

Introduction

The final part of this chapter considers what the future prospects for New Right think-tanks might be, given Margaret Thatcher's departure as Prime Minister and Leader of the Conservative Party. Before doing this, however, it is important to recognize that there are several theoretical issues which continue to divide the New Right. The purpose of the first part of this chapter is to explore these issues. As we shall see, a useful way of doing this is to consider a number of key publications produced by New Right think-tanks in the late 1980s and early 1990s.

Limited versus Minimal Government

The first issue is that of 'limited' *versus* 'minimal' government. In essence, the argument here is about the true extent of 'public goods'. All New Right neo-liberals agree that the writ of government in capitalist countries such as Britain has grown too far. The key question is how - and how far - it should be reduced (Seldon 1990). In this connection, the case for 'limited' rather than 'minimal' government (the alternatives that form the key difference between New Right neo-liberals) has been outlined by John Gray (1989).

As John Gray suggests, the proper extent of the activity and authority of the state is the key question in political theory. In this connection, Gray's first claim is that the project of limiting government in Britain stands today in urgent need of reassertion; government must relinquish a paternal role in the economy and society, substantially withdraw from the sphere of civil life and assume again its true office as defender of the peace and guardian of civil society. The Oakeshottian view of the office of government as 'the umpire whose business it is to administer the rules of the game or the chairman who governs the debate according to known rules but does not himself participate in it', Gray argues, has been conspicuous by its absence in recent years from political discourse in Britain (Gray 1989: 15).

Gray's second, and more contestable, claim is that a government which is limited has nevertheless an important positive agenda to fulfil. In this connection, Gray argues that although government is presently vastly inflated in its activities, a century or more of interventionism has built up needs and expectations which must be addressed; what is needed is not a minimum state but a limited government with significant positive responsibilities. A limited or framework government 'should go beyond its most essential role as umpire and peace-keeper' in three chief areas. Government has a duty to emancipate the poor and the underclass from the culture of dependency and thereby enable them to act as full participants in civil society (see Chapter 7). It has an obligation to protect or promote independence and freedom of choice by enabling all those who wish to do so to acquire a decent modicum of wealth and to exercise personal control over their health, education and provision for old age. It is also, Gray argues, a responsibility of government to facilitate the transmission of valuable cultural traditions across the generations. In this regard, he writes, it behoves government in Britain to acknowledge the fact of cultural diversity by providing each tradition with opportunities and even resources whereby it can express and reproduce itself in peaceful coexistence with its neighbours (Gray 1989: 16).

For Gray at least, the scope and limits of government cannot be determined *a priori*. Time, place and historical circumstance are of crucial importance in determining both the range and character of intervention by the state in civil society. The minimum state is defined as that in which the sphere of government intervention is exhausted by the protection of *negative rights* only; a limited government, on the other hand, is said to have *positive duties* in respect of encouraging the relief of poverty, supporting services such as health and education, and in protecting valuable cultural traditions. Moreover, Gray argues, a limited government has good reason to concern itself with the 'distributive implications' of its systems of taxation and welfare. Government is entitled and obliged to provide a range of positive services as 'means to the ends of greater independence, freedom of choice and diversity in communal life'. A limited government does most to achieve these ends, however, when it acts both to repair and renew the fabric of civil society - namely, the institutions of private property and contractual exchange on which a market economy, and thereby all the autonomous institutions of free persons, finally depend (Gray 1989: 16).

Following Hobbes, Gray argues that the primordial obligation of government is to make and keep peace, where this encompasses both forging and maintaining in good repair the institutions of civil society whereby persons and communities with incompatible values may peaceably co-exist. Yet, discharging this duty will nevertheless commit government to activities that go far beyond the provision of the 'public goods' of national defence and law and order. The renewal of civil society demands that the state do more than be patiently attentive to the rules of the game of the market. This may entail government 'supplying families and communities with the means whereby their distinctive values and ways of life may be affirmed and renewed across the generations [and will] require concern for the health of the autonomous and intermediary institutions which stand between the individual and the state'. Trade unions, universities and professional bodies, he argues, should be assured a protected sphere of 'independence' under the rule of law (Gray 1989: 22-23).

For Gray at least, government activity should be confined to the production of 'public goods'. In a Hobbesian perspective, he argues, the greatest of these is peace, the pursuit of which involves government in the provision of goods that go far beyond those comprehended in the maintenance of law and order. Concern by government for a civil society free from destructive conflict should lead it to be concerned with the distribution (and not just the efficient production) of wealth. Universal literacy, whatever disadvantages it may have, is of benefit to everyone, and government may legitimately act to promote it. Similarly, though more controversially, government may act to 'promote a common culture' by supporting the arts, and by other measures. Moreover, because people 'sometimes need resources' in order to participate fully in a market economy, a limited government may act to provide those with small resources with 'the wherewithal to make good use of market freedoms'. A limited government may thus legitimately act to provide a variety of public goods. In this connection, Gray specifies as 'public goods' not only those indivisible and non-excludable items that are either produced by government or not at all, but any good that has weighty positive 'externalities' (Gray 1989: 32).

The alternative neo-liberal approach (the case for 'minimal' government) emerges from the work of several followers of Mises and other 'Austrian' economists (Rothbard 1970, 1973), and from the anarcho-capitalist writings of David Friedman (1973, 1978). Both in effect mount a root-and-branch attack on the notion of maximalist or unlimited government based on variants of social choice. Advocates of minimal government reflect the anxiety that the role of government should be confined to 'indispensable' functions that cannot be performed in any other way. As Arthur Seldon (1990: 185) argues:

> The difficulty with limited government that liberals have yet to resolve is that its functions must be exercised through the imperfect political process that distorts and manipulates individual preferences. Who makes the rules that politicians are to enforce in the public interest if not the politicians themselves? *Quis custodiet ipsos custodes?* Limited government implicitly supposes that government will perform faithfully the main functions allotted to it even though it is judged incompetent in performing other functions.

For Seldon at least, the notion of 'limited' government 'lacks the indispensable instinctive scepticism of government taught by the classical liberal economists that led them to want government confined to its unavoidable minimal functions of public goods rather than to the indeterminate limited functions that could be decided by government itself'. In particular, Seldon argues, if government cannot be expected to perform acceptably the services it can leave to the market, 'it cannot be expected to devise neutrally the rules that decide the services it must perform itself' (Seldon 1990: 185).

New Right neo-liberals, then, differ on the optimum use of the state. West German economic liberals who continue the tradition of Ludwig Erhard generally see a state active in the avoidance of inflation and the control of monopoly, as argued in their journal *Ordo*. Other neo-liberals have become more sceptical of the state, even in these functions. These 'libertarian' neo-liberals have been reinforced by the writings of Anthony de Jasay (1985) and other thinkers in Europe, in the United States and in Australia, whose writings have newly emphasized the extravagant claims made for the beneficence or competence of the state and which further reinforce the intellectual argument for 'the irreducible minimal functions of government under capitalism as it could be' (Seldon 1990: 243).

The Market versus the Social Market Economy

A second (and related) issue is that of the market *versus* the social market economy. In this connection, it is the burden of John Gray's argument that the market economy is not a self-sustaining order, but 'depends crucially on an undergirding culture of liberty', whose vitality presupposes a good distribution of resources and opportunities, so that all sections of society can benefit from, and participate in, market institutions (Gray 1989: 10). A limited government, for Gray at least, has a vital role in transmitting the values upon which a market economy depends; thus a limited government which rejects or is indifferent to the culture which underpins the market neglects one of the conditions of its own existence (Gray 1989: 74).

For Gray at least, the argument for limited government and a market economy is not in the end economic, but ethical. It is the burden of his argument that, in the conditions of a modern society, only market institutions can give practical effect to the values of liberty and human dignity. The argument for the market, for Gray, is not that government be conceived of as an economic enterprise, but rather the contrary. It is that only market institutions allow free individuals to opt into, or out of, enterprise. The long-term survival of the free market, in Britain at least, is said to depend finally on an intellectual realignment in which the acceptance of market liberalism is at the heart of a new public consensus. In this connection, Gray argues, a limited government should restrict itself to setting the framework of market capitalism - a framework 'encompassing policy which will address the distributional and cultural preconditions of a stable market order' (Gray 1989: 75).

This argument has since been developed by Gray in two further publications. In the first of these, he argues that a limited government has tasks that go well beyond keeping the peace. It has also a responsibility to protect and shelter the vulnerable and defenceless, to promote the conservation and renewal of the natural and human environment and to assist in the reproduction of the common culture without which pluralism and diversity may become enmity and division. The role of a 'limited' government is thus other and larger than that specified in the libertarian dogmas of contemporary neo-liberalism. The free market economy is not something free-standing, primordial or self-moving. It rests upon the foundations of a common culture of liberty, and has to support it the institutions of a strong state tempering its excesses and sheltering those - the very old, the disabled and the chronically sick, for example - who may be without the resources or the skills to flourish in a market economy (Gray 1991: 11-12).

The free market, for Gray at least, is not a self-sustaining order, but presupposes as its matrix a network of intermediary institutions animated by a culture of liberty. The 'political legitimacy' of a free market economy is said to depend on such institutions being in good repair and where necessary on their being tended and nurtured by government. Vital as it is as an expression of individual freedom, he argues, the market is but one dimension of society in which individuals make choices and exercise responsibility; individuals also live in families and 'belong' to churches and other voluntary associations in which market exchange is inappropriate or peripheral, and it is this cultural and institutional matrix of the free market that must now be addressed. Nor is it wise to attribute to the market a perfection British Conservatives have learnt not to ascribe to government; like any other human institution, Gray argues, the market is imperfect and, in certain areas of policy, exclusive reliance on it is a recipe for failure. One need only look to Germany or Japan, Gray argues, to see how markets may be supplemented by the constructive engagement of government (Gray 1991: 31).

More recently still, Gray has outlined the case for a social market economy, as theorized in the Freiburg school of Eucken and Erhard and as it might be realized in the specific context of contemporary Britain. For Gray at least, the free market is emphatically not a natural social phenomenon, but a creature of law and government. The free market is not free-standing or self justifying, but is part of a larger nexus of institutions, with whom it shares a justification in terms of 'the contribution it makes to human well-being'. Thirdly, he argues, the market will lack ethical and political legitimacy unless it is supplemented or constrained by institutions that both temper its excesses and correct its failures, such as an enabling welfare state. For Gray at least, the theory of the social market economy is that market institutions are 'always embedded in other social and political institutions that both shape them and legitimate them' (Gray 1992: 82).

In this connection, Gray argues that market institutions in Britain 'require for their legitimacy a range of governmental policies and institutions' - including the institution of 'an enabling welfare state'. (It is not claimed that an enabling welfare state, *per se*, was a part of the German social market economy; only that, in Britain today, it best complements the institutions of the market, and so captures the spirit of the social market economy.) Freeing up the market, for Gray, and reducing the invasive state, thus requires a positive and not only a negative agenda of government policy; this is affirmed against the background of a prior affirmation that government should 'intervene' only where private provision and voluntary association are demonstrably inadequate. In other words, the principle of *subsidiarity* - the principle that government should not 'usurp functions that can be well discharged by intermediary institutions' - ought to be observed throughout policy (Gray 1992: 84).

Gray's topic in *The Moral Foundations of Market Institutions* is that of 'the limits of market institutions', the question of the areas in which market provision is either 'inappropriate or requires supplementation'. For Gray at least, the most obvious area in which the limits of market institutions are revealed is that of 'public goods' (goods that, being neither partionable nor excludable, must be supplied to all or none). Yet Gray focuses not on goods such as clean air, but on those *inherently* public goods (Raz 1986) which are associated with a public culture in which autonomous individuals have a rich array of options to choose from. In general, Gray argues, 'valuable autonomy' presupposes a stock of 'roles, statuses, institutions and social forms' and a structure of 'intermediary institutions embodied in a common culture, from which individuals can derive worthwhile options'. A liberal government, Gray argues, has a positive responsibility to tend and nurture these intermediary institutions and ought never to make policy on the model of the atomistic individual related to others only by a variety of contractual agreements (Gray 1992: 78).

For Gray, then, an individualist order is 'not free-standing, but depends on forms of common life for its worth and its very existence'. Equally, he claims, autonomy is valueless if it is exercized in a community denuded of the inherently public goods that create worthwhile options and which thus make good choices possible. One of the basic needs of human beings, Gray argues, is membership in a community; such membership will be stable if, and only if, that 'community' is seen to be meeting basic human needs, through the institutions of the market and, where these fail, through other institutions, such as those of an enabling welfare state (see later). A market economy without a commitment to measures which protect both the 'well-being and autonomy of the vulnerable and defenceless', Gray argues, will lack both ethical and political legitimacy. The argument of his paper is that a humane 'social market economy' is both the only sort of free economy likely to survive in the years to come and the only sort that deserves to survive (Gray 1992: 93).

In outlining the 'constitutive features' of the social market economy, Gray rebuts the standard objections, made by classical or fundamentalist liberals, to the very expression. Often, Gray notes, it is maintained that the phrase is tautologous, because markets are *themselves* social institutions which presuppose and generate 'a host of social relationships - not all of which are economic in the narrow sense'. Alternatively, he notes, though incompatibly, it is often argued that the phrase is oxymoronic, because markets do not exist to serve any social or collective end, but only to satisfy the disparate purposes of *individuals*. Finally, he writes, it is commonly alleged that the expression has no clear meaning at all (Gray 1992: 81).

In a 1991 article, the first of these objections to the term 'social market economy' was powerfully argued by Ralph Harris. For Harris at least, the competitive market is *necessarily* a social instrument. It is, he maintains, nothing less than a network of local, national and international links, enabling people to trade together freely for their mutual benefit, as workers, consumers, producers, dealers, savers, borrowers or investors. The market, he writes, could also be regarded as 'social' in a second sense. It operates within a developing framework of laws, customs and standards. These extend from approved weights and measures to help in cash or in kind for those who cannot help themselves. Supporters of the market, Harris argues, differ on the scope for reforming this legal framework but for true free marketeers the test is to avoid sapping the market's efficiency in maximizing output or its flexibility in adapting to changes in resources, technology, competition and consumer preferences (Harris 1991).

Again, in *The Fatal Conceit* and elsewhere, Hayek rehearses the allegation that the expression 'social market economy' has no clear meaning at all. The word 'social', he argues, has acquired so many different meanings as to become useless as a tool of communication and to empty the nouns it qualifies of their meaning. The word 'social', he argues, has become a 'weasel word'. Just as a weasel is supposed to be able to empty an egg without leaving a visible sign,

Hayek argues, the word 'social' deprives of content any term to which it is prefixed. The phrase 'social justice', for example, is on this view 'a semantic fraud' (Hayek 1988a: 117-8).

For Hayek at least, while the abuse of the word 'social' is international, it has taken perhaps its most extreme forms in West Germany, where the constitution (1949) employed the term *sozialer Rechtsstaat* (social rule of law), and from where the concept of the 'social market economy' (popularized by Ludwig Erhard) has spread. Citing Professor Erhard's own view that the market economy did not have to be *made* social but was so already as a result of its origin, Hayek argues that whereas the rule of law and the market are, at the start, fairly clear concepts, the attribute 'social' 'empties them of any clear meaning' (Hayek 1988a: 117). Thus, Hayek writes: 'While I know what a market economy is intended to mean, I have no idea what "social market economy" can possibly mean - except that the rules of the market are not to be followed' (Hayek 1988b: 50).

Markets versus Community?

A further issue that the New Right and its think-tanks have yet to resolve is that of markets *versus* community. For, it is the burden of John Gray's argument that the 'legitimacy of the free market in the political realm' depends not only on its capacity to deliver economic growth but also - and more importantly - on its being both contained and sustained by the common allegiances nurtured by traditional Toryism and tempered by a liberal social policy that is 'in harmony with the spirit of the age'. Only in this way, Gray suggests, can 'conservative individualism' have a political future (Gray 1991: 12).

For over a decade, Gray observes, the policy agenda of British Conservatism has been dominated by the goal of liberating market forces, and according the market economy its rightful legitimacy. For Gray at least, this direction of Conservative policy has had impressive results and has produced a shift in the stance of the state in regard to the market that is perhaps irreversible. Nor is the agenda of marketisation yet exhausted. Conservatives, he argues, have much further to go in extending market institutions into hitherto sacrosanct areas, reducing taxation, inflation and government expenditure, and privatizing industries and services. For Gray at least, there is a strong case for introducing market choice in many social and welfare services. In all these areas, he argues, conservatives will be building on the achievements of the past decade (Gray 1991: 30).

Yet, in all likelihood, Gray argues, only a reassertion of the traditional 'Tory' concern for compassion and *community* can hope to sustain the free market which the last decade of conservative government has achieved. For Gray at least, conservative policy which neglects, or seems to neglect the vulnerable and needy, or which is so committed to market freedoms that it leaves to its own devices the human and natural environment in which markets operate will provoke a revulsion in which the traditional Tory concern for the health of the community is captured by socialist egalitarians and collectivists. Accordingly, he argues, if this danger is to be averted, Conservative policy needs a major shift in orientation, from overriding concern with the market economy to concern with its social and cultural preconditions (Gray 1991: 30).

As we saw in Chapter 3, it is the burden of David Willetts' argument that economic liberalism, although it offers a host of valid insights into the operation of the economy, just will not do as a complete political philosophy. Thus, free markets need conservatism. For Willetts at least, economic liberals may see all of life as being like shopping, but this leaves unexplained the question of what we are shopping for - and why. What makes us the 'shoppers' that we are? For Willetts at least, economic liberals have fought an 'admirable battle' for the interests of consumers to be given priority over the interests of producers, but this leaves unexplained the question of who these consumers are; what there is to them apart from their immediate appetites; what they are loyal to; what duties they believe they have. An understanding of our position in historic communities, Willetts argues, is essential to answer these deeper questions (Willetts 1992: 93).

Secondly, Willetts argues, a 'conservative' understands the importance of the institutions and affiliations which sustain capitalism. The instinct to 'truck, barter and exchange' may indeed be universal, but it only generates a modern, advanced economy if it is expressed through a particular set of social institutions, such as private property, a law of contract, an independent judiciary and legislation ensuring that consumers have accurate information. For Willetts at least, these institutions need to be sustained by ties of loyalty and sentiment. The law of 'contract' cannot rest simply on a social contract, because that begs the question of where contracts come from (Willetts 1992: 93).

Thirdly, Willetts argues, conservatives do not accept markets and the price mechanism everywhere. 'You cannot sell your children. You cannot sell your vote. The state does not seek to raise revenue by auctioning places on a jury. Royal weddings are not commercially sponsored (yet)'. The market system, for Willetts at least, is constrained and limited by other values. A pure economic liberal, he argues, cannot explain what these values are or why individuals subscribe to them (Willetts 1992: 93-4).

Individualism, as Hoover and Plant (1989: 78) argue, is the guiding value of classical liberal political thought. New Right neo-liberals who borrow from this tradition, though, discard the nuances. The ideal of individual freedom is unencumbered by any of John Locke's concern for equity in the distribution of scarce goods, or of Mill's understanding that the individual pursuit of pleasure must be disciplined by a regard for the social consequences of others making the same choice in the same case. While classical liberals placed individual liberty at the top of their. scale of values, there was always at least a secondary regard to the welfare of the community (Hoover and Plant 1989: 78).

Classical liberalism, for Hoover and Plant, has been altered by New Right neoliberals in that they elevate private self-interest to a position of dominance over almost every form of the public interest. Classical liberal thinkers in general, and Hayek and Friedman in particular, do in fact acknowledge a slightly wider role for public authority than the 'free-market' preference for simply enforcing the law, delivering the mail and defending the shores. Classical liberals such as Locke and Mill, however, at least acknowledged human need as a principle in distribution, a concern that is absent in Hayek and Friedman; for individualist conservatives such as Hayek and Friedman, community is 'but the consequence of individual choices made for whatever reason, and the only limit allowed is protection from coercion' (Hoover and Plant 1989: 9 and 78).

Modern conservatism, for Willetts at least, aims to reconcile free markets with a recognition of the importance of community. If markets and communities are alternatives, we have to give one precedence over the other. Socialists back their concept of the community over the market. Libertarians, on the other hand, opt for the free market (Willetts 1992: 92-3):

> The rigorous free-marketeer (or 'economic liberal'), without a trace of conservatism in him, will think that this concern with communities is all agonizing about nothing. What matters is giving people the greatest practical amount of freedom; that means markets. People want increasing prosperity, and that too requires markets. He is not worried if markets erode traditional social ties - seeing it as good riddance. If ties to a firm, or a spouse, or a neighbourhood are more conditional and more tenuous then, the libertarian says, that may be no bad thing. If a business or a marriage is going badly, it is right for people to break free so they can fulfil themselves elsewhere. He sees life as a giant supermarket in which we are free to choose between a range of different lifestyles and values, as well as jobs and possessions. He cannot understand why conservatives put so much stress on irrational brand loyalty.

At stake here, as we have seen, is the issue of the legitimacy of the free market in the political realm. Indeed, in one sense this is a clear tension between free -

market and more traditional forms of conservatism. Many conservative traditionalists, after all, have long taken the view that the free market cannot secure its own legitimacy, and that other values crucial to society may be threatened by free markets. In the late 1970s, the point was argued powerfully by Sir Ian Gilmour, a dissenting member of the first Thatcher administration, when he argued (Gilmour 1978: 118) that:

> The preservation of freedom is a complex business. But if people are not to be seduced by other attractions, they must at least feel loyalty to the State. This loyalty will not be deep unless they gain from the State protection and other benefits. Homilies to cherish competition and warnings against interference with market forces will not engender loyalty ... Complete economic freedom is not therefore an insurance of political freedom. Indeed, it can undermine political freedom. Economic liberalism because of its starkness and its *failure to create a sense of community* is likely to repel people from the rest of liberalism.

More recently, Robin Harris has argued in a pamphlet for the CPS that, in full-heartedly embracing capitalism, Conservatives have seen more clearly what it can and cannot achieve. Harris goes on to argue (Harris 1989: 33) that:

> It has been claimed for democratic capitalism that it relies upon, and indeed encourages, fraternity and co-operation in many ways: and this is probably true. But, the mobility and flexibility which a successful capitalist economy requires is bound, in some degree, to militate against the sense of community in neighbourhoods and the solidarity of the extended family.

Again, there is the argument developed by the German philosopher and social theorist, Jurgen Habermas, in his book *Legitimation Crisis*, that capitalism, because of its individualism and the demands of mobility, reduced traditional values, on which it actually rests for its own legitimacy in a broader sense. Thus, from the point of view of both the traditionalist right and the 'communitarian' left, the values of the market are placed in jeopardy by the unconstrained market. Both stress those forms of values and integration which must not be undermined by markets, and for the left this requires attention to distributive justice (Hoover and Plant 1989: 235).

Moreover, as we saw in Chapter 7, there is quite a deep issue here in terms of the coherence of the market-capitalist outlook. As noted in Chapter 1, part of the strategy is to argue that in modern society there is insufficient moral agreement to seek to constrain market outcomes through public policy. Such policies would have to embody end-state or patterned principles of distributive justice and the market theorist will deny that these can be agreed in a free, morally pluralistic society. And yet, so far as personal morality is concerned, the conservative capitalist will typically argue in favour of the maintenance of certain sorts of traditional values, and indeed, there has been on the right an interest in restoring Victorian values (Chapter 3). What is not at all clear is that this is a coherent project - given the New Right's strictures on the impossibility of moral agreement to guide public policy in the distributive arena. As Hoover and Plant (1989: 235) argue:

> The project depends upon an unargued and very implausible view that agreement is possible so far as personal values are concerned, and that these could be encouraged by government, while at the same time the degree of moral pluralism in modern society could be stressed as a way of undermining distributive politics.

For Hoover and Plant at least, we see here a clear case of the way in which traditional conservative preoccupations 'sit very uneasily with free-market assumptions'.

Community versus Communities

A final area of controversy and of continued debate within the think-tanks concerns the issue of community *versus* communities. For David Willetts at least, reconciling the pursuit of self-interest with duties to the community is perhaps the fundamental issue of moral and political philosophy (Willetts 1992: 96). In this connection, he argues, a successful and coherent conservatism has to 'tie together' free-market economics and a sense of community (Willetts 1992: 11-12). The principles of free markets aligned with a strong sense of community are, Willetts argues, fundamental conservative principles (Willetts 1992: 51-2). Conservative thought at its best, he argues, conveys the mutual dependence between the community and the free market (Willetts 1992: 182).

For Willetts at least, understanding of the importance of our ties to a community leads the conservative to value what modern sociologists call the mediating structures - the family and the trade union, the neighbourhood and the firm, the 'club' and the church; Burke, he argues, captured this element of conservatism in a famous passage:

> To be attached to the subdivision, to love the little platoon we belong to in society, is the first principle (the germ as it were) of public affections. It is the first link in the series by which we proceed towards a love to our country and to mankind.

For Willetts at least, our identity comes from our language, our beliefs, our experiences and histories - not all of which we can control. Thus we do not choose our parents, our language or the place of our birth. We cannot stand outside ourselves and judge our whole lives. There are, Willetts argues, 'limits to what we can reason about' (Willetts 1992: 68).

For Willetts at least, this conservative account of what it is to be a person offers a powerful account of the origins of moral obligations. They follow from the social roles we occupy. The leap from is to ought (from factual descriptions, to statements about how we should act) is bridged by understanding the duties that come with our roles: father, employee or (more ambitiously and controversially) citizen. These serve both as descriptions of who we are and also carry with them obligations which we cannot escape. Duties do not come from contracts which are voluntarily entered into, but are inescapable parts of our life history as members of a community. Moral obligations are not abstract and universal (*Moralitat*) but embodied in particular social relations (*Sittlichkeit*). There are duties such as to our children, to our neighbours, and even more specific ones, such as participating in the legal system through jury service. They could not be expressed or understood outside a particular set of institutions or a culture. These are duties which only make sense because of particular social institutions which already exist. We are, in a sense, born into them (Willetts 1992: 68).

For Willetts, however, there is still a need to be clear about the relationship between such shared values and the nation-state. Does the conservative believe in the 'community' embodied in the nation-state, or rather in an intricate, overlapping 'network of communities' in which the nation-state has a 'special, but not a commanding role'? This question of *community or communities*, he notes, is not usually presented in so raw a form in conservative thought. It is 'more a matter of degree' than of 'two exclusive options'. But there are different conservative views which can be distinguished, and the dilemma 'does suggest some theoretical tensions' (Willetts 1992: 71 and 105).

On the one hand, he argues, there is the tradition of Burke - the conservative community of the nation-state - carried forward into the nineteenth century by romantic nationalism. This is what one might call *macro-conservatism*, with a particular set of values embodied in the over-arching national community. In this connection, he suggests, Burke must be regarded as a believer in the national community (Willetts 1992: 71):

> Many conservatives who cite his famous remark on the little platoons assume that they are setting out a conservative vision of a civil society in which the neighbourhood, the family or firm are all valued for themselves; but on closer

inspection, the assumption behind Burke's argument may be rather different. A platoon is part of an army directed by a general towards a particular objective. And, he does not actually praise these [little] platoons for their intrinsic qualities, but because they are a means of love of the state.

The alternative, for Willetts at least, is what one might call *micro-conservatism*. This emphasizes the particular network of communities which gives each individual life its meaning, from the family and the firm to the neighbourhood and to friends or relatives or colleagues who may come from another country. In this connection, he argues (Willetts 1992: 105) that:

> The nation-state has a role, but a much more modest one in sustaining a political order in which this multiplicity of communities can thrive. The nation-state can command our loyalty as the protector of these communities but we certainly cannot look to it as one organic whole embodying detailed moral purposes which we all share. If we look at what we love and gives our lives meaning, we find that the nation-state is but one among many.

As far as *macro-conservatism* is concerned, it is the burden of Robin Harris's argument that 'individuals can attain sanctity if not security, purpose if not prosperity, *outside* the State. But that is the exception'. For the vast majority, he argues, it is only through the State that individuals can flourish - that they can live the 'good life' (Harris 1989). In this connection, he quotes Burke for the view that 'He who gave our nature to be perfected by our virtue willed also the necessary means of its perfection - he willed therefore the State'. When Burke wrote, he argues, the state was clearly Christian, and there existed a large degree of consensus about moral values. Now, this is threatened. However difficult it may be to achieve the objective, Harris argues, for the Conservative it can never be other than true that government is the steward of a moral system, eternally and everywhere valid (Harris 1989: 18).

For Harris in particular, the most important element in the Conservative community which must be strengthened is religion. Again, he quotes Burke for the view that for the sources of culture and civilization, we should look to 'the spirit of a gentleman, and the spirit of religion'. The religion of the Conservative, he argues, is not just any religion, but rather Christianity (Harris 1989: 49):

> This is not to say that all Conservatives are Christians, which would be absurd; it is, most emphatically, in no way to ignore the wisdom and virtue of the many non-Christians, particularly Jews, who share fully in liberal, democratic, Western values. It is to do no more than state that the tradition and the values from which Conservatism has sprung, and which continue to inspire it, are Christian.

In this connection, Harris argues not against the pursuit by people of all faiths and none of the way of life which they desire for themselves and for their children, but for the assertion of the 'dominance [but not total dominance] of Christianity throughout the national community' (Harris 1989: 50).

It is, on the other hand, a cardinal point of Gray's 1991 argument that we in Britain live in a culture that is in very large part post-Christian and post-religious - and in which a 'sceptical and secular' conservatism is therefore appropriate. In Britain, Gray argues, 'secularization' is far advanced and likely to be irreversible, so that the culture and traditions that bind people together 'cannot any longer be distinctively Christian or informed by any shared transcendental faith'. A sound conservative policy, he argues, cannot be nostalgist in inspiration; once the cake of custom is broken, he writes, we must 'do our best' with what is left; it cannot be baked anew. For Gray at least, this means a policy that aims to infuse an 'irreducibly pluralist, self-critical' society with coherence, self-confidence and stability (Gray 1991: 10).

Similarly, Gray argues, the project of restoring an organic national community, as advocated by Roger Scruton, is a 'distraction from serious policy-making' in a society that is irreversibly pluralist. For Gray at least, this project of restoring an organic national community in Britain is a vain, chimerical and perhaps even a harmful one. The pursuit of a vision of nationhood which has no purchase on our historical traditions is, for Gray at least, an aberration, a distraction from the task of sustaining the bonds we do share and which do hold us together (Gray 1991: 20).

In Britain today, Gray argues, allegiance cannot express a deep community of shared values. The communitarian ambition of making political loyalty 'coterminous' with membership of a single moral community, he writes, could not be more inappropriate (Gray 1991: 20-1):

> We are, none of us, what in the jargon of recent philosophy are called 'radically situated selves' [i.e.] persons whose identities are defined by [our] membership of a single, all-inclusive community. We are each of us members of many and sometimes conflicting communities: we are (in Fulke Greville's phrase) 'suckled on the milk of many nurses'. With such a plural inheritance, we cannot reasonably expect that political allegiance will express a thick culture of common values. What we must hope, nevertheless, is that we have in common enough respect for the ruling ideas of civil society - ideas of tolerance, of responsibility and of equality under the rule of law - for the diversity that we harbour to be fruitful rather than an occasion for division among us.

For Gray at least, the pursuit of a delusive national community is but a distraction from the humbler but indispensable task of filling out that 'thinner' common culture of 'respect for civil society' that presently enables us to co-exist in peace (Gray 1991: 24).

> Building up that common culture, in turn, effectively enfranchises us all as active citizens in a polity to which we can all profess allegiance. A conservative policy, rightly conceived, is not one which seeks to renew old traditions by deliberate contrivance - which is (in Wittgenstein's phrase), 'as if one tried to repair a broken spider's web with one's bare hands'.

The proper policy, Gray argues, is to nurture the traditions we share while respecting the variety of practices whereby we hold them in common (Gray 1991: 25).

Moral Foundations of Market Institutions

The argument thus far has been that there are several theoretical issues which continue to divide the New Right and its think-tanks in Britain. Having said this, it remains for us to consider what the future prospects for the think-tanks might be, given Margaret Thatcher's departure both as Prime Minister, and as Leader of the Conservative Party. Before doing this, however, I want to return now to the argument of John Gray's *The Moral Foundations of Market Institutions* (Gray 1992), a paper which has been the subject of much lively discussion at the IEA and which is in important respects strongly critical of the standard positions in neo-liberal thought. In so doing, my purpose is to emphasize a number of points of remaining disagreement as between left and right in British politics and to indicate from a position to the left of John Gray's where I think his argument needs further development to be fully plausible.

In this study, John Gray examines the moral legitimacy of the market economy. The position he advocates has as its central notions satiable basic needs, including that in autonomy, and the rich diversity of options provided by a good community. The view presented by Gray is that of a liberal market economy constrained (or supplemented) by an enabling welfare state: in other words, a social market economy, as understood in the Freiburg School of Eucken and Erhard, freely applied by the author to the current situation in Britain. The argument developed by Gray diverges from the standard position of contemporary classical liberals in that it is avowedly an ethical argument and not an amoral appeal to the prosperity that market institutions deliver; this is said to reflect the author's conviction that market institutions work well only where their practitioners accord them moral legitimacy. For Gray at least, this last point is relevant especially in the emergent post-communist societies of Eastern Europe where the ethical properties of market institutions are little understood and where an amoral defence of the market advocated by many contemporary liberal and libertarian economists only reinforces popular suspicion of it (Gray 1992: 2).

For Gray at least, the ethical standing of the market lies in its indispensable role as one of the chief preconditions of the autonomy of the individual. The free market, for Gray, enables the individual to act upon his own goals, values, objectives or plan of life, without subordination to any other individual and without subjection to any collective decision procedure. It is from its role as *an enabling device* for the protection and enhancement of human autonomy that the ethical justification of the market is ultimately derived (Gray 1992: 19).

For John Gray, the intrinsic value of negative liberty *per se* is negligible. The value of negative liberty must therefore be theorized in terms of its contribution to 'something other than itself which does possess intrinsic value'. In this connection, Gray argues that the chief value of negative liberty is in its contribution to the positive liberty of autonomy. By autonomy is meant the condition in which a person can be at least part author of his life, in having before him a range of worthwhile options, in respect of which his choices are not fettered by coercion, and with regard to which he possesses the capacities and resources presupposed by a reasonable measure of success in his self-chosen path among these options (Gray 1992: 22).

In this connection, Gray argues, the defence of the market as an 'enabling' institution for individual autonomy has important implications for the matrix of claims which people possess when they enter the market economy. If, as Gray argues, the morally unsatisfactory idea of negative freedom cannot account for the ethical standing of the market, then it is plausible to suppose that the entitlements or claims which people possess as they enter the market cannot coherently be restricted to those which grant them immunity from coercion by others. They will also be positive claims that guarantee a decent array of worthwhile options and which confer upon people entitlements to resources. For Gray at least, the argument which justifies free markets as enabling devices for autonomy also, and inexorably, justifies the institution of an *enabling welfare state*, where this is among the conditions of autonomous choice and action (Gray 1992: 30).

For Gray, then, the same considerations of individual autonomy that justify market institutions also mandate the institution of an enabling welfare state to be defended not in terms of justice or rights but in terms of the promotion of individual well-being and autonomous choice among the worthwhile options provided by a rich and deep community. In this connection, it is important not to confuse John Gray's rejection of a rights-based defence of the welfare state with the objections to welfare rights that are part of the received conventional wisdom of latter-day classical liberals (Gray 1992: 58):

> Welfare rights, unlike the traditional negative, passive liberal rights against coercion and force, demand more than the non-interference of others for their protection: they impose obligations on others to act to supply goods and services. Further, welfare rights are extremely sensitive to resource scarcity and conflicts among them can easily arise: welfare rights therefore do not possess the property of non-conflictability or compossibility held by negative rights against aggression. As a related point, welfare rights are highly indeterminate, their content being under-determined by any easily ascertainable body of hard empirical fact.... For this last reason, welfare rights are not easily justiciable. And, since they presuppose a level of wealth that is historically rare, they cannot claim the property of universality that is usually associated with basic rights.

For Gray at least, none of these arguments has any significant force (Gray 1992: 59):

> Negative rights, like welfare rights, impose obligations on others and make demands on resources in any real world in which rights are not afforded protection by the enforcement of sanctions for their violation.... Not only does the protection of negative rights demand the appropriation by the state of scarce resources, it is also true that there may be competition and conflict among negative rights in their claims upon resources.... Negative rights are no more compossible, that is, no less likely to conflict with each other, in the real world than are welfare rights. Finally, all rights are conditional - rights to life or liberty may be withdrawn, overridden or forfeited by imprisonment or capital punishment if their holder's conduct justifies such abridgement. In all these respects, negative rights and welfare rights enjoy full moral parity.

In advocating an enabling welfare state, John Gray rejects as rationally indefensible and morally superficial the libertarian view that the scope of a limited government is confined to the sphere of 'passive rights to negative liberty'. Instead, Gray advocates a position which aims to empower or enable people in the satisfaction of their basic needs. In this connection, he argues, a *basic need* is one whose satisfaction is essential to the possibility of a worthwhile life, and whose frustration renders impossible the living of a good life. Basic needs are needs whose satisfaction 'contributes to, or enhances autonomy, such as needs for food, housing, health care, education and so forth' (Gray 1992: 63).

It is at this point in his argument that Gray puts to work Raz's seminal exploration of the 'satiability' of most basic needs (Raz 1986). For Gray at least, such needs are basic, inasmuch as their satisfaction is a 'precondition' of a worthwhile human life, and they are satiable, in that the welfare claims they generate can be met completely, and without remainder. Gray believes that Raz's account of the satiability of most basic needs is relevant here:

> Raz [he argues] illuminates a fundamental property of basic needs, as distinct from wants or preferences, when he notes that, most of them - in principle - are capable of complete satiation. The needs of the disabled, or of the illiterate, though sometimes perhaps expensive to meet, can be met completely - that is to say, to the point at which they can lead reasonably autonomous lives. The crucial conceptual distinction is made by Raz, when he notes that happiness is a satiable value, whereas pleasure is not. A person with a happy life need have no reason to seek to improve his life, whereas someone devoted to pleasure always has reason to seek more pleasure. Most basic needs have the property of satiability which means that once they are met, the content of the welfare claim which guarantees their satisfaction is exhausted.

The enabling welfare state advocated by Gray, then, differs from others in that its ethical foundation is not in ideas of justice or distribution (see later) but in providing for the satisfaction of basic needs, including that in autonomy (Gray 1992: 31).

Gray's argument, then, aims to empower or to enable people in the satisfaction of their basic needs. It stops short, however, of accepting equality of well-being or of the value of autonomy as a legitimate goal of public policy. The normative principle that individuals' well-being, or the value of their liberty, be equalized, neglects, for Gray at least, the satiability of most basic needs - including those connected with autonomy - and has the flaws of all distributional principles that are designed to have a foundational role in a political morality. Autonomy, he argues, is best theorized as a basic need that is satiable; the level at which its satiation occurs may vary between - and even within - societies but nothing in the nature of things prevents us from specifying the conditions under which the basic need of autonomy has been satisfied. For Gray at least, the example of the severely disabled person is instructive here:

> If, let us say, we consider two people with the same, severe disability, where one is a millionaire and lives in the Ritz Hotel, and the other lacks resources and is provided for by disability benefits, but where both persons enjoy the conditions necessary for a dignified, meaningful, and autonomous life, then in my view the difference in the level of resource-provision of the two disabled persons has no moral significance. If both have good lives, why should the difference between them in terms of wealth concern us at all?

Secondly, Gray argues, the empirical argument that empowerment has a necessarily distributive dimension rests on a conceptual fallacy in that it assimilates the empowerment of the poor and the needy to the model of political power. Empowerment or, as John Gray prefers, 'entablement' means conferring on people the opportunities and the resources they need to live autonomously. For Gray at least, it is thoroughly unclear - and there is no reason to suppose that enabling one person necessarily - or even commonly - entails disabling any other:

> How do welfare benefits for the disabled, perhaps framed in terms of voucher schemes, limit or disempower the able-bodied? In general, such schemes will have the effect of enhancing autonomy in the population, without incurring any cost in the heteronomy of others. Because it is a satiable good, autonomy - the basis of many of the welfare benefits that are defended here - is rarely, if ever a positional good.

The welfare benefits defended by Gray, then, are defended not by reference to any distributional principle, but instead by appeal to the well-being of their holders. In instituting benefits for the congenitally handicapped, Gray argues, we are not seeking to compensate them for their bad luck in the genetic lottery but to protect and promote their well-being. For Gray at least, there is no distributional principle at stake in these, or in similar policies (Gray 1992: 36).

Autonomy, Social Rights and Distributive Justice

There are several important issues at stake here which need to be treated carefully. As Gray suggests, it is the burden of Raymond Plant's argument (Plant 1990) that a commitment to egalitarianism is necessitated by any liberal position which aims, as Gray's does, to empower or to enable people in the satisfaction of their basic needs. In this connection, Gray and Plant agree that autonomy is a basic need or interest of human beings. Where they disagree is over the set of conditions necessary for the achievement of autonomy and I shall explore these a little in what follows.

Gray argues in his latest study for the inadequacy of negative liberty taken on its own, a view with which Raymond Plant agrees and has argued for elsewhere (Plant 1984). Gray and Plant agree then, that negative liberty understood as freedom from coercion cannot be a basic value on its own. As Plant (1992: 121) argues:

> To see why this might be thought to be so, we might ask the defender of negative liberty why we want to be free from coercion. The most plausible answer to this

question would be that when we are free from coercion, we are then free to live a life shaped by our own values, purposes, and plan of life. That is to say, freedom from coercion is valuable to us because it is an indispensable condition for us to be able to live an autonomous life shaped by our own purposes and values.

If, however, as Gray and Plant agree, autonomy is the central value, to which negative freedom makes a central contribution, then autonomy cannot be separated from ability, resources and opportunities (Plant 1992: 123). For Plant at least, this is a point of quite central political importance:

> Once there is a recognition that negative freedom can only be justified in terms of the contribution that it makes to autonomy (if not, why is liberty valuable to us?) then the claim that there is a sharp distinction to be drawn between being free to do something and being able to do it is not all that clear cut. We value negative liberty because it secures a sphere in which we are then able to do things. However, if what makes liberty valuable is its link with what we are able to do, then we cannot sharply separate liberty and ability.

For Plant at least, negative liberty is not crucial taken on its own or as an intrinsic value but has to depend on our conception of the Good and the abilities which we think that people need in order to achieve what we regard as valuable in human life (Plant 1992: 125).

Plant also believes that Gray is absolutely correct to argue that there is no sharp distinction between civil and political rights and welfare rights, having used similar arguments in an attempt to establish this point from a position to the left of John Gray's (Plant 1988). To some extent, he suggests, the position here mirrors the debate about negative and positive liberty. Plant (1992: 132) goes on to argue that:

> If rights are supposed to protect liberty and to impose obligations on others in terms of respecting my freedom, then if what grounds the importance of negative liberty is autonomy and that in turn implies both freedom from coercion and access to resources, the rights to protect liberty will be both negative (to protect me from coercion) and positive (to guarantee me access to resources - a guarantee which cannot be secured within the market).

For Plant, however, Gray's version of the symmetry of negative and positive rights can be taken one stage further in terms of the idea that there must be a right to the protection of civil and political or negative rights. For Plant (1992: 132) at least, this is because:

Rights have to be enforceable, if they are to be rights at all. It is the legitimate enforceability and thus a right to the protection of such rights that counts and this will be a positive right to the enforcement of rights, and thus will necessarily involve both costs and resources.

A further issue, as we saw in Chapter 7, is whether or not the welfare rights John Gray does want to defend should be linked to obligations of a workfare or learnfare type. As we have seen, the conditional approach to welfare rights for the able-bodied requires them to discharge concomitant obligations. However, if, as Gray and Plant agree, there is no categorical difference between welfare rights and negative (or, civil and political) rights, then it is unclear on what kind of principle welfare rights are being made conditional on virtue being shown while civil and political rights are not. As Plant (1992: 136) argues:

> Is [Gray's] willingness to entertain a conditional basis for welfare rights perhaps symptomatic of an assumption that these are not, in fact, genuine rights? However, all of Gray's arguments in this study suggest that there is not a difference of principle between them. It is largely because I believe there is no way of distinguishing them, that I am more inclined than I was to think that they should not be ascribed on a conditional basis any more than civil and political rights are.

As Plant suggests, the concept of needs looms quite large in Gray's argument for social rights. Before going on to discuss this point in detail, however, it is important to consider the economic liberal's critique of the idea of needs, because Gray himself - as he acknowledges in the present study - has in the past shared this critical standpoint in relation to needs. In 1983, for example, Gray argued as follows (Gray 1983: 182):

> The objectivity of basic needs is equally delusive. Needs can be given no plausible cross-cultural content, but instead are seen to vary across different moral traditions. Even where moral traditions overlap so as to allow agreement to be reached on a list of basic needs, there is no means of arriving at an agreed schedule of urgency among conflicting basic needs. Again not all needs are in principle satiable. Think only of medical needs concerned with senescence. These are surely basic needs in that their nonsatisfaction will result in death, or worthless life ... there is no natural limit on the resources that could be devoted to satisfying them. There is an astonishing presumptuousness in those who write as if hard dilemmas of this sort can be subject to a morally consensual resolution. Their blindness to these difficulties can only be accounted for by their failing to take seriously the realities of cultural pluralism in our society; (or what comes to the same thing) to take as authoritative their own traditional values. One of the chief functions of the ideology of social justice may be, as Hayek intimates, to generate an illusion of moral agreement, where in fact

there are profound divergencies of values.

As Plant argues, most of the elements of the liberal critique are to be found in this passage - the vagueness and open-endedness of needs; the lack of a clear account of what would satisfy them and whether this is subject to a clear limit; disagreement in society over what needs actually are; the incommensurability of needs and the fact - only implicit in this passage - that, because of their vagueness and open-endedness, interest-group pressures can always expand the sphere of needs and hence the scope of government, not to mention public expenditure (Plant 1992: 127).

John Gray has now retracted some of this radical critique - but not all of it. As we have seen, the vital issue that has changed his mind lies in his adherence to a view set out by Joseph Raz in *The Morality of Freedom* (1986) that there is a set of definable satiable needs and that this can be used as a basis for a society to confer social rights in respect of such 'limited' needs. This argument is central to Gray's thesis both in terms of meeting the economic liberal critique of social rights, and in distinguishing his position from both social democracy and socialism which would take a more redistributive view of social rights. As Plant (1992: 128) notes:

> If Raz's principle is well grounded, then it would be absolutely central to meeting the economic liberal's critique of needs-based welfare rights - in the sense that (*pace* the economic liberal) needs would be satiable rather than open-ended, and the obligations and resources to which these needs would give rise would be clear and limited. It is also central to distinguishing his position from those further to the Left in that if most needs are satiable then they do not have a tendency to grow and thus this would put a clear limit on the extent to which they are to be seen as redistributive.

The idea, then, that needs have natural limits of satiability is the key element in John Gray's attempt to differentiate his more restrictive view of welfare rights - and the needs on which they rest - from a more expansive, redistributive, and egalitarian or at least social democratic one (Plant 1992: 129).

As Plant notes, however, the principle that needs are satiable, while crucial to Gray's argument at many places, is vague and, as Gray admits, is subject to some central exceptions. For Plant at least, if John Gray is not able to limit needs by the satiability constraint, then it seems the issues of needs, welfare rights and some conception of fairness and social justice come together. As Plant (1992: 130) argues:

If not all needs are satiable ... the content of welfare rights will have to be negotiated in a way that embodies some conception of what a fair degree of provision for a particular set of rights is going to be. Instead of the limit to provision being set by, as it were, an internal conception of satiation, it will have to be settled by a negotiation of what we regard as fair provision in a particular society against a background of limited resources. However, this necessarily links up the idea of social or welfare rights with the distributive notion of fairness which Gray wants to avoid. It also links it to the idea of a fair value of liberty defended by John Rawls in *A Theory of Justice*. If welfare rights and the needs that underpin them are necessary conditions of autonomy as Rawls, Gray and myself argue, and if the goal of a liberal political order is securing the basis of autonomy for all citizens, then either these conditions are limited by the fact of satiability as in Gray, or by distributive fairness as in Rawls' conception. Thus if the argument about the satiability of needs cannot be made, then it does seem to me that Gray's argument will turn into the distributive one he wants to avoid and is the main principle which distinguishes his view from a social democratic one.

For Plant at least, if needs are not satiable, we have to work out a degree of fairness to meet such needs since, as Gray and Plant agree, these have to achieved through rights rather than through the market (Plant 1992: 140).

Gray also argues that Plant has a defective view of empowerment in which empowerment is seen as having a necessarily distributive dimension. For Plant at least, this is the case because power is a positional good in that it declines in value the more widely it is distributed, and disappears altogether if distributed equally. In Plant's view, therefore, empowerment has to be concerned with distribution, in that empowerment is in crucial respects a zero-sum business with individuals being empowered only by a transfer of power from other individuals or groups. For Plant at least, empowerment is positional for certain goods, and can be achieved only by disempowering others (Plant 1992: 137-8).

For Gray, however, empowerment (or, as he prefers, entablement) means conferring on the poor and the needy the opportunities and resources they need to live autonomously. For Gray at least, it is thoroughly unclear - and there is no reason to suppose - that the entablement of a person necessarily, or commonly, entails the disablement of any other. On this crucial issue, Gray argues as follows (Gray 1992: 34):

How do welfare benefits for the disabled, perhaps framed in terms of voucher schemes, limit or disempower the able-bodied? In general, such schemes will have the effect of enhancing autonomy in the population, without incurring any cost in the heteronomy of others. Because it is a satiable good, autonomy - the basis of many of the welfare benefits that are defended here - is rarely, if ever, a positional good.

For Plant, on the other hand, conferring rights, entitlements, or vouchers, and the whole movement in respect of Citizen's Charters (now popular across the political spectrum), is essentially about empowering citizens, consumers, patients and so forth *vis-à-vis* professional groups in the public sector. It is not about some limited level of entablement which leaves power relations intact, but about a redistribution of power from professional groups to the consumer of professional services outside the market sector. Social rights are thus essentially redistributive, because they are involved in redistributing power (Plant 1992: 139-40):

> Part of Gray's argument for thinking that social rights or entitlements enhance autonomy is that they do give greater power to the person bearing the rights in respect of professional administrators of welfare and social resources. This has certainly been part of the liberal case for vouchers that Gray himself cites in the passage just quoted. On the public choice view of the behaviour of public sector bureaucracies, vouchers are a way of empowering the recipient of the voucher, not just in the sense of entablement but rather empowering the bearer of the entitlement [or] voucher against the public sector official who might otherwise determine the nature, the terms and the level of service offered according to the ... discretion of the official, whether social security official, consultant, G.P., teacher, social worker or whatever. This seems much closer to my view of empowerment as a positional good than Gray's view about entablement which disempowers or disables no-one else. Take [John] Gray's own example of vouchers for the disabled. In giving this choice-enhancing measure to individuals, it seems me that the power of professionals who are in charge of resources and services for the disabled would be diminished. It may be true - as Gray says - that resources for the disabled do not limit or disempower the able-bodied but that surely is not the point. The people from whom the power is being redistributed are the professional groups in question. Hence I believe that the empowerment of the poor and needy through rights and entitlements is essentially redistributive, that this power is a positional good and that what is at stake is a zero-sum game, in that the power of the needy enhanced through rights is at the expense of others, not to be sure the general group of the able-bodied, but rather the professional groups with responsibilities in this area.

Hence, for Plant, once we are in the business of satisfying basic needs through rights in the public sector, then conferring rights is a zero-sum or distributive business, and involves a systematic disempowerment of producer interests in the public sector (Plant 1992: 140).

Prospects

It remains for us to consider what the future prospects for New Right think-tanks might be, given Margaret Thatcher's departure as Prime Minister and Leader of the Conservative Party. Writing in *The Socialist Register* in 1979, Andrew Gamble argued that the long post-war period of expansion and stability had come to an end during the previous ten years and that there had been (Gamble 1979: 2):

> a real intellectual change, a remarkable revival of liberal political economy through the elaboration of the doctrine of the social market economy, a doctrine which, under different labels, has made increasing headway within the Conservative Party in the last ten years. The Conservative Government elected in 1979 had a group of ministers in the crucial economic ministries (Treasury, Industry, Trade, Energy), who were all adherents of the doctrine and prepared to govern in accordance with its prescriptions.

For Gamble at least, Britain was living through the 'crisis that should never have happened, the crisis that Keynesian techniques and social democratic policies and institutions were supposed to have banished forever, because they had overcome the tendency of the capitalist economy towards deficient demand and under consumption. The slow-down in the pace of accumulation ... provided the opportunity for a widespread rejection of Keynesian political economy - and an onslaught on the policies, values and organizations of social democracy' (Gamble 1979: 1-2). Given this background, it is at least *plausible* to suppose that the IEA, in particular, 'played an important role in changing the climate of opinion from the mid-1970s onwards and ... in turn *profited from the change in climate*' (Kavanagh 1990: 83).

As we have seen in this chapter, however, there are several issues which continue to *divide* the New Right and its think-tanks. The reasons for this have to do with the changing nature of both the intellectual debate and the political agenda. As Plant suggests, the intellectual debate after Thatcher, Reagan and the changes in Eastern Europe is no longer about central economic planning or the case for markets *per se*, but much more about the range of social and political institutions within which markets are embedded, the scope and purposes of these institutions (and their relationship to the market economy), along with a debate about the range of goods which ought to be treated as commodities. For Plant at least (1992: 120):

> This second task of trying to work out the appropriate moral limits to markets is also centrally important because the market is only likely to appear to be legitimate and command loyalty if it is seen to have a definite sphere of legitimacy and that it is

constrained from spilling over into spheres of human life within which we do not wish to see goods treated as commmodities. Given the degree of inequality which will naturally arise from free market exchange, and the fact that these will be influenced by morally arbitrary factors such as natural endowment, fortunate upbringing and just sheer luck, it is important to work out some consensual view about where appropriate limits lie for an institution which embodies these features.

As the former Director of the IEA, Graham Mather, has argued 'twenty years ago, it was enough for a free-market think-tank to say "why not try the market?" But the very success of that technique means that it is no longer enough' (Castle 1991).

A second factor which has arguably enhanced the 'influence' of New Right think-tanks in Britain in recent years concerns what one commentator has referred to as the 'privatization' of policy-making (Oakley 1989). Of particular importance here was Mrs Thatcher's decision to abolish the Central Policy Review Staff (CPRS) in 1983 and the strengthening of her own Downing Street Policy Unit thereafter. As Hennessy and Coates (1991: 14-15) argue:

> Mrs Thatcher used the opportunity of the ... demise [of the CPRS] to strengthen her own Downing Street [Policy] Unit. It was seen as a quick-dash, politics-driven outfit: brash where the CPRS had been stolid, partisan where they were neutral, often short-term where they were long-term.... [The Policy Unit] was *hers*, she valued it and used it on central issues, like the Health Service review.... Under Mr Major now, as under Mrs Thatcher, [the Policy Unit is] the place where outside think-tanks can already find a *potential* conduit to inside influence.

As Hennessy and Coates point out, however, Britain, unlike the United States, has a permanent, career civil service which 'sails serenely on whatever set of ministers - with their handful of special advisers - the electorate may install or remove from time to time' (Hennessy and Coates 1991: 10). As far as outside 'think-tanks' are concerned, they argue, this essential feature of the nature and operation of British government has important negative implications (Hennessy and Coates 1991: 15 and 19):

> Convincing the little cell in Number 10 is one thing. Shifting any entrenched departmental orthodoxy is another.... Whitehall, even with a Freedom of Information Act in place, will still be very different from Washington.... Departments - the Queen's own pressure groups - will remain tough citadels to storm, the price we pay for having a career Civil Service.

Bibliography

Adam Smith Institute (1990), *The First Hundred*, ASI, London.

American Enterprise Institute (1987), *A Community of Self-Reliance: The New Consensus on Family and Welfare*, AEI, Marquette University, Milwaukee.

Anderson, D. (ed) (1980), *The Ignorance of Social Intervention*, Croom Helm, London.

Anderson, D. *et al.* (1981), *Breaking the Spell of the Welfare State*, SAU, London.

Anderson, D. *et al.* (1982), *Educated for Employment?*, SAU, London.

Anderson, D. (ed) (1984), *The Kindness that Kills*, SPCK, London.

Anderson, D. (ed) (1986), *A Diet of Reason*, SAU, London.

Anderson, D. (ed) (1988), *Full Circle?*, SAU, London.

Anderson, D. (1991), *The Unmentionable Face of Poverty in the Nineties*, SAU, London.

Anderson, M. (1978), *Welfare*, Hoover Institution, Stanford University, California.

Barnett, C. (1986), *The Audit of War*, Macmillan, London.

Barry, N. (1986), *On Classical Liberalism and Libertarianism*, Macmillan, Basingstoke.

Barry, N. (1987), *The New Right*, Croom Helm, London.

BBC (1989), 'Morals Made to Measure', *Analysis*, BBC Radio 4.

Beattie, A. (1987), *History in Peril*, CPS, London.

Blaug, M. (1984), 'Education Vouchers: It All Depends on What You Mean', in J. LeGrand and R. Robinson (eds), *Privatization and the Welfare State*, Allen and Unwin, London.

Bogdanor, V. (1976), 'Education', in R. Blake and J. Patten (eds), *The Conservative Opportunity*, Macmillan, London.

Bosanquet, N. (1983), *After the New Right*, Heinemann Educational Books, London.

Bradley, I. (1981), 'Intellectual Influences in Britain: Past and Present', in A. Seldon (ed), *The Emerging Consensus...?*, IEA, London.

Brophy, M. *et al.* (1984), *Trespassing?*, SAU, London.

Brown, A. (1985), *Trials of Honeyford*, CPS, London.

Brown, G. (1989), *Finding Fault in Divorce*, SAU, London.

Brown, M. *et al.* (1985), *No Turning Back*, Conservative Political Centre, London.

Brown, M. *et al.* (1986), *Save Our Schools*, Conservative Political Centre, London.

Buchanan, J.M. *et al.* (1978), *The Economics of Politics*, IEA, London.

Buchanan, J.M. and Tullock, G. (1981), 'An American Perspective', in A. Seldon (ed), *The Emerging Consensus...?*, IEA, London.

Burrows, L. (1988), 'Missing Mothers: The Effects of Women Working', in D. Anderson (ed), *Full Circle?*, SAU, London.

Butler, E. *et al.* (1985), *The Omega File*, ASI, London.

Butler, E. and Pirie, M. (1988a), *Health Management Units*, ASI, London.

Butler, E. and Pirie, M. (1988b), *The Health of Nations*, ASI, London.

Castle, S. (1991), 'Coup's wake casts pall on think-tank', *Independent on Sunday*, 1 September.

Centre for Policy Studies (1975a), *Objectives and Style*, CPS, London.

Centre for Policy Studies (1975b), *Why Britain Needs a Social Market Economy*, CPS, London.

Centre for Policy Studies (1987), *The Welfare Challenge*, CPS, London.

Centre for Policy Studies (1989a), *Aims and Achievements*, CPS, London.

Centre for Policy Studies (1989b), *Exertion and Example*, CPS, London.

Chitty, C. (1989), *Towards a New Education System*, Falmer Press, Basingstoke.

Clark, C. (1977), *Poverty before Politics*, IEA, London.

Cowling, M. (1990), *Mill and Liberalism*, Second Edition, Cambridge University Press, Cambridge.

Cox, C. and Marks, J. (1981), 'Educational Allowances: Power to the People?' in A. Flew *et al.*, *The Pied Pipers of Education*, SAU, London.

Cox, C. and Marks, J. (eds) (1982), *The Right to Learn*, CPS, London.

Cox, C.B. and Dyson, A.E. (eds) (1969a), *Fight for Freedom: A Black Paper*, Critical Quarterly Society, London.

Cox, C.B. and Dyson, A.E. (eds) (1969b), *Black Paper Two: The Crisis in Education*, Critical Quarterly Society, London.

Cox, C.B. and Dyson, A.E. (eds) (1970), *Goodbye Mr Short: Black Paper Three*, Critical Quarterly Society, London.

Cox, C.B. and Boyson, R. (eds) (1975), *Black Paper 1975*, J.M. Dent, London.

Cox, C.B. and Boyson, R. (eds) (1977), *Black Paper 1977*, Temple Smith, London.

Culyer, A.J. (1981), 'The IEA's Unorthodoxy', in A. Seldon (ed), *The Emerging Consensus...?*, IEA, London.

David, M. (1989), 'Education', in M. McCarthy (ed), *The New Politics of Welfare*, Macmillan, London.

Deuchar, S. (1987), *History - and GCSE History*, CPS, London.

Edgar, D. (1986), 'The Free and the Good', in R. Levitas (ed), *The Ideology of the New Right*, Polity, Cambridge.

Elwell, H. (1986), *NHS: The Road to Recovery*, CPS, London.

Enthoven, A. (1985), *Reflections on the Management of the National Health Service*, Nuffield Provincial Hospitals Trust, London.

Fisher, A. (1974), *Must History Repeat Itself?*, Churchill Press, London.

Flew, A. *et al.* (1981), *The Pied Pipers of Education*, SAU, London.

Flew, A. (1985), *The Philosophy of Poverty*, SAU, London.

Flew, A. (1990), *Self-Improvement and Social Action*, SAU, London.

Flude, M. and Hammer, M. (eds) (1990), *The Education Reform Act 1988*, Falmer Press, Basingstoke.

Friedman, D. (1978), *The Machinery of Freedom*, Arlington House, New Rochelle.

Friedman, M. (1953), 'The Methodology of Positive Economics', in M. Friedman (ed), *Essays in Positive Economics*, University of Chicago Press, Chicago.

Friedman, M. (1962), *Capitalism and Freedom*, University of Chicago Press, Chicago.

Friedman, M. and Friedman, R. (1980), *Free to Choose*, Pelican Books, Harmondsworth.

Gamble, A. (1979), 'The Free Economy and the Strong State', in R. Miliband and J. Saville (eds), *The Socialist Register 1979*, Merlin Press, London.

Gamble, A. (1986), 'The Political Economy of Freedom', in R. Levitas (ed), *The*

Ideology of the New Right, Polity, Cambridge.

Gamble, A. (1988), *The Free Economy and the Strong State*, Macmillan, London.

Gilmour, I. (1978), *Inside Right*, Quartet Books, London.

Goldsmith, M. and Willetts, D. (1988a), *Managed Health Care*, CPS, London.

Goldsmith, M. and Willetts, D. (1988b), *A Mixed Economy for Health Care*, CPS, London.

Graham, D. and Clarke, P. (1986), *The New Enlightenment*, Macmillan, London.

Gray, J. (1983), 'Classical Liberalism and the Politicisation of Poverty', in A. Ellis and K. Kumar (eds), *Dilemmas of Liberal Democracies*, Tavistock, London.

Gray, J. (1984), *Hayek on Liberty*, Blackwell, Oxford.

Gray, J. (1989), *Limited Government: A Positive Agenda*, IEA, London.

Gray, J. (1991), *A conservative disposition*, CPS, London.

Gray, J. (1992), *The Moral Foundations of Market Institutions*, IEA Health and Welfare Unit, London.

Green, D. (1987), *The New Right*, Wheatsheaf, Brighton.

Green, D. (1988), *Everyone a Private Patient*, IEA, London.

Green, D. (1990), 'Introduction: A Missed Opportunity', in D. Green (ed), *The NHS Reforms: Whatever Happened to Consumer Choice?*, IEA Health and Welfare Unit, London.

Green, D. (1992), 'Liberty, Poverty and the Underclass', in D. Smith (ed), *Understanding the Underclass*, Policy Studies Institute, London.

Greenleaf, W.H. (1983), *The Ideological Heritage*, Vol. 2 of *The British Political Tradition*, Methuen, London.

Griffiths, B. (1984), *The Creation of Wealth*, Hodder and Stoughton, London.

Griffiths, B. (1985), *Monetarism and Morality*, CPS, London.

Griffiths, B. (1989), *Morality and the Market-Place*, Hodder and Stoughton, London.

Halcrow, M. (1989), *Keith Joseph: A Single Mind*, Macmillan, London.

Harris, Ralph (ed) (1965), *Freedom or Free-for-all?*, IEA, London.

Harris, Ralph (1986), *Morality and Markets*, CPS, London.

Harris, Ralph (1991), 'High Price of a Social Market', *Sunday Telegraph*, 17 February.

Harris, Robin (1989), *The Conservative Community*, CPS, London.

Hartwell, R.M. *et al.* (1974), *The Long Debate on Poverty*, IEA, London.

Haviland, J. (ed) (1988), *Take Care, Mr Baker!*, Fourth Estate, London.

Hayek, F.A. (1967), *Studies in Philosophy, Politics and Economics*, Routledge and Kegan Paul, London.

Hayek, F.A. (1976), *The Mirage of Social Justice*, Vol. 2 of *Law, Legislation and Liberty*, Routledge and Kegan Paul, London.

Hayek, F.A. (1988a), *The Fatal Conceit*, Routledge, London.

Hayek, F.A. (1988b), 'The Weasel Word "Social"', in R. Scruton (ed), *Conservative Thoughts: Essays from the Salisbury Review*, Claridge Press, London.

Hennessy, P. and Coates, S. (1991), 'Little Grey Cells: Think Tanks, Governments and Policy-Making', Strathclyde Analysis Papers No. 6, University of Strathclyde, Glasgow.

Heseltine, M. (1987), *Where There's A Will*, Hutchinson, London.

Hexham, I. (1985), *The Bible, Justice and the Culture of Poverty*, SAU, London.

Hillgate Group (1986), *Whose Schools?*, Hillgate Group, London.

Hillgate Group (1987), *The Reform of British Education*, Claridge Press, London.

Himmelfarb, G. (1987), *Victorian Values and twentieth-century condescension*, CPS, London.

HMSO (1989), *Working for Patients*, Cm. 555, London.

Hoover, K. and Plant, R. (1989), *Conservative Capitalism in Britain and the United States*, Routledge, London.

Howell, R. (1991), *Why Not Work?*, ASI, London.

Hutt, W.H. (1971), *Politically Impossible...?*, IEA, London.

Institute of Health Service Management (1988), *Alternative Delivery and Funding of the NHS*, IHSM, London.

Jenkins, P. (1989), *Mrs Thatcher's Revolution*, Pan Books, London.

Jones, K. (1989), *Right Turn*, Hutchinson Radius, London.

Joseph, K. (1975), *Reversing the Trend*, Barry Rose, Chichester and London.

Kavanagh, D. (1990), *Thatcherism and British Politics*, Oxford University Press, Oxford.

Kedourie, H. (1987), *Errors and Evils of the New History*, CPS, London.

King, D. (1987), *The New Right*, Macmillan, London.

Kirzner, I. (1976), 'On the Method of Austrian Economics', in E.G. Dolan (ed), *The Foundations of Modern Austrian Economics*, Sheed and Ward Inc., Kansas City.

Kirzner, I. (1980), 'The Primacy of Entrepreneurial Discovery', in A. Seldon (ed), *The Prime Mover of Progress*, IEA, London.

Knight, C. (1985), 'The New Right and Education', in A. Seldon (ed), *The 'New Right' Enlightenment*, E and L Books, Sevenoaks.

Knight, C. (1990), *The Making of Tory Education Policy in Post-War Britain 1950-86*, Falmer Press, Basingstoke.

Lawlor, S. (1988a), *Away with LEAs*, CPS, London.

Lawlor, S. (1988b), *Correct Core*, CPS, London.

Lawlor, S. (1988c), *Opting Out: A Guide to Why and How*, CPS, London.

Lawson, N. and Bruce-Gardyne, J. (1976), *The Power Game*, Macmillan, London.

Lees, D.S. (1961), *Health Through Choice*, IEA, London.

LeGrand, J. (1982), *The Strategy of Equality*, Allen and Unwin, London.

Letwin, O. (1988), *Aims of Schooling*, CPS, London.

Letwin, O. and Redwood, J. (1988), *Britain's Biggest Enterprise*, CPS, London.

Lister, R. (1989), 'Social Security', in M. McCarthy (ed), *The New Politics of Welfare*, Macmillan, London.

Littlechild, S.C. (1986), *The Fallacy of the Mixed Economy*, Second Edition, IEA, London.

Lynn, R. (1988), *Educational Achievement in Japan*, SAU/Macmillan Press, London.

Maclure, S. (1988), *Education Re-formed*, Second Edition, Hodder and Stoughton, London.

Marenbon, J. (1987), *English, Our English*, CPS, London.

Marsland, D. (1981), 'Education: Vast Horizons, Meagre Visions', in A. Flew *et al.*, *The Pied Pipers of Education*, SAU, London.

Maynard, A. (1975), *Experiment with Choice in Education*, IEA, London.

Mead, L. (1986), *Beyond Entitlement*, Free Press, New York.

Minford, P. (1984), 'State Expenditure: A Study in Waste', *Economic Affairs*, April-June.

Mitchell, B. (1989), *Why Social Policy Cannot Be Morally Neutral*, SAU, London.

Mitchell, W. (1988), *Government As It Is*, IEA, London.

Morley, R. (1988), 'Charities, Single Payments and the Social Fund', in R. Cohen and M. Tarpey (eds), *Single Payments: The Disappearing Safety Net*, CPAG, London.

Murray, C. (1984), *Losing Ground: American Social Policy 1950-80*, Basic Books, New York.

Murray, C. (1990), 'Underclass', in C. Murray *et al.*, *The Emerging British Underclass*, IEA Health and Welfare Unit, London.

Novak, M. (1990), *Morality, Capitalism and Democracy*, IEA Health and Welfare Unit, London.

Oakley, R. (1991), 'Privatized Policy-Making for the Tory Right', *The Times*, 17 February.

O'Hear, A. (1986), 'Education Beyond Present Desire', *Salisbury Review*, April.

O'Keeffe, D. (1981), 'Labour in Vain: Truancy, Industry and the School Curriculum', in A. Flew *et al.*, *The Pied Pipers of Education*, SAU, London.

O'Keeffe, D. (ed) (1986), *The Wayward Curriculum*, SAU, London.

Parker, H. (1982), *The Moral Hazard of Social Benefits*, IEA, London.

Paton, C. (1989), 'The Prime Minister's Review of the National Health Service and the 1989 White Paper Working for Patients', in N. Manning and C. Ungerson (eds), *Social Policy Review 1989-90*, Longman, Harlow.

Peet, J. (1987), *Healthy Competition*, CPS, London.

Pirie, M. (1982), *The Logic of Economics*, ASI, London.

Pirie, M. (1988a), *Micropolitics: The Creation of Successful Policy*, Wildwood House, Aldershot.

Pirie, M. (1988b), *Privatization: Theory, Practice and Choice*, Wildwood House, Aldershot.

Plant, R. (1988), 'The New Consensus on Family and Welfare: A View from the Left', unpublished.

Plant, R. (1992), 'Autonomy, Social Rights and Distributive Justice', in J. Gray *et al.*, *The Moral Foundations of Market Institutions*, IEA Health and Welfare Unit, London.

Pugh, R. (1987), 'Financial Nightmares: Legacy of an Unsocial Fund', *Community Care*, 10 December.

Raz, J. (1986), *The Morality of Freedom*, Clarendon Press, Oxford.

Redwood, J. (1988), *In Sickness and in Health*, CPS, London.

Rothbard, M. (1970), *Power and Market*, Sheed Andrews and McMeel, Kansas City.

Rothbard, M. (1973), *For a New Liberty*, Collier-Macmillan, New York.

Russel, T. (1978), *The Tory Party: Its Policies, Divisions and Future*, Penguin Books, Harmondsworth.

Sacks, J. (1985), *Wealth and Poverty: A Jewish Analysis*, SAU, London.

Sadowsky, J. (1985), *The Christian Response to Poverty*, SAU, London.

Segalman, R. and Marsland, D. (1989), *From Cradle to Grave: Comparative Perspectives on the State of Welfare*, SAU/Macmillan, London.

Seldon, A. (1968), *After the NHS*, IEA, London.

Seldon, A. (1977), *Charge!*, Temple Smith, London.

Seldon, A. (1980a), 'The NHS: Success? Still on Trial? Failure?' in A. Seldon (ed), *The Litmus Papers*, CPS, London.

Seldon, A. (1980b), 'Preface', in A. Seldon (ed), *The Prime Mover of Progress*, IEA, London.

Seldon, A. (1981a), 'Preamble: The Essence of the IEA', in A. Seldon (ed), *The Emerging Consensus...?*, IEA, London.

Seldon, A. (1981b), *Wither the Welfare State*, IEA, London.

Seldon, A. (1986), *The Riddle of the Voucher*, IEA, London.

Seldon, A. (1989), 'Economic Scholarship and Political Interest: IEA Thinking and Government Policies', in A. Gamble *et al.*, *Ideas, Interests and Consequences*, IEA, London.

Seldon, A. (1990), *Capitalism*, Blackwell, Oxford.

Sexton, S. (1987), *Our Schools: A Radical Policy*, IEA Education Unit, Warlingham.

Shand, A. (1984), *The Capitalist Alternative*, Harvester Press, Brighton.

Steinfels, P. (1979), *The Neo-Conservatives*, Simon and Schuster, New York.

Tomlinson, J.R.G. (1989), 'The Schools', in D. Kavanagh and A. Seldon (eds), *The Thatcher Effect*, Clarendon Press, Oxford.

Tullock, G. (1976), *The Vote Motive*, IEA, London.

Wilby, P. and Midgley, S. (1987), 'As the New Right Wields its Power', *Independent*, 23 July.

Wilcox, B. (1989), 'The Education Reform Act 1988: Implications for Schools and Local Education Authorities', in M. Brenton and C. Ungerson (eds), *Social Policy Review 1988-89*, Longman, Harlow.

Wilkinson, M. (1977), *Lessons from Europe*, CPS, London.

Willetts, D. (1989), *Reforming the Health Service*, Conservative Political Centre, London.

Willetts, D. (1992), *Modern Conservatism*, Penguin Books, Harmondsworth.

Worsthorne, P. (1988), *The Politics of Manners*, CPS, London.

Young, H. (1990), *One of Us*, Pan Books, London.